T5-ASM-309

LABOR
☆ U ☆ S ☆ A ☆
TODAY

LABOR
⋆U⋆S⋆A⋆
TODAY

By LESTER VELIE

HARPER & ROW, PUBLISHERS

NEW YORK, EVANSTON,

AND LONDON

[1964]

TO FRANCES,
WHO HELPED PRODUCE THIS BOOK,
AND ALAN AND FRANKIE

Contents

Foreword: Labor U.S.A. Revisited   ix

CHAPTER 1   When Machines Don't Need Men—
             What of the Unions?   1

CHAPTER 2   Electricians' Hours   5

CHAPTER 3   The Union That Automation Built   9

CHAPTER 4   Dave McDonald Has a Plan   15

CHAPTER 5   Hurrah for the Gray, White and Blue!   20

CHAPTER 6   George Meany: Plumber with His
             Finger in the Dike   24

CHAPTER 7   The Hoffa Phenomenon, Part 1:
             Dead End Kid with a Plus   40

CHAPTER 8   The Hoffa Phenomenon, Part 2: The
             Strange Saga of James Hoffa, Banker   57

CHAPTER 9   Why They Hate Walter Reuther   63

CHAPTER 10   David Dubinsky: He Bosses 400,000
              Women   80

CHAPTER 11   The Boys from Seventh Avenue   91

CHAPTER 12   Wherein a Negro David Staggers
              a Union Goliath   100

CHAPTER 13   Journey to the Underworld   107

CHAPTER 14   The Corrupters   123

CHAPTER 15   You Can't Steal a Union Any More   135

CHAPTER 16   How to Get a $100,000,000 Raise   143

CHAPTER 17   Labor U.S.A. vs. the Kremlin   156

CHAPTER 18   Samuel Gompers: Father with Labor
              Pains   171

CHAPTER 19   John L. Lewis: Labor's Rogue
              Elephant   193

CHAPTER 20   Six Days That Shook the Union
              World   213

Index   223

Foreword:
Labor U.S.A. Revisited

Unions are a necessary part of a free society—a force that keeps other forces from dominating a country. The Bolsheviks, the Nazis, the Franco Falangists—all took the same first step toward creating a goosestep society. They abolished the free trade unions. Conversely, when General Douglas MacArthur sought to bring democracy to occupied Japan, one of his first moves was to legalize and encourage the organization of unions.

Back in 1935, a quarter-century before Negro sit-ins were heard of, Congress passed the most significant of all civil rights laws— the Wagner Labor Relations Act. It protected the right of wage earners to form unions and so win a voice over their wages and working conditions.

As millions of men and women poured into new unions and flooded the old, there came to power a diverse array of leaders: men of genius like John L. Lewis and men of greed like Dave Beck; men of ideas and ideals like Walter P. Reuther and David Dubinsky and primitives like William E. Maloney of the Operating Engineers, who ran his first union with the help of gangster guns.

Today there are as many kinds of union leaders as there are

unions to lead. Harry Van Arsdale, Jr., of the New York electricians, who pioneered the twenty-five-hour week and orders his members to improve themselves "or else," is a union leader. And Anthony "Tony Pro" Provenzano, boss New Jersey Teamster found guilty of extortion, is a union leader. Joseph A. Beirne, president of the telephone workers, who writes thoughtful books on labor's automation dilemma, is a union leader. And so is James R. Hoffa, who maintains so many lawyers to fight prosecution that they are known as the Teamsters Bar Association.

While writing some fifty magazine articles on unions and union leaders during recent years, I was surprised to find there are virtually no books on this fascinating field for the general reader. Scholarly works on labor problems and history, yes. A book that might interest, say, an intelligent newspaper reader, no. I have tried to provide such a book.

When *Labor U.S.A.* was published in 1959, the unions' chief problem was corruption of the few that could discredit the many. Today, it is the new industrial revolution—automation. The first section of *Labor U.S.A. Today* is devoted to it. Five chapters, including "The Hoffa Phenomenon," deal with the problem children of the union family.

Labor U.S.A. Today makes no attempt to be all-inclusive, and perhaps some leaders—good or bad—who might be in an encyclopedic book won't be found here. I have tried, instead, to introduce the reader to the men who give our unions their special flavor—and to take a look at what the unions do.

While this book is not a history, it does tell—through the lives of two men, Samuel Gompers and John L. Lewis—how the American unions got where they are today. Lastly, I have tried to picture the role the unions play in the tidal changes that are sweeping down on all of us.

Kings Point, New York   LESTER VELIE

LABOR
☆ U ☆ S ☆ A ☆
TODAY

CHAPTER 1

When Machines
Don't Need Men—
What of the Unions?

A technology explosion rocks our country and reshapes our education, our leisure, our training for earning a living. Hammered hardest and earliest on this anvil of change are the labor unions. For the backbone of the unions is the blue-collar industrial worker. And to see what is happening to him, let's look in on some of the new intelligent machines.

At Winston-Salem, North Carolina, in a onetime wagon works where blacksmiths hammered out iron tires only a decade ago, an intelligent machine does the work of men's eyes and brains, as well as their hands. It is the world's first computer-directed automatic assembly line. Created by Western Electric engineers, it produces an electronic resistor for missiles, computers and telephone switching systems—by the tens of millions. Yet only two men in white coats are on hand along the two seventy-foot assembly lines. The computer, at one end, schedules the month's work, directs the producing devices, corrects them if they go off course, tests the products and rejects them if they are faulty.

At mineheads in Wyoming, crewless trains flow along stretches of automated railway, never stopping even while loading. One man, at the electronic controls, supplants a dozen once used in the traditional railroad operation. And in New York City, a crewless subway train, shuttling between Times Square and Grand Central Station, gives a preview of the automated, city-wide transit systems planned by San Francisco and other cities.

In 180 plants across the country, a machine called the Milwaukee-Matic does virtually any machining job by itself, selecting the necessary tool from a battery of 961 it controls. The machine spots defects and replaces tools if necessary. Wherever it goes, the machine displaces half the machine operators and 40 percent of the machine-tool men once needed.

With intelligent machines like these, we make more steel than a decade ago, but with 25,000 less workers; mine more coal, but with only one-half the workers; produce more cars than we did a decade ago and twice as much chemicals, but with a shrinking work force. To sum up, industrial production is up more than 20 percent since 1957, but there are 775,000 less jobs in industry.

As a result, some of labor's biggest powerhouses—the industrial unions that organize an entire plant or a mine or an industry— have lost members.

The United Mine Workers, 600,000 strong in 1949, had thinned to 400,000 by 1963. (Changes in fuel use played a part in this.)

The United Auto Workers, with 1,500,000 members in 1955, now has some 1,100,000 dues payers. (Decline in airplane production is partly responsible.)

The Textile Workers Union of America, 375,000 strong in 1951, has shrunk to 192,000.

One union, the Brotherhood of Locomotive Firemen and Enginemen, is threatened with something new in labor history—sudden death. The railroads contend that its members who once shoveled coal into the iron horse are no longer needed in the oil-using diesel locomotive.

Does this mean that the unions are finished—that it is only a matter of time before they'll dry up and blow away? Not at all.

While industrial jobs are declining, other kinds of jobs are increasing and so offer opportunities to some unions.

A few simple figures explain why. Back in 1919 when there were only 105,000,000 of us, we needed some 26,000,000 workers to grow our food, dig our metals, make the goods we need. In 1963, when there were 189,000,000 of us, the workers needed to perform similar chores remained virtually the same—26,000,000. Where did the jobs come from, then, for the 80 percent increase in population? They came from a higher standard of living, from additional services to the American people. The 14,000,000 Americans who worked in service industries in 1919—selling goods, moving them, nursing, doctoring, entertaining, banking—stood at 36,000,000 by 1963.

To the unions, this tidal shift from industrial to service workers or technicians poses an historic opportunity and a headache, for the white-collar, middle-class-oriented worker is harder to organize.

At Whiting, Indiana, in the instrument control room of a twenty-story petroleum distillation tower, I talked to four new technicians, all in their twenties, bred by the intelligent machine. They were checking the computer that ran the entire operation.

As mechanically minded youngsters, they once would have gone into some skilled craft, that of electrician, say. They would have finished their education at high school, worn dungarees at their work and joined a craft union. Now they worked in white shirts and business suits for a salary instead of an hourly wage. They had the equivalent of two years' college training and called themselves maintenance engineers—although they had no degree. And they were hostile to unions.

"How could we strike?" one maintenance man asked. "This system must be kept going twenty-four hours around the clock."

Along with the challenge of organizing workers like these, automation confronts unions with the problem of going along with the introduction of the new intelligent machines, yet at the same time finding some way to keep union members off the industrial ash heap. This poses a dilemma within a dilemma. For to save jobs when machines don't need men requires cooperative schemes between managers and union leaders. And this, in turn, requires a new kind of collective bargaining. For the stakes are no longer a few cents more per hour as they once were. Now the stakes are men's livelihoods.

"I'm forty-five," a striking printer told me in New York, "but it's the slag heap for me if we don't do something about these new typesetting machines that operate by tape instead of human fingers." This fear shut down New York's newspapers for four months while publishers and union leaders sought—but did not find—a way to let the boss have his new machine yet let the worker keep his job.

Who in labor will cope with these new problems?

If you look to Labor's summit—the twenty-nine-member Executive Council of the AFL-CIO—you see older men, average age sixty-two years, who made their mark in other times, the 1930's, fighting other problems, subsistence wages, sweatshop hours.

This aging leadership, coupled with the erosion of industrial union membership, stirs talk about the "Decline of the Labor Movement." But it is premature to talk of labor's decline when unions can shut down the steel industry for 116 days, as they did in 1959, or immobilize East Coast docks, as they did in early 1963.

Furthermore, crises seem to bring forth the men to solve them. New ideas, new leaders and even new kinds of unions are emerging to fit the new times.

We shall now meet some of the more significant of these.

CHAPTER 2

Electricians' Hours

If you are a union electrician in New York City, you go to work at 8 A.M., and at noon take an hour off for lunch. Returning at 1, you work another hour—total workday, at regular pay, five hours. Then you work another hour at time and one half overtime. Bankers may have bankers' hours, but you have something more exclusive—electricians' hours.

The man who invented them is Harry Van Arsdale, Jr., a broad-shouldered New Yorker of fifty-six with wise old eyes, a tired, gravelly voice and hair that turned gray years ago. Van Arsdale is business manager of Local No. 3 of the International Brotherhood of Electrical Workers which embraces 9,000 skilled electricians and 21,000 workers in lampshade and other factories. Back in 1933, when Van Arsdale assumed his local's leadership, he espoused a philosophy then radical in labor. He told his men: "You produce more, and I'll get you more."

So his members have been knocking themselves out ever since to discover timesaving devices. They vie for prizes—offered by their own union—to discover a machine that enables one man to do a job that once required seven. They fire their own loafers and train their own incompetents to produce more.

A Local No. 3 vice president once guided me through a newly rising New York skyscraper where his men were installing cables and fixtures.

"Look at this automatic pipe threader," the union man said. "Used to take a man an hour to thread a length of pipe by hand.

5

Now the machine does the job, untended, in a few minutes." He pointed to a winchlike device pulling cable through a conduit. "Used to take seven or eight strong men to pull wire by hand," he said. "Now one man and this machine can do it. One of our members invented it when we put on a drive for ideas."

Employers of Local No. 3's electrician members have retaliated with free college scholarships for the dues payers' children, bargain-priced apartments, interest-free loans to buy homes or cars, and hourly earnings of $5.20 plus $1.40 in benefits: $6.60 total! The benefits include, besides $250 monthly pensions (with Social Security), a unique additional annuity payment of $150 monthly.

In 1962, Van Arsdale and Local No. 3, always in the avant-garde of union ideas, made themselves the bellwether for the entire Labor movement. Van Arsdale achieved a twenty-five-hour standard work week for his electricians. The radically abbreviated week startled and distressed the Washington headquarters of the AFL-CIO, whose leaders feared that this radical idea would hurt the Federation's more modest drive for the thirty-five-hour week. The White House, too, was opposed, for fear that such a work week would inflate costs and prices.

In New York City, an impressive army lined up against Van Arsdale. The city's chamber of commerce and other employer groups and the big builders put pressure on the electrical contractors with whom Van Arsdale deals not to yield. The New York press attacked the twenty-five-hour week as unconscionable.

Chief union argument for a shorter work week was that it reduces unemployment, and Van Arsdale's union, in 1962, was just about the last in America that could complain about members' idleness. Not only were they working overtime during New York's building boom, but electricians had to be imported from other cities to meet the demand. Furthermore, automation devices used by electricians are of a limited variety, and can't be said to displace workers wholesale.

But Van Arsdale wasn't thinking of his men alone. He is also president of the New York City AFL-CIO council and as such is spokesman on legislative, political and other matters for the city's 1,000,000 unionists. As a labor statesman he had brooded long about hard-core unemployment and the human cost of automation.

Unperturbed by the storm he had stirred, Van Arsdale waged an eight-day strike and won it. But being Van Arsdale, he kicked up another frontier idea to go with the twenty-five-hour week. He proposed an Office of Impartial Review to be named by New York's Mayor Robert F. Wagner, to check on labor-union practices and costs and so serve as a kind of watchdog for the public interest. The highly respected arbitrator, Theodore H. Kheel, was named to head the Review Office.

Reporting on the twenty-five-hour week, some ten months after it began, Kheel noted that Van Arsdale's union had worked harder than ever to reduce labor costs, and had taken new steps to reduce overtime. Except for the period between July and September, when union members take vacations and so increase the overtime of those who remain on the job, Kheel reported that "The twenty-five-hour week has not had the drastic effects [in boosting costs] predicted for it."

Van Arsdale compares a union leader's calling with that of a clergyman. He lives no better than his members and does not count the hours he puts in for his flock. Van Arsdale's pay for a seven-day week is little more than the $170 his rank-and-filers earn for a five-day week, although his members are willing to pay him more. His home is a modest cottage he helped his father, an electrician's union member for fifty years, to build.

Van Arsdale's day begins at 8 A.M. when he shows up at construction sites to ferret out loafers. It ends at the union near midnight. But wherever Van Arsdale is, the wheels are spinning inside his head.

Many of Van Arsdale's innovations have helped win security for his men that he never had in his own childhood. His men had pensions, free dental care and medical check-ups years before the rise of welfare funds and fringe benefits. They were the first building trades men to get paid vacations. Van Arsdale asked the employers to form a pioneering Joint Industry Board of the Electrical Industry to administer welfare funds. Union men and bosses on the board took to calling themselves "The Team."

Employers vied with union men to advance new ideas. Out of it came low-cost apartments for Local 3 members, financed from pension funds. When Van Arsdale suggested a convalescent home for union members, the Team borrowed from its pension funds again to buy a three-hundred-acre Long Island estate. The sixty-room mansion had been empty for years and required a basement-to-attic cleaning and outfitting. An employer took over the job.

Once the cradle-to-the-grave security of his men was assured, Van Arsdale turned his innovating to education, both for his members and for his members' children.

Members take a week's course to stimulate interest in reading and thinking at the union's Long Island estate. The union pays the members $140 for a week's expenses. The Team foots the tuition and maintenance charges. Van Arsdale feels that the introduction to education has so helped members think better and get along better with people that he dreams of another innovation: a full-fledged, union-sponsored university. Meanwhile, he keeps after his members to take advantage of New York as a "City of Noble Culture" and to visit museums and libraries and Shakespeare productions in Central Park.

One Van Arsdale innovation brought no benefits to his members, and in fact cost them money. This was Van Arsdale's decision some years ago to extend the powerful hand of his union to workers in subsistence-wage factories. Van Arsdale sent his organizers into factories making electrical components where wages often were the minimum under the federal law. Some of these nonelectrician members earn less than $1.50 an hour; Local No. 3 charges them no dues, but give them protection and leadership.

CHAPTER 3

The Union That
Automation Built

Joseph A. Beirne, a quiet man who heads the country's newest major union—the Communications (telephone) Workers of America—could paraphrase Shakespeare. "Out of this nettle, automation," Beirne might say, "we pluck this flower, a strong union."[1]

For, of all union leaders, Beirne is the one to whom automation has been a boon, not a bane. The insecurity it created among American Telephone & Telegraph Company employees as far back as two decades ago gave Beirne's then fledgling union something special to do. By being one of the first union leaders to work closely with an employer to retrain, transfer or otherwise stave off wholesale automation dismissals, and by learning how to organize white-collar workers, Beirne created militant unionists out of middle-class-minded women telephone operators. With telephone maintenance technicians and clerical workers, he battled the biggest employer in the world, the A.T. & T. system, to build a union 300,000 strong. Out of its unique experience with an employer who pioneered in automation, the Communications Workers of America emerged as the union which other unions may have to copy to survive. Its leader, Joe Beirne, in turn, has achieved influence that reaches beyond his own union.

For a year he talked on a hundred-radio-station hookup on

[1] What Shakespeare's Hotspur said: "Out of this nettle, danger, we pluck this flower, safety."

9

problems ranging from aiding Latin America to the unions' role in helping productivity. He has written a book, *New Horizons for American Labor,* to launch a "dialogue that will get labor moving." Increasingly, his name crops up among the two or three presidents of international unions who are mentioned as potential successors to AFL-CIO president, George Meany.

To understand CWA's significance as a bellwether union, it is necessary to look for a moment at the employers with whom it deals. The Bell system of telephone operating companies, stretching from Maine to California, has been described as one vast, sensitive computer. From the Bell Telephone laboratories came the transistor and the circuits that paved the way for the computer and much of modern electronics. In the late twenties, the Bell system made the fateful decision to change from manual to dial telephones, thus plunging into automation years before the word had even been invented. Telephone workers were the first, then, to feel automation's impact. In the decade from 1947 to 1957, the number of Bell system telephones almost doubled (from 28,500,000 to 52,300,-000), yet the increase in employees needed to service the 83 percent rise in telephones was only 17 percent!

Actually, telephone operator jobs declined. But gains in maintenance and clerical openings led to a small net increase in Bell system jobs.

As uncertainty clouded telephone operators' jobs, they turned to the CWA for protection. Joe Beirne and his union developed a working arrangement with Bell system companies in which the company would give the union confidential notice, as much as three years in advance, that new, automated equipment was planned for for a specific community. Thus when dial telephones supplanted manual operation in one Chicago suburb, the union studied the list of 482 affected operators, checked their backgrounds to see who among them was capable of being retrained, who would accept new assignments in other communities. With the union playing this kind of role, almost one-third of the operators won new jobs in the Bell system. Others chose to retire or take termination pay. Those who felt they had grievances could appeal to the union.

The mechanical nature of the telephone operator's job gave Beirne's union a further opportunity to attract members.

"When we began organizing," Beirne recalls, "the telephone operator had to work under a disciplinary system a slave would object to. The operator had to sit in rigidly prescribed manner, without any rest periods in the morning. She had to memorize seventy-five different responses and give these back automatically to telephone customers, while a supervisor listened in on her conversation to check up on her.

"We wanted to know why telephone operators broke down, and why they had to go to rest homes to recuperate," Beirne recalls.

In time, the CWA won morning "breaks" for the telephone operators. For those working on night shifts, the union achieved working weeks as low as twenty-eight hours.

Yet to attract members, the CWA had to do more than merely minister to employee grievances. Most of the operators, as well as many of the linemen and other telephone service technicians, harbored middle-class suspicions of unions. To attract them, Joe Beirne had to make the CWA respectable and responsible.

Beirne took ads in the local newspapers to explain to small townsfolk—normally hostile to unions—that CWA members were "their brothers and sisters," whose improved welfare was bound to help everybody in the community. But most of all, Beirne's CWA never lost a chance to show a community that it was an organization that cared for its own. Once when a telephone company refused to give a pregnant telephone operator maternity leave, the CWA local hired an ambulance to stand by in the street outside the telephone office—suitably placarded to show the union's concern.

When the union scandals erupted in the late 1950's, Beirne waged his own crusade against James R. Hoffa. Union leaders generally fear to tangle with the Teamster president, because of his power to hurt or help in a strike. Beirne, however, urged the AFL-CIO to form a new Teamsters union to lure Hoffa's members away.

The outraged Hoffa retaliated by raiding Beirne's CWA locals, urging Beirne's members to defect to the Teamsters, which, he said, had the union muscle to deal with the country's biggest corporation. In one attempt to woo away a Western Electric maintenance local affiliated with Beirne's CWA Hoffa spent $750,000 (in vain).

Ironically, despite its quest for respectability, the CWA has had to wage bitter strikes, some accompanied by considerable damage to company property, to establish itself.

A.T. & T. system companies encouraged company unions to stave off independent unionization. And when these defected wholesale to the CWA, the A.T. & T. system companies signed contracts. But, so the union charged, they resorted to grudging bargaining, or no bargaining at all.

Thus, in 1947, a decade after other big unions had established themselves in steel, autos and other industries, the CWA was waging a national strike, which it described as a fight for its life. Strikes against telephone companies in West Virginia, Indiana and elsewhere continued into 1955, when CWA members laid so effective a siege on supervisory personnel who were operating telephones in a West Virginia office that food had to be dropped to them by helicopter. Some fifty thousand CWA members were involved in the strike against Southern Bell Telephone. Here destruction of company property was so widespread that the CWA, disclaiming any responsibility, nevertheless paid the telephone company $3,500,000 in an out-of-court settlement.

In these strikes, Beirne faced one of automation's biggest posers: how does a union achieve bargaining power when it can't shut the boss down with a strike?

"Although our people went off the job in the 1955 strike," Beirne recalls, "the company's automated system went on working hour after hour, day after day. Local calls went through. Most long distance calls went through. Striking was like throwing a rock at the Queen Mary as she sailed down the harbor."

Yet CWA won many of its demands. Beirne accomplished this with a new kind of union bargaining power: community good will.

As a public utility, a telephone company is highly sensitive to community opinion—and to that of the state legislature and state public service commission that regulates it and sets its rates. Telephone companies work hard, then, to earn a reputation as good citizens. They select employees who will be courteous on the telephone and who, as repairmen, can be trusted in customers' living rooms—and even in their bedrooms. Job candidates are screened with FBI thoroughness; character and home life are looked into. (In southern Florida, a telephone company personnel man, checking one lady applicant, was met at her door by her boy friend—clad in shorts. P.S.: she didn't get the job.)

Telephone company employees are thus among the most respected people in town. They enjoy status. Neighbors seek their opinions. Starting with such human material, Joe Beirne worked hard to outdo the public relations-conscious telephone companies. Under his prodding, CWA members became the busiest joiners and doers of good works in the 800-odd towns where the union has locals. A recent check of CWA members turned up half a dozen mayors, scores of city councilmen and members of state legislatures. Beirne sets the pace as a vice president of the United Community Funds and Councils of America.

If such pillars of the community go on strike, the manager of the local bank may ask his friend, the local telephone company manager, why some of his bank's best customers are on a picket line. Neighbors are likely to show sympathy. During the 1955 strike, CWA women members recall, "little old ladies with tears in their eyes would approach us on the picket line and press dollar bills into our hands." Food merchants and restaurants supplied coffee and sandwiches for the pickets, and city commissions passed resolutions supporting the union.

Both sides seem to have shown a greater respect for each other after this strike. Collective bargaining in the telephone industry, as Beirne put it, "became a conversation between equal forces."

Stabilization of relations with Bell system companies is about the only stable fact about CWA life, for the union is in a constant turmoil of change. For one thing, some 20 to 30 percent of the Bell system work force changes yearly as women leave to get married or have babies. So CWA has to organize like mad, draw in a vast stream of new faces yearly, merely to stand still. Then, too, the character of union membership is changing drastically. In 1945, switchboard operators constituted 52 percent of the Bell system work force, but by 1958 this had dwindled to 32 percent. Higher-paid craftsmen and technicians, on the other hand, increased to such an extent that today there are more men than women in CWA. The union thus has become an industrial union (which, by defini-tion, organizes everybody in a plant or an industry) composed to a large extent of skilled craftsmen and technicians who ordinarily belong to a craft union.

Joe Beirne has had to live with change, then, and to think hard about change. He has thus become an important spokesman for change in the labor movement: for change to new organizing methods, for new slogans, for new union services to members and to communities. He has even suggested a new kind of peace-keeping relationship between union and boss.

Big nations, argues Beirne, no longer put armies in the field to test each other's strength. Now they play war games on a computer, putting all the facts of their own and their adversary's power into the computer and letting the machine tell them who won the war. He urges employers and unions to do the same, and make demands and concessions accordingly.

CHAPTER 4

Dave McDonald
Has a Plan

David J. McDonald, the sixty-one-year-old, still photogenic president of the United Steelworkers of America, is a union leader whom other leaders not long ago might have voted as "the man least likely to succeed."

Unlike virtually every other president of an international union, McDonald did not come up from a "job in the plant" and an apprenticeship in local union politics. He started as a stenographer for Philip Murray, then a vice president of the United Mine Workers. (McDonald remained with Murray when he became head of the Steelworkers.) For years, McDonald couldn't make up his mind whether to be a union leader or an actor.

Although he heads a union melting pot of Negroes, Hungarians, Poles, Irish and other plain folk, McDonald affects a studied, custom-tailored garb, a theatrical air and a turgid rhetoric, and so probably has less communication with his members than any other national union leader. In fact, he spends much of the year at a home in posh Palm Springs, California, just about as far away from the big steel plants and union halls as one can get.

Because of his union's size—it is the country's second biggest with 1,152,000 members—McDonald is entitled to an important voice in the counsels of Labor. So McDonald is a vice president of the AFL-CIO, a member of its top Executive Council and of the Council's executive committee. But McDonald's is a quiet voice.

Yet, for all that, McDonald's Steelworkers union has been a leader among big unions in devising important firsts for accommodating to change.

In the Long Range Sharing Plan, negotiated with the Kaiser Steel Company, the Steelworkers union has been the first in a manufacturing industry to come up with a contract that guarantees that no man shall lose his job because of the introduction of new machinery.

The Steelworkers have broken ground, too, with a Human Relations Committee composed of union representatives and steel executives which supplements contract negotiations with a nonstop talk fest and unhurried search for solutions to automation problems. Lastly, the Steelworkers have won thirteen-week vacations with pay, once every five years, for long-term employees.

For these solid achievements, good marks must go to McDonald and to the brilliant "thinking men" on his staff. One was Arthur J. Goldberg, lawyer and negotiator for the Steelworkers before he became Secretary of Labor and, later, a Justice of the U.S. Supreme Court. Goldberg's mantle as "brain" for the Steelworkers has since largely fallen to the union's able economist, Marvin J. Miller.

At the end of the bitter steel strike of 1959, the first big test of strength over featherbedding, Edgar Kaiser, chairman of the Kaiser Steel Company, had a talk with Arthur Goldberg, then the Steelworkers' lawyer.

"There must be some better way, Arthur, to work things out," Kaiser said.

"Let's form a long-range committee," Goldberg suggested. "And let's put some public members on it."

It took almost three years for company and union, with public member guidance, to come up with a plan that was to come to grips with automation firings and share the benefits of more efficient operation with the worker. This was the "Long Range Sharing Plan."

At the cement and glass union hall of the Kaiser Steel Company Steelworkers local at Fontana, California, I listened one night as union leaders explained the plan to suspicious members. Some four hundred union members had come, some in their Sunday best, many with their wives. All hung on every word.

"What's there in it for us?" one steelworker shouted.

Union Economist Marvin Miller, a chief architect of the plan, assured the men, "You have had no protection against technological change. Now you have it. That's what's so important about this plan. No one goes out the gate [gets fired] because of a new machine."

"But doesn't anyone get laid off?"

"When times are bad, yes. Because of automation, no. If a new machine cuts out a man's job, he's shifted to an employment reserve. His pay and seniority stay the same. As soon as a job opens elsewhere in the plant, he's shifted to it, even if the company has to train him. We don't expect new machines to displace men faster than attrition shrinks the work force. But even if it does, *no one's going to lose his job.*"

Miller also explained how the company shared with the men when more efficient operation brought savings.

The next day, in a plantwide union election, the men voted three-to-one to accept the plan.

(P.S. The first monthly cost savings bonus, paid in March, 1964, yielded an average of $26 for each of the four thousand eligible employees.)

McDonald's automation security and sharing arrangement with the Kaiser Steel Company has as yet found no takers among other steel producers. But the Human Relations Committee not only has become part of the labor-management machinery of the entire steel industry; it is being copied in other industries as well.

The Human Relations Committee, too, like the Kaiser Long Range Sharing Plan, was born as the result of a "Never again" vow, taken after the 1959 steel strike.

It was clear from that disaster that some kind of hot line would have to be set up between employers and union to keep them in touch with each other between the periodic confrontations known as contract negotiations. It was no longer possible to maintain a silent aloofness for two or three years, then seek to settle, within the space of a month or so, such vexing new problems as the size of work crews, the boss's right to trim forces without consulting the union, the length of the work week.

Nothing less than a permanent summit meeting to exchange opinions, dig out facts on which solutions could be based, would do.

The tableau of togetherness that union and management members of the committee present at their sessions would startle anyone who remembers the once bloody union organizing struggles in the industry.

Side by side at the head of the conference table sit the two co-chairmen: for the union, Steelworkers President McDonald, pipe in hand, his sparkling platinum-gray hair parted and brushed impeccably; for the eleven steel companies, R. Conrad Cooper, executive vice president of U.S. Steel, long of leg and face, chomping on a cigar.

Below the summiteers on opposite sides of the table are three industry men and five union men.

Traditionally, union and management meet on neutral ground, neither in a union hall nor in a company's executive suite. But the Human Relations Committee meets in the skyscraper offices of the U.S. Steel Corporation in Pittsburgh. The meeting room is narrow with walls of paneled gray steel, with steel chairs to match. It is a severe room, suggesting that emotional tantrums, common to contract negotiations, are out of place here.

In fact, if any emotion is to be shown, it can be shown by only one person at a time. Such are the rules of this summit game. If tempers flare between two conferees, they are adjured to "remember the spirit of 4024"—the number of the room in which they meet. The spirit is one of informality. Nothing that one conferee says at one moment will be held against him if he changes his mind and says something different the next. A union man may support an industry man's argument or vice versa. Nothing said inside 4024 will get out, to embarrass a conferee with his colleagues, whether in the union or in a company.

While the summit group meets periodically—there have been some fifty meetings in forty-two months—subcommittees charged with special missions, the study of medical plan costs, for instance, meet almost continuously. Six broad areas are under constant exploration, among them wage incentives, training, what work a foreman or outside contractor can do.

Because of the nonstop explorations of the Human Relations Committee, many problems were so well in hand by the time contract negotiating time came around early in 1963 that a contract was signed with time to spare before the expiration of the old. It was an exhilarating change from the breakdown of the negotiations four years before.

Permanent peace-keeping machinery similar to the Human Relations Committee has spread to automobiles, rubber, clothing, meat-packing, electrical manufacture. Automation, posing a survival challenge to unions and employers alike, is bringing some of them closer together than ever before.

CHAPTER 5

Hurrah for the Gray
White and Blue!

For years, James A. Suffridge, the tall, handsome and carefully groomed president of the Retail Clerks International Association, has toiled in one of labor's less rewarding vineyards: the white-collar folk who mind the nation's stores.

Then, presto! Along with the automation revolution came a technological upheaval in retailing which operated with a reverse twist. The new distribution factories known as supermarkets and discount houses displaced the white-collar salesperson with a gray-collar-type goods handler and checker—who does blue-collar work.

Since the gray collar is easier to organize than the white, Jim Suffridge's Retail Clerks have become the wonder and the envy of the labor world. While automation causes other leaders to wonder where their next union member is coming from, Jim Suffridge has upped his membership 25 percent in the last four years alone to 400,000. Unlike other giants like the Steelworkers and the Auto Workers, who have largely exhausted the possibilities of their jurisdictions, the Retail Clerks have only begun to tap theirs. Jim Suffridge's organizers talk of a union of two million, which would make it the nation's biggest.

To achieve this goal, the Retail Clerks plow back about thirty cents of every dues dollar on organizing. The methods are suitable to the Retail Clerks' role as a union of the future. The Retail Clerks cultivated public goodwill with TV commercials on the

"Today" network program, and with radio commercials on a network radio show. Once, during a city-wide attempt to organize department store workers in Milwaukee, Wisconsin, the union tried a "saturation" campaign, flooding the town with billboard and streetcar ads, with television and radio sales pitches.

Yet organizing isn't easy, even among the new gray-collar workers, and the Retail Workers have to fight for new members. One reason is that retailing, perhaps more than any other business area, is infested by a species of middleman who is a throwback to the "union busters" of pre-Wagner Act days. These provide a variety of espionage and other services to fight union organization, and—when all else fails—serve as go-betweens to bring in a crooked union leader who will make a sweetheart contract with store owners.

To cope with conditions created by such go-betweens (see Chapter 14, "The Corrupters"), the Retail Clerks have developed countermeasures, among them a *Devil's Dictionary,* in which the devil, of course, is the boss who uses unfair labor practices. Starting with "A" for Arbitrariness—"When the employer dictates working conditions and rates of pay as he pleases"—the dictionary goes on to "B" for Brainwashing, "C" for Coercion and so on. In this "dictionary," "M" is for Money—defined as "A medium of exchange in plentiful supply among customers and employers, but in short supply among store workers." The dictionary is suitably illustrated with cartoon caricatures to make its points. As a number of victorious struggles with big league department stores have proved, the employer who hires antiunion specialists to fight the Retail Clerks is in for a long war with a tenacious and resourceful opponent.

As a union that accentuates organizing, it is natural that the Retail Clerks should have an exhaustive manual of instruction for organizers. In launching a new discount house the store owner races to build and stock his store so as to get goods moving and money working in the shortest possible time. The most hectic part of the race may involve the new work force. Some employers seek to sign them up hurriedly into company unions or into compliant independent unions. So, on the store's opening day, Suffridge's organizers have had to buttonhole new store employees as they leave the bus that brings them to work, then sign them into the union as they walk the short distance to the store. All as directed in the organizers' manual.

The Clerks' sales pitch can be attractive, for the union can show some impressive collective bargaining gains, particularly in fringe benefits. If you are a member of the Retail Clerks Los Angeles local, for instance, you need never worry about a doctor or hospital bill for yourself or family. The employer contributes to a hospital plan that pays for everything—including psychiatric care!

Because of his burgeoning power base (membership), and the respectability of his union, Suffridge is a rising power in labor. Suffridge is a vice president of the AFL-CIO and as such sits on the Executive Council, where, until now, he has bided his time, saying little, except to follow the leadership of George Meany. But he obviously has a future. His face is seen whenever a handful of top union presidents confer at the White House or participate in some law-signing ceremonial with the President. When President Lyndon B. Johnson, then Vice President, made a foreign goodwill trip, Jim Suffridge was the labor leader whom the late President Kennedy tapped to go along with him.

Suffridge has developed a close friendship with George Meany, who likes to refer to the younger man as "My Jimmy." Suffridge lives at North Arlington, Virginia, not far from Meany's home at Bethesda, Maryland. They play golf together, visit at each other's homes and are together at parties, such as on New Year's Eve.

It is traditional that union leaders, particularly presidents of a federation, like the AFL-CIO, don't retire, but die in harness. George Meany is no exception, and it is an open secret that he intends to hold his office, knowing that his retirement would precipitate a knockdown and drag-out fight for the succession. While Walter Reuther was once regarded as the logical successor to Meany, he is now given only an outside chance because of the bitterness created inside the Federation over jurisdictional struggles between the old AF of L and the old CIO unions.

Jim Suffridge, who has not been involved in the jurisdictional struggle, is regarded as a man who would be acceptable to both wings of the merged Federation.

When the Retail Clerks' convention voted in 1963 to give Suffridge the title of president emeritus should he wish to retire, the move inevitably stirred conjecture that preparations were being made for Suffridge to step up to an AF of L post—probably that of secretary-treasurer—where he would be in a strategic position ultimately to succeed George Meany.

The gossip might have been premature, but it indicated that Jim Suffridge is a man of increasing importance in Labor.

CHAPTER 6

George Meany:
Plumber with His
Finger in the Dike

When George Meany, president of the AFL-CIO, was named a delegate to the United Nations in 1957, one of the first things he did on reaching the UN Headquarters on New York City's East River was to head for the building's subbasement.

There, in the maintenance men's locker room, Meany shook hands all around with electricians, plumbers, carpenters, and said, "I guess you're wondering what a Bronx plumber is doing upstairs instead of down here?"

The question as to what (and how) ex-plumber George Meany is "doing upstairs" has been asked with increasing wonder in and out of the unions ever since Meany moved "upstairs" to the AF of L presidency in 1952—and immediately exploded with massive energy all over the union map. The wonder didn't arise because of Meany's humble origin; most every labor leader begins modestly, is self-taught and self-made. It was because there was little in Meany's past on which to predict a brilliant or crusading future. He was already fifty-six when he took over the leadership of the AF of L, an age when men have dreamed their dreams and leave the making and shaking of new worlds to younger men. Meany, besides, had evolved from that section of the Labor movement—the building trades unions—where corruption was extensive. And,

24

although honest himself, Meany, on the face of it, had been the typical New York labor politician, saying nothing and doing nothing about the corruption that sent key union bosses, including a friend, to jail.

For fourteen years, George Meany—as secretary-treasurer of the old AF of L—was frustrated by President William L. Green, who, the older he got, the more he delighted in keeping responsibility from the younger man. Only the leaders at the Federation summit could see occasional flashes of the leadership that was to emerge later.

Many veteran observers, sizing up Meany, were dubious.

"Why doesn't Meany denounce union racketeers?" one writer asked nine years before Meany became AF of L president. "If some people hope that he is just biding his time waiting to be president before undertaking to delouse the Federation's unions, they're going to be disappointed," the writer predicted.

If there was any union idealism in George Meany, it lay locked inside him, behind the casual grammar and West Side New Yorkese in which he expressed himself. To some, he was the perfect embodiment of the AF of L bureaucrat, who would go along with the Federation's essential philosophy: what the bosses of the constituent unions did was their own business.

Yet, in five turbulent years, Meany made history. He united the AF of L and CIO, so creating a merged Federation of 131 unions with 13,500,000 members. He created the image of a moral union movement. He turned the unions into a major unofficial force that fights Communism on a world-wide front.

When Anastas Mikoyan, the Russian deputy premier, visited here early in 1959, he asked to see the American "union trade center"—the AFL-CIO headquarters. Arrived at the new $4,000,-000 structure, a stone's throw from the White House, Mikoyan pressed his nose like a little boy against the cold glass of a lobby door and peered inside. This was as close as he, or any other Soviet official, could get to the AFL-CIO. None has yet been invited in. To George Meany, Soviet unions are not bona fide labor organizations, but instruments of the Communist party.

Meany is the human hinge on which virtually every recent crucial event in the Labor movement has turned and must continue to turn. These have not only involved the fight on corruption. Although merged, the craft unions of the old AF of L and the industrial unions of the CIO were locked in a subterranean struggle for empire—who shall organize whom—that threatened the very life of the Federation. It has been Meany's Solomon-like job to make and keep the peace.

Sam Gompers founded the unions; John L. Lewis mushroomed them from a minority to a major force in American life. George Meany united them and made of them the social conscience of the country: a force in the struggle for Negro rights and against poverty. Under Meany the unions enjoy greater influence than ever before. He drops over to the White House for chats with President Johnson—who says that Meany is a man to whom he listens. Meany is a guest at virtually every White House state dinner.

The tools Gompers used were a scholar's intellect and a diplomat's wiles. John L. Lewis had the grand manner of the leader who stirs the multitudes. George Meany has the strength to make the lonely decisions.

When George Meany lowers his 230-pound bulk into the president's chair at the great oval table around which the AFL-CIO's Executive Council meets, he—more than any other of the leaders—looks the part of a laboring man.

Jacob S. Potofsky of the Amalgamated Clothing Workers, sensitive-faced, handsomely bearded and fond of walking canes and homburg hats, could easily pass for a professor of medicine. David McDonald of the Steelworkers, with his wavy platinum hair, finely chiseled nose with flaring nostrils, looks an aging matinee idol. George M. Harrison, conservatively tailored and self-assured, is a picture of the big business executive (which is not far wrong, for his Railway Clerks union pays him $61,700 yearly for his services).

But there is no mistaking the onetime journeyman plumber in

massive George Meany. The great neck that's too big for the biggest standard-sized collar; the large bald head; the snub-nosed Irish face with the mouth turned down belligerently, from which a ten-cent cigar protrudes; the great, meaty hands. Put them all together, and they spell Mr. Labor.

Meany looks like a rock and is a rock. He is incapable of, and indifferent to, subtleties. For him, it is all truth, and to hell with the consequences.

Once in Washington, French officials wined and dined Meany while plying him with sweetly reasonable arguments that the French colonial policy in North Africa was good for the natives.

"Any questions, Monsieur Meany?" his hosts asked when the brandy was being served. "Only one," said "Monsieur" Meany in his gravelly New York accent. "When are you going to stop kicking the Algerians around?"

Much has been made of Meany's bluntness. It is a clue to inner resources and a fierce independence which may even border on contempt of what others think. Even if one of the others happens to be the President of the United States.

When labor leaders called on President Harry Truman during the Korean War to protest the minor role they had been given in the mobilization agencies, the President promised that he would do something about it.

Both the late William Green, as president of the AF of L, and the late Philip Murray, as head of the CIO, said that was good enough for them. Then Meany spoke up from in back of the room.

"That doesn't take care of it, Mr. President," he said. "The trouble is there's not enough responsibility in the agencies themselves—they're run by businessmen."

Somewhere along the way, Meany acquired the feeling that the best one to rely on is yourself. So he has played the role of loner. This breaks every rule of politics, including labor politics, where a man has to develop friends, a coterie, a following on his way up. Instead, Meany told off the men who had his future in their hands. He is one of the few men who stood up to the formidable

John L. Lewis. The picture of these two massive-faced, bulldog
men glaring at each other was a memorable one, but it was Lewis
who retreated.

Lewis had proposed that labor leaders refuse to sign the Taft-
Hartley non-Communist affidavit and so defy and defeat the Act.
None dared take him on, until Meany rose. He began by accusing
Lewis of palship with "stinking America haters who love Mos-
cow." Said Meany, "I'm prepared to sign a non-Communist affida-
vit. I'm prepared to sign an affidavit that I was never a comrade
of the comrades." Lewis (a lifelong Republican) never forgave
Meany.

Meany, when secretary-treasurer of the old AF of L, so antago-
nized Boss Dan Tobin of the Teamsters that Tobin, riled, sought to
make George Harrison of the Railway Clerks president—rather
than Meany. Harrison refused to go along, and so Meany made it
anyway.

Today, as head of the Federation, Meany is still the loner. An
aide has said, "George doesn't build power. He is a power himself."
Another president might build a personal political machine and
have a corps of press agents to build him up. Meany has no
personal machine, no bloc of unions on which he can rely during
a showdown in the Executive Council. And no press agents.

Having no personal machine, Meany doesn't count noses on an
issue in advance of a Council meeting. He lays the biggest problems
on the table without advance warning—and bulls through his point
of view.

Much of the credit the unions today enjoy for fighting the racketeers stems from Meany's blunt, black and white, no-compromise
decisions.

When Meany threw the gangster-infiltrated Longshoremen's
Union out of the old AF of L, an aide brought Meany a message
from the late Tony Anastasia, boss of the Brooklyn dockers, and
brother of the late Albert Anastasia, onetime head of Murder, Inc.

"Let me and my local come back into the AF of L," said Tony, "and I'll drive out the gangsters in the rest of the union."

"O.K.," said Meany. "We'll let Tony Anastasia's local back in. But he can't come with it." Tony's local—and Tony—stayed out.

But the bluntness which helps save the good name of the Labor movement is hard on the men around Meany.

Although union men talk of "solidarity" and call each other "brother," there's a curious lack of manners among the labor leaders, and little or no compassion for each other. During the early days of the merger, Executive Council meetings often left bruised feelings and sometimes came close to leaving bruised heads.

There was a good deal of rancor between George Meany and Walter Reuther. Once, Meany—who can be brutal—startled Labor's elders by shouting at Reuther, "I don't trust you."

Reuther was so shaken by this that he considered resigning his AFL-CIO vice-presidency, but friends talked him out of it.

Another time, Meany and big Joseph Curran of the National Maritime Union indulged in a cold and unsmiling exchange of insults in which Meany shouted "Liar!" at Curran.

"If you were fifteen years younger," the ham-fisted Joe Curran stormed, "I'd climb over this table and beat the hell out of you."

Troubled Elders

When Meany failed to arrive for the first day of the Executive Council meeting at Puerto Rico in early 1959, Walter Reuther won initial support for a pet project: a march on Washington to dramatize unemployment.

George Harrison bitterly opposed the scheme as a leftist tactic. Bested by Reuther, he took his troubles to Bill Schnitzler, the AFL-CIO's secretary-treasurer. Schnitzler, ex-head of the Bakers Union, is a jolly man, more given to making peace than to stirring up storms. But he had his own personal gripe against Reuther and the CIO faction. That morning—with Meany absent—Jim Carey and Walter Reuther had upset the usual seating arrangements at Execu-

tive Council meetings. To Schnitzler, it was as if the CIO faction
were symbolically taking over the Federation while Meany was still
president.

George Harrison, too, like Schnitzler, is an equable man, and has
often conciliated warring Federation factions. Now peacemakers
Schnitzler and Harrison hastened to the airport to meet Meany as
he flew in from Washington and to stir him up with tales of the
morning's doings.

Strained feelings exploded with a bang at the next day's Executive Council meeting.

"You little bastard," Meany shouted at one vice president. "I've
leaned over backwards to be fair!" Then Meany turned to Reuther,
and the two men went at it hammer and tongs over Reuther's
march on Washington plan. Here Meany won, and the scheme was
modified.

Executive Council meetings have become quiet and even gentle-
manly affairs. For one thing, Meany's hold on the united Federation is now so strong that few leaders from old CIO care to tangle
with him as they once did. Too, the old divisive jurisdictional
struggles have abated. Furthermore, automation's erosion of factory
jobs tends to draw the union leaders together into a common,
frustrated brotherhood.

One labor historian has compared the solid Meany to a fullback
who is good for five yards with every plunge. But to Meany's critics,
the time has passed for bowling over opposition. In the face of the
new unemployment problem, imagination and vision are needed.

Meany's aggressiveness and inflexibility get him into trouble as
an administrator, too.

As president of the AFL-CIO, Meany is somewhat of an
employer himself, bossing a staff of seven hundred economists,
editors, clerical workers and others. These include some one hundred union organizers who help unions affiliated with the Federation. When these organizers wanted to form their own union and
bargain with the boss, i.e., George Meany, the Federation president
reacted like some of the employers he'd often excoriated. Meany

argued that his organizers were "part of management" and shouldn't have a union. He was accused of discriminating against ringleaders and was dragged reluctantly before the National Labor Relations Board where a pro-union vote by his employees forced him to accept and bargain in good faith with a union.

To his rugged qualities Meany adds a muscular mind of surprising intellectual power—surprising because of the casual grammar in which his ideas are sometimes couched. In the midst of a skilled exposition of an international problem, for instance, Meany will say, "I'll tell you what he done."

Meany owns a flypaper memory which seems incapable of letting go a name, a time, a fact. "When I got my plumber's apprentice papers on January 17, 1917," Meany will reminisce in the most matter-of-fact way. This gift Meany has used to store his mind with a scholar's knowledge of union history. Meany is, in fact, one of the best-read men in Labor. He likes to reveal that he's read every speech Sam Gompers, the founder of the AF of L, ever made, which means thousands of speeches.

With the passion of a Ph.D. researcher, Meany has made his way through the massive archives of the Federation, absorbing in punishing detail the published discussion of problems now forgotten, by labor elders long dead. The facts that Meany has mined he uses effectively in a type of speech-making that is strictly his own. Meany's talks consist of incisive, jabbing sentences and are free of any flourish or oratorical side.

When Meany was negotiating the AFL merger with the CIO, Walter Reuther made a long, opening statement of principles that had his listeners shifting in their seats. Meany, in his turn, took only four sentences to get to the heart of the merger problem. They were:

"We can go after unity the long way or the short way. The short way is to merge into one trade union center which will protect the integrity of all affiliates. The long way is to solve all of our problems before merging. Which will it be?"

When delegates to the AFL-CIO Atlantic City convention of

1957 debated the expulsion of the Bakers Union, Meany asked for the floor with his usual modest introduction: "I'd like to say a few words." It was the end of a grueling convention day. Yet Meany, hoarse with weariness, talked for forty-five minutes without a note, drawing on memory to marshal the facts that crushed all opposition to the expulsion move. To those who were seeing Meany in action for the first time, it was an astounding intellectual feat.

"George Meany is a new man," one witness marveled. "He's like a moth emerging from a chrysalis"—a shorthand reference to Meany's evolution from Plumbers' business agent to labor statesman.

Away from the official labor world, Meany is oddly warm and sensitive. It is as if he puts on a gruff mask while acting the role of top Laborite and takes it off at home or with his friends. One aide believes that the real Meany is shy and insecure, assuming an aggressive posture to hide this.

In private conversation, the unofficial Meany will put his big paw on his listener's arm—warm Latin style—to establish closer communication. He loves companionship and will lose himself happily for hours in a game of gin rummy—preferably with his old friend and counselor, Dave Dubinsky of the Garment Workers. Unlike the ascetic Walter Reuther or the all-work-and-no-play George Harrison, Meany manages to move mountains of work—but lives the good life, too, on his forty-five-thousand-dollar yearly salary. He is a diligent trencherman, as his Falstaffian girth proves. And, with his magnet memory, it is a cinch for him to be an expert on place-names and years of vintage wines. As a graduate of the old AF of L, whose leaders treated themselves well, Meany sees nothing wrong in the leisure pastimes of the upper-middle class. He plays golf in the low eighties. But propriety dictates that he doesn't go across the road from his Bethesda, Maryland, home to play. For the golf course there is the Burning Tree Club where high Republicans disport.

Meany used to play the piano, something he learned to do, like his vast reading, in his own undisciplined way. When agreement was reached on merging the AFL and CIO, the elated Meany descended on the grand piano in the hotel lobby and there belted out several choruses of the lilting French tune *"La Seine."* In recent years Meany has taken to playing an electric organ in his home. And lately he has taken to painting—mostly landscapes which remind one of Grandma Moses.

The Meany household used to be a lively place when his three daughters were home. But now Meany and his wife, the former Eugenia McMahon, whom he met when she was a Garment Center worker and member of the International Ladies Garment Workers Union, are rarely home nights. For the Meanys are among the most sought-after guests at diplomatic and other Washington social functions.

"I'm Not Bragging About It"

Cynics inside Labor like to see in Meany's early New York career a "past" that he is living down today. And it is true that the labor world that produced George Meany was not one that on the face of it would produce a labor reformer.

Meany was born in 1894 into a stanchly union family in the Harlem section of West Side New York, then middle class. His father, Mike Meany, a chunky plumber foreman, headed the second biggest local (three thousand men) of the United Association of Journeymen and Apprentices of the Plumbing and Pipe Fitting Industry of the U.S. and Canada—the Plumbers Union to you and me.

Young Meany, known as "Brother" to his family and the kids on the block, parted company with formal book learning at the first year of high school and, after several jobs, turned to plumbing. The husky George was a good enough athlete to earn $7.50 to $10 a Sunday as catcher for a semi-pro team. He was also a serious fellow who pledged himself at confirmation not to drink until he was twenty-one—and the strength this gave to his will lasted the rest of his life, for he still drinks sparingly.

At twenty-two, Meany, a full-fledged journeyman plumber, worked on such big jobs as Grand Central Station and the Commodore Hotel, to care for his widowed mother and seven brothers and sisters. But, sad to say, he was the sort of union member he today deplores. During his first two years in the union, Meany went to no meetings. When he did take an interest in the local, fellow dues payers recognized in "Mike Meany's boy" the leadership qualities they had seen in the father, and elected George business agent. So, at twenty-eight, Meany put away his Stillson wrench and pipe fittings and took up the trade he was to follow the rest of his life: that of union civil servant or labor politician.

Meany's own local, as he revealed with his usual unsparing candor later,[2] "was a closed union, closed in the fact that it didn't take in any new members. It would supply plumbers "only to our own contractors"—who, in turn, belonged to a closed employers' association that barred other contractors from work.

"We even went so far," Meany said, "that we wouldn't take clearance [transfer cards] . . . and so shut out union members of our own craft from other cities."

"I am not bragging about it. I am not proud of it." said Meany. "That was what we did thirty-five or forty years ago."

Deals in which the union polices and protects the employers' monopoly over contracts in the area (by withholding labor from outsiders) usually mean graft for the union official. And, while there was never a hint of scandal about George Meany, the fact remains that he was part of, and remained discreetly silent about, a system that invited corruption and exploded, from time to time, in sensational scandals.

The notorious Pier Carpenter boss, Robert P. Brindell, went to prison for extortion the year before George Meany became a Plumbers' business agent in 1922. "Brindellism" became a generic term for widespread building trades corruption. Later, the equally notorious Joe Fay of the Operating Engineers, whose members

---

[2] In a speech to the Building and Construction Trades Department of the AFL-CIO, at Atlantic City, December, 1957.

drive heavy earth-moving equipment, went to Sing Sing Prison in a $400,000 extortion that rocked the country.

In the middle thirties, when Meany had advanced to the presidency of the New York State Federation of Labor, he played golf with Fay and later said that Fay was "a nice guy to be with—except when he got drunk." Yet Fay had other important friends besides Meany. One Fay buddy was the New Jersey gangster boss, Longy Zwillman. In fact, in his day Fay was the underworld's back door to the unions. When a mild antiracketeering resolution was introduced at the AF of L convention of 1940, Fay caught up later with the busybody who introduced it—David Dubinsky of the Garment Workers—and sought to beat him up.

The assault became page-one news. Yet Meany raised no protest, sent no solacing word to Dubinsky—which caused Dubinsky more anguish than the blows, for he stayed away from the next year's AF of L convention in protest. And when Joe Fay went to jail, George Meany went to visit him.

The labor boss who dominated the New York City scene when Meany was coming up the labor politics ladder in the thirties was Joe Ryan, president of the International Longshoremen's Association, who left the Labor movement in disgrace later. Ryan, in 1934, was head of the powerful New York City Central Labor Trades Council, and so had the delegate strength to influence State Federation conventions. For that reason, Meany critics such as John L. Lewis like to assert with satisfaction that "Joe Ryan made George Meany president of the New York Federation of Labor."

These are the bare facts of Meany's early rise. If left to stand by themselves, they could provide a dramatic contrast between an early, discreetly silent Meany and the reformer he later turned out to be.

But, as always in life, the picture is a mixed one.

For instance:

Young Meany's Plumbers local was no better in its dealings with employers than it should be. But, internally, it was a clean and democratic union. When Meany came to Wednesday night meetings, the union hall chairs would be lined with mimeographed sheets giving the local's monthly expenditures for paper towels, drinking cups, stamps, officials' wages and expenses. There were yearly elections, and candidates lined up before the ballot boxes where the voting dues payers could look them over and question them—and where, I suppose, the office seeker could keep an eye on the voting.

Concerning his friendship with Joe Fay, George Meany once was asked, "Is it valid to compare your visit to Joe Fay in prison with Harry Truman's controversial trip to Kansas City for Boss Tom Pendergast's funeral?"

"No, it isn't," Meany shot back. "Truman owed his early rise to Pendergast. I owed nothing to Joe Fay."

As for his relations with Joe Ryan of the Longshoremen, soon after he (Meany) became president of the New York State Federation, he tangled with Ryan over the mayoralty election in New York City and forced Ryan to quit his post as head of the New York City Central Trades Council. If Meany had any obligations to Joe Ryan, he didn't show it.

Ryan, as a supporter of the old, corrupt Tammany Hall political machine, had backed its Democratic candidate for Mayor. Meany worked for the election of the reform candidate Fiorello La Guardia —so breaking with the old-line labor leaders.

At Albany, as a State Labor Federation official, Meany worked with and came under the influence of the New Deal liberals who had been swept into power by the Roosevelt landslides of 1932 and 1936. An important part of Meany's job was that of lobbyist. He established a record of 141 bills passed. Meany's friendship with the then Governor, Herbert H. Lehman, helped. So did his skill in marshaling facts and driving them home before legislative committees.

An old friend summed up Meany's New York career:

"Sure, he came from the building trades. That was his world, and he spoke for it. But he also lived and worked in the liberal New York climate. He had a ringside seat at the pioneering work of such progressive unions as the Garment Workers and Amalgamated

Clothing Workers, with their cooperative housing and medical plans.

"George doesn't show he's absorbing anything," his friend went on. "So, in some ways, he was like Franklin Roosevelt, who didn't shine as a Governor.

"Meany didn't show much as head of the State Federation. But once he got to be president of the AF of L, and had responsibility —then you saw you had before you a man!"

George Meany became the third president of the American Federation of Labor in late 1952. William Green, his predecessor, had clung to the presidency until his death at age eighty-four; he had sat like a mountain on all notions for change, and the House of Labor was in disrepair. Meany, as new head of the House, had several urgent tasks. Racketeering termites had gotten into the foundations. More urgent still was the need to end the twenty-year war with a rival house, the CIO.

To end this civil war meant negotiating with Walter Reuther, who had just been elected president of the CIO. Meany and Reuther had sized each other up for the first time at a labor dinner back in 1949. Fellow labor leaders, observing them, began to make book as to who would emerge as top man on the labor totem pole.

The two men were different in temperament and in union background. Yet when they met in 1953 to talk merger, there was a bond between them. They needed each other. Reuther had only a shaky hold on the CIO, and there were threats of secession by big member unions. Meany could wait and pick up the pieces into the AF of L, or he could make an honorable peace. Meany chose a merger of equals.

Into the new Federation's constitution were written some new ground rules which member unions had to observe. These bore the fancy title of Ethical Practice Codes, but some of the language bore Meany's blunt stamp: "No person should hold or retain office in the

AFL-CIO or in any of the affiliated unions who is commonly known as a crook or racketeer."

To cleanse the unions, Meany had to purge his own mind of the union beliefs of a lifetime. Meany had grown up with the belief that a union is a voluntary organization like a lodge or a church. It was bred into his bones, too, that the Federation had no right to reach into and interfere with the internal affairs of its member unions.

Meany had to change the beliefs of his colleagues on the Executive Council, too. Many of these were aging men, well over sixty— a time of life when men aren't eager for change. Harry Bates of the Bricklayers was seventy-five. George Harrison was sixty-two. Others, younger, might not take kindly to change either. Maurice Hutcheson, president of the 800,000-man Carpenters, had inherited his union and a million-dollar fortune from his father, the late Big Bill Hutcheson, and was soon to be indicted in a land scandal.

Yet Meany won two crucial tests involving revolutionary change.

First, Meany proposed that union officers who took refuge in the Fifth Amendment, to conceal possible union skulduggery, should be booted from their jobs. This was a radical invasion by the Federation of member union self-rule. Yet all except one Council member voted with Meany. The nay, prophetically, came from Dave Beck, the Teamster boss. When Beck pleaded the Fifth Amendment before a Senate committe soon after, Meany promptly called a special Council meeting and ousted him as AFL-CIO vice president.

Several months later Meany asked the Council to suspend the Teamsters—as a prelude to their expulsion at the coming convention.

It was a bitter ordeal for Meany and for the Council members.

Cutting away the then 1,500,000-member union—which paid $1,000,000 of taxes into the AFL-CIO yearly—meant putting asunder the union empire Meany himself had joined together. The Council members, fearing union civil war, sought a face-saving device that would keep the Teamsters in. Al Hayes, president of the

Machinists and head of the Ethical Practices Committee, checked up with his own officials and found them two to one against suspension.

On the eve of the meeting, Meany could be sure of only one vote to suspend. His own. But the Council backed him.

George Meany's cleansing operation—by an odd twist of history —came none too soon. The unions were entering a period of wrenching change in which they would need every resource of public goodwill. A new industrial revolution threatens to shrink the unions' size and influence, unless George Meany and other leaders find a way out.

Early in 1959, as the recession began to wane, it became clear that despite booming production hundreds of thousands of laid-off workers would never get their jobs back again.

Goods were being produced with less human effort. Electronic brains, directing mechanical muscles—automation—were taking the place of the unskilled wage earner.

He was being replaced in part by engineers, technicians, computer clerks—white-collar technical and professional workers.

The character of the work force was changing. To labor leaders, this historic shift is a nightmare. For fully 85 percent of the 17,500,000-odd members of unions are blue-collar wage earners.

Every year, some 1,400,000 persons pour into the country's work force. To maintain their relative position of influence, the unions have to recruit new members just to stand still.

That is why "Organize the unorganized" has been the key slogan of the unions. Until now the organizing was done chiefly among blue-collar workers. Now it must be done among workers who have resisted unionism—among white-collar and professional employees.

The picture of plumber Meany with his finger in the dike—holding back a sea of union troubles—is not an exaggerated one.

CHAPTER 7

The Hoffa Phenomenon, Part 1: Dead End Kid with a Plus

The Teamsters Union—more formally, the International Brotherhood of Teamsters, Chauffeurs, Warehousemen and Helpers of America—is Big Brother to all the unions. Not only is it the biggest —some 1,500,000 strong at the last count—but, with its power over deliveries, the Teamsters can make or break the organizing drives and strikes of other unions. Some, like the Laundry Workers, have depended on the Teamsters for their very lives.

In fact, the Teamsters Union is a labor federation all by itself, a vast catch-all whose constitution claims virtually everything that some other union hasn't nailed down, and much that it has.[1]

Today, only one-third of the Teamsters are drivers. The man who wrestles crates in a warehouse is a Teamster, and so is the girl who works in a mattress factory. Brewery workers wear Teamster union buttons, and so do girls who pound typewriters. Dairy farmers and dairy workers are Teamsters also. Store clerks? Gas station attendants? Jukebox repairmen? They may be Teamsters, too.

[1] An excerpt: "This organization has jurisdiction over all teamsters, chauffeurs, warehousemen and helpers; . . . all classes of dairy employes; brewery and soft drink workers; workers . . . in ice cream plants; all other workers employed in manufacturing, sales and distribution of food, milk, dairy and other products; all cannery workers; *and other workers where the security of the bargaining position of the above . . . requires the organization of such other workers.*" (Emphasis mine.)

40

The man who heads the Teamster empire is one of the Labor movement's biggest wheels. Indeed, the hand that rules the Teamsters can rock the nation. This hand is the hand of James Riddle Hoffa.

For three weeks, during the summer of 1958, Senators bombarded Jim Hoffa with questions as to why he didn't get rid of the criminals in his union. But it seemed to me as I watched Hoffa that the Senators couldn't establish communication with him. The Senators and Hoffa were men from two different worlds.

"Have you checked up on business agent Joe Mug who took bribes from employers?" a Senator would demand.

"Yes, I've checked up on him," Hoffa would reply.

"What did you find out?"

"I found out he didn't do it."

"How did you find this out?"

"I asked Joe, and he denied it."

Was Hoffa a supercynic? Or did he have the scale of values and moral outlook of the underworld?

I have sometimes felt in following the career of a Frank Costello or an Albert Anastasia that these were atavistic throwbacks to an earlier tooth-and-claw time where men had not yet developed— inside their heads—the governor over their actions that is known today as conscience.

Could this explain Hoffa, too?

It is hard for Hoffa to understand, for instance, that a man's actions may spring from other motives than the desire to make a quick buck.

For years, Hoffa referred to Walter Reuther and his dedicated Auto Workers across town in Detroit as "them squares from Milwaukee Avenue."

"Jimmy thinks every man has a price," a friend has said of him. And Hoffa's first close brush with disaster stemmed from a McClellan Committee investigator's charge that Hoffa had hired him to pry out committee secrets. (Hoffa, tried, was acquitted.)

There is, finally, within Hoffa the seeming underworld solidarity with those who are in trouble with the cops. A lamster (fugitive), an ex-convict emerging from jail, and even the fellow caught red-handed and serving time can expect union money and union jobs from Hoffa, it was testified before the McClellan Committee.

"Hoffa will always be in trouble," one observer summed it up. "Not in jail necessarily, nor even under indictment—just in trouble. This is a man at war in his heart with orthodox society. He was probably a cop-hater as a kid, and he has not changed; but the cop image has changed for him. Today it is the Senate, the courts, the press, the whole sprawling, occasionally majestic apparatus of the social order."[2]

Hoffa is, in other words, Labor's Dead End Kid.

But a Dead End Kid plus inner authority, plus an outsized drive for power and great creative organizing talent. These he has used to help make the Teamsters the big and brawny union it is today, and the Teamster one of America's highest paid unionists. So, if Hoffa is a man at war with society, he's also a man divided against himself: part legitimate trade unionist—part condoner and supporter of labor racketeers. This contradiction, packaged within one human wrapper, makes for just about the most complex and fascinating character in Labor. And not the least of Hoffa's fascinating facets is that, for his top aides, tough guy Hoffa has been helped by a coterie of once-radical intellectuals.

Face to face, Hoffa looks so boyish that everyone calls him "Jimmy." This is because of his size, a chunky five feet five inches, his disarmingly direct manner of speech and his muscular face which becomes animated and young with talk. But the face that can be engaging, as when Jimmy grins, can become glacier-cold and hard, as when Hoffa is pushed into a corner by questions. And the open blue eyes can harden into icy-cold, shiny little marbles.

[2] Eric Sevareid in a broadcast over CBS radio.

Hoffa's strength emerges at once.

Although Hoffa is usually the smallest figure in a room, he's likely to be the biggest man in it.

At an employer-Teamster conference for settling workers' grievances, I once heard the employers and the drivers state their case. Then all heads would turn expectantly to Hoffa.

"This is my decision," he'd say with finality. And, as he put it, "That's it, brother!"

When I first interviewed Hoffa in Chicago in 1955, Harold Gibbons, long his top aide, sat in. Gibbons is a Teamster power in his own right in St. Louis and is used to giving orders. Yet his demeanor toward Jimmy, who comes to his shoulder, was that of a respectful junior clerk to the senior partner of the firm.

With the inner authority goes toughness.

As a tough kid, it was testified before a Congressional committee, Hoffa lashed a rival union man across the back with chains. As a tough guy, Hoffa was still at it a few years ago, fighting it out with his fists in a street brawl that followed contract negotiations in the South.

The fist has played an important role in Hoffa's union life.

It was used, first, as a means of survival when Hoffa was a young organizer in Detroit—and had to cope with thugs hired by anti-union employers.

"Our cars were bombed out," he has said. "Somebody broke into our office and destroyed our furniture. There was only one way to survive—fight back. And we used to slug it out in the streets."

Later, the fist was used for survival of a different sort.

"Why do you keep hoodlums on the union payroll?" reporter Clark Mollenhoff asked Hoffa, referring to a local in Tennessee.

"To kick those hillbillies around and to keep them in line," Hoffa replied. (Questioned on this by Robert Kennedy, then counsel for the McClellan Committee, Hoffa would neither affirm nor deny the statement.)

When the International Association of Retail Clerks discovered that its Detroit local was dominated by Hoffa,[3] and sent an aide to the Teamster headquarters building to retrieve the records, Hoffa pointed to a hulking aide in a corner.

"See that guy? He'd just as soon shoot you as look at you," Hoffa said, according to the Retail Clerks' aide. Hoffa denied this.

Being tough, to Hoffa, also means feats of endurance of body—and mind—that lesser men could only marvel at. This Dead End Kid is no loafer.

Once, after an all-day grilling before the McClellan Committee that would have wilted another man, Hoffa flew from Washington to West Virginia for an evening meeting with a local there. That done, Hoffa boarded a plane for Detroit, arriving close to midnight to preside over a cheering rally of his home local. He then returned to Washington, winding up at 4 A.M., a working day that had started as usual at seven the morning before.

"He just ain't human," one critic cried.

As for toughness of mind and seeming nervelessness, here is what Hoffa endured, and survived, in a nine-month period that began in late 1957. He was tried twice on criminal charges and acquitted. He was haled before the Executive Council of the AFL-CIO, and was told that his union would be booted from the Federation if he, a corrupt influence, remained a power in it. (I saw Hoffa emerge from this meeting, grim-faced but hurling a defiant "No comment" at the pack of reporters that closed in on him, symbolic of a hostile world closing in for the kill.)

"How much can a man take without breaking?" an observer asked.

A good deal apparently, if that man is Hoffa. For soon after, he battled his way with equal defiance through three weeks of McClellan Committee grilling. Unperturbed, and unrested, Hoffa launched a whirlwind barnstorming campaign around the country to mend his union political fences.

Hoffa, the hard-working Dead End Kid, doesn't drink or smoke, being as abstemious as Walter Reuther in this regard. He eats

[3] Hoffa had organized the local and turned it over to a nephew to run.

modestly, concentrating on a virtually all-meat diet, and stays clear of rich desserts. He rounds out his meal with tea.

For all his dabblings in business, Hoffa doesn't seem to have accumulated many goods, nor does he care to make a splash. His clothes are store bought, and in summer he's likely to be seen in a short-sleeved shirt open at the neck, in ill-cut slacks and cheap white cotton socks. Where Hoffa's predecessor, Dave Beck, lived in a $150,000 mansion with swimming pool and private movie projection room, Hoffa lived, until he moved to Washington, in a modest brick house for which he paid $6,800 in 1939.

Beck traveled in his own private plane and junketed often abroad. The only recreation that Hoffa takes from his murderous early morning to midnight workday are two fishing and hunting trips yearly with his son, Jim, Jr. For the Dead End Kid is also a model, even sentimental family man.

Empire Builder

A friend of Hoffa's referred to him as Napoleon, noting with mock seriousness that Jimmy looks like the "Little Corporal," has his oversized drive for power and even has a wife by the name of Josephine.

Hoffa is, in fact, an empire builder of considerable proportions. The Teamsters, when Hoffa was getting started in the early thirties, had only 5 percent of the members they boast today (75,000 in 1932 as against 1,500,000 in 1963). The union embraced drivers and helpers almost exclusively. The word "warehousemen" had not even been added to the union's name. The Teamster Brotherhood consisted of isolated locals that bargained their own contracts and paid little mind to the then president, Dan Tobin.

In a quarter-century, the Teamsters Union not only mushroomed in size, but changed its character and assumed a unique power. Federal laws helped spur the Teamsters' growth. But for much in the Teamsters' reconstruction, Hoffa must be regarded as a chief architect.

Run, Jimmy, Run!

Jim Hoffa began his hard journey through life on a sentimental day—Valentine's Day, 1913. The place was Brazil, Indiana, a drab mining town and last stop of Jim's father John, a coal driller. John Hoffa had followed his trade through Kentucky and Illinois, had brought four kids into the world—then died when Jimmy was seven, leaving the brood to his widow to feed and shelter as best she could.

Hoffa's official biography has this to say:[4] "Jimmy, running barefoot, strung clam lines in the river for food, stole green apples, and shot rabbits."

Jimmy has been running ever since.

Brought to Detroit at twelve, young Hoffa left school at the seventh grade to help make ends meet—and at eighteen struck his first blow for the workingman.

His job, at thirty-two cents an hour, was to unload produce from freight cars during a night shift that began at 4:30 P.M. In between cars, young Hoffa and his friends sat out the night hours—without pay.

"We got tired being kicked around," he said later. And he organized his first union by signing up the men around him—so winning better conditions from the boss, a chain store.

Hoffa's feat so impressed union men that he was soon entrusted with a Teamster charter.

The man who controls a Teamster local is a power in Labor and in the community. For in Hoffa's own words, "Everybody fears the Teamster, and he fears him because there is no successful strike vote that a union doesn't have to come and see the Teamster business agent to help them win the strike."

The syntax may be casual, but Hoffa's words embrace a truth and a secret to power.

Soon, at nineteen, Hoffa reached for a higher rung, the leadership

[4] *The Name Is Hoffa,* published in 1956 in connection with a testimonial dinner to Hoffa.

of the Joint Detroit Teamster Council, which in those days controlled the town's three Teamster locals.

Hoffa got only four of the twenty Council delegates' votes. But he made himself president anyway. "I just went in and took over," he later boasted. Inside the Teamsters, there was a more plausible explanation. The chunky, fist-swinging kid had support behind him which even the hard-bitten Teamsters in the Joint Council had to respect.

I once asked Hoffa about reports by Detroit union men that he had taken over the Council with the help of hoodlum muscle.

"They did the same thing to me then that you're doing now," Hoffa shot back.

"What am I doing now?" I asked.

"You're trying to put me in the mob."

Mob or no mob, Hoffa knows a good idea when he sees one. Back in 1933, Hoffa watched with great interest as a union idea fought for its life. The idea, improved and expanded by Hoffa and Beck, was to change the Teamsters.

The idea belonged to a band of men who controlled Teamster Local 574 in Minneapolis, Minnesota. In the midst of a depression which had reduced union membership by 50 percent, and had the unions gasping for their lives, the brothers Vincent, Grant and Miles Dunne, and Farrell Dobbs had a vision.

The Teamsters, they felt, were destined to dominate the labor scene as trucks replaced railroads in handling freight. The dreamers already held the crucial control of truck terminals and the unloading in Minneapolis. By insisting that Minneapolis union men would not unload incoming trucks unless Teamsters were driving them, they forced truck owners outside Minneapolis to recognize and deal with the Teamsters. These newly organized union drivers could then organize other terminals—and this "leapfrogging" process could go on and on, to the greater power and glory of the Teamsters.

The Minneapolis Teamsters did something else that was new. They recruited into the union workers who weren't drivers. They signed up workers in warehouses.

Jimmy Hoffa, then in his twenties, watched, fascinated, from Detroit as the Minneapolis group expanded its domain far beyond Minneapolis.

The Dead End Kid perceived that the Teamsters there had fashioned an economic fist against which few employers could stand up. Inside this fist were the wheels that move goods and the warehouses that shelter them.

Hoffa put it this way, "If you can't take it in or out [because the Teamsters control the trucks], and if you have no place to put it [because the Teamsters control the warehouses], what are you going to do with it?"

Rather than find out, employers usually signed up.

Hoffa pushed out beyond Detroit. He organized a statewide Teamster Conference, the first of its kind. This turned the isolated Teamster locals of Michigan into a powerful mutual-assistance network. Hoffa went on to form a loose association of Teamster locals in twelve states.

Out in the Far West, another rising star in the Teamsters, Dave Beck, was also extending his influence in the Teamsters by forming a regional organization which he called the Western Conference of Teamsters. But Hoffa went one step further and so topped Beck. He invented the regional or area-wide agreement. Even under the ambitious Beck, the Teamsters bargained, at most, on a city-wide basis. Now Hoffa negotiated revolutionary single contracts embracing employers and drivers in as many as twenty-three states.

By the mid-1950's, no matter how you looked at it, Jimmy Hoffa had run far.

He could swing enough weight to elect Dave Beck president of the Teamsters and himself a vice president. He became head of the newly formed Central Conference of Teamsters—and master of 650,000 dues payers.

Hoffa was also a big man outside his union. Around him clustered a growing group of satellite unions, mostly tainted. George Meany could be the head of all organized labor, but when leaders of the Hotel and Restaurant Workers, or Laundry Workers, or

Bakery or Distillery Workers, needed organizing or strike help, they called Jimmy Hoffa. Gangsters who needed union charters to set up in labor racketeering called Hoffa, too. He became the underworld's back door to the unions—the powerful "Man to See" who could pick up the phone and order some union to do a favor for a friend —or lose Jimmy's all-important friendship.

Hoffa became a political power in Michigan. At a meeting of the state's Democratic Committee, Hoffa's lawyer and business partner, George Fitzgerald, became the National Committeeman from Michigan, with power over patronage dispensed in the state by Harry Truman's administration.[5] Hoffa ran his own man for Lieutenant Governor. Although he lost here, he contributed generously to campaigns and helped elect judges. And just as a Congressional investigation was beginning to question him where it hurt, it ended. Representative Wint Smith (Republican) of Kansas said, "Pressure came from so high that I can't even discuss it."

Then, at the height of his unique power, Hoffa was plunged into a struggle for survival.

Like a man who has incurred a debt, Hoffa was presented with a bill at a time it was most embarrassing for him to pay it. The debt was exposure. And the collectors were the journalists and the Congressional investigators who began to lift some rocks under which a curious breed of union life proliferated.

The McClellan Committee itemized eighty-two charges against Hoffa—ranging from acceptance of favors from employers to the harboring of criminals, and the protection of rackets and use of terror against members.

Under fire, Dave Beck and other offenders quit their unions. But not Hoffa. Not only did he survive, but he went on to greater power still.

Why?

The answer lies partly in Hoffa's own tough hide. It lies also in one of the strangest rescue expeditions in labor annals. To the aid

[5] For a fuller account of Hoffa, the politician, see Chapter 9: "Why They Hate Walter Reuther."

of tough guy Hoffa, in his time of need, came two intellectuals from the other side of the union movement's tracks. One was a once-dedicated Socialist who is still involved in liberal causes, Harold J. Gibbons. The other was the late Eddie Cheyfitz, who had been a Communist in his youth. As idealists, both had entered the union movement to change the world. They had the organizing and propaganda skills acquired in early leftist union days. They had ideas. And they had the understanding of men's strengths and weaknesses that they acquired as practioners of the class struggle. All these they put at the service of Hoffa to help pull him through.

Two Eggheads in Yoke for Hoffa

Gibbons is a rangy, handsome man with the thoughtful face and disciplined speech of an English professor. When the McClellan Committee questioned Gibbons about violence in St. Louis—where Gibbons is Teamster boss—his press agent handed out a mimeographed biography to reporters.

Gibbons is a "student of economics and history and the Labor movement," said the handout, and a thinker who had lectured at five universities, including Harvard.

The twenty-third child of a Pennsylvania coal miner, Gibbons came up from that part of the union movement which Hoffa most despised, the CIO part that produced Walter Reuther. A protége of Chicago Socialists, Gibbons was the vice president of the American Federation of Teachers at twenty-five, then gravitated to Sidney Hillman's Amalgamated Clothing Workers. At thirty-one he came to St. Louis, where he started with a clerks' union and wound up as head of a Teamster local under circumstances that caused Robert F. Kennedy, then counsel to the McClellan Committee, to describe Gibbons as buying his way into the Teamsters.

When the St. Louis underworld blocked Gibbons' further rise in the city-wide Joint Council of Teamsters, he took a trip to Detroit. There he met and talked with Jimmy Hoffa.

"Hoffa made a few phone calls," a friend explained later. Whom

Hoffa called and what he said are not precisely known. The gist, however, was that anyone who tangled with Gibbons would have "trouble with Hoffa." Gibbons returned to St. Louis and was soon master of all the Teamsters there.

The Hoffa-Gibbons acquaintanceship ripened. Hoffa had the shirttails on which a clinging Gibbons could ride to great Teamster power. Gibbons had the brain and propaganda savvy that could help Hoffa cope with the chain reaction of crises exploding about his ears.

So close did the two become that, during the day, Hoffa and Gibbons were continually in each other's adjoining offices in the marble Teamster headquarters in Washington. At night they shared a suite of rooms in the Woodner Hotel. Wherever Hoffa goes, in his constant travels, Gibbons is sure to go. With Hoffa, Gibbons shares all the decisions.

"Together," a friend said of Hoffa and Gibbons, "they are the International."[6]

Eddie Cheyfitz, who until his death was the other close adviser to Hoffa, had been a brilliant mathematics major at the University of Michigan and a member of the Young Communist League. He made a pilgrimage to Moscow, then returned to become a boy-wonder union leader (like Hoffa and Gibbons). He became disenchanted with Communism in his twenties, and later left union work altogether and took up the trade of counseling employers on how to deal with unions. Later, he picked up a law degree to help him with his work.

While serving Hoffa, Eddie Cheyfitz also plied a little-understood, behind-the-scenes trade. He was, as one prominent labor lawyer described it, a "channel." When employers' and unions' bargaining negotiations faltered, Eddie was the channel through which confidential compromise proposals would pass.

---

[6] In late 1963, Gibbons and several other top Hoffa aides resigned their headquarters jobs, but retained their local offices. This, apparently, anticipated Hoffa's conviction on Federal jury tampering charges several months later. Should Hoffa, now appealing an eight-year sentence, go to jail, Gibbons could spearhead a move to remove him from office.

To be a successful "channel" required wide acquaintance among labor leaders—which Eddie Cheyfitz had—and access to the Teamsters, which means Hoffa. This is how Cheyfitz came to the Teamsters:

As a onetime adviser to Eric Johnston of the Motion Picture Association, Cheyfitz was asked one day for a solution to a problem. Dave Beck, newly elected president of the Teamsters in 1952, was going to Europe and unashamedly had asked the movie industry to send along some cameramen with him to record his trip.

"Just give him the cameras, and let him take his own pictures," suggested idea man Cheyfitz. Then Cheyfitz tipped the story to columnist Victor Riesel, who had a column's worth of fun with it. When Dave Beck protested this bit of *lèse-majesté*, Cheyfitz had another idea. He called Riesel, with further material, and now another column appeared, less damaging.

This palship with newspapermen so impressed Beck that he invited Cheyfitz to come with him and be his press agent. This Cheyfitz did, managing to hold on to his employer clients as well. As Beck's good boy, Cheyfitz inevitably met Hoffa, who, impressed with Eddie's fast talk and fast thinking, took to having dinner with Cheyfitz when he came to Washington. Cheyfitz became the man to see for reporters who wanted stories from Hoffa—and for labor men who wanted favors. From Dave Beck's sinking ship, Ed Cheyfitz leaped easily to Jimmy Hoffa's bandwagon.

Hercules once had the strong man's job of cleaning out the Augean stables. Gibbons and Cheyfitz were confronted with a similarly Herculean (and redolent) task: the job of cleaning up the Teamsters and repairing Jimmy's reputation.

The surest way would have been surgery. If Hoffa would submit to cutting away the hoodlums, he'd be cleansed.

But Hoffa couldn't or wouldn't get rid of the hoodlums.

So Harold Gibbons turned instead to press-agent gimmicks. He engineered a 2,500-guest testimonial dinner for Jimmy at the Michigan Fair Grounds Coliseum. The guests came by the carload.

As a crowning piece of cynicism, the dinner had as a chairman a Chicago department store owner who had fought unions all his life.

Everything about the dinner was big. Even the menu proclaimed: "Jumbo shrimp, Colossal green olives, Mammoth ripe olives."

And there was at each table—to set matters straight about Hoffa —an authorized pamphlet biography: *The Name Is Hoffa.*

Not long after this, "the name Hoffa" appeared on a U.S. indictment charging bribery. The FBI arrested Hoffa, charging he had Senate committee documents on him. Now Hoffa needed more than respectability. He needed to stay out of jail. So to his rescue came Eddie Cheyfitz.

Shortly before his arrest, Hoffa had been a guest at a most curious dinner. Eddie Cheyfitz was the proud host in his own home. And he could indeed be proud, for he had as his other guest Washington's lion of the moment, Bob Kennedy, then counsel for the McClellan Committee.

Only in America, as Harry Golden might have put it, could there have been such contrast in guests. On one side of the table was Kennedy, just thirty-one, but looking no more than twenty-five— multimillionaire's son and product of Harvard University. Facing him was Jimmy Hoffa, also boyish at forty-four, cynical product of Detroit's streets. The two men sized each other up. Inside Hoffa's head, so he thought, was locked a secret, the secret that—so a later indictment charged—he had hired a Kennedy staff member to find out what the McClellan Committee had on Hoffa.

But the man Hoffa hired had told all to the FBI and to Kennedy. So in Bob Kennedy's head, at that very moment, raced the thought that Hoffa would soon be arrested on bribery charges.

When this came about soon after, dinner host Cheyfitz swung into action. First he procured for Hoffa the gifted Washington lawyer, Edward Bennett Williams, a courtroom strategist and spellbinder in the grand tradition of a Clarence Darrow. Cheyfitz had known Williams at Georgetown University, and had set up law offices with him.

Hoffa was tried before a jury of eight Negroes and four whites.

One spectator at the trial was ex-heavyweight Joe Louis. The Negro ex-champion followed the proceedings with conspicuous interest, and during the breathers in the trial would, just as conspicuously, chat with Hoffa. Joe Louis' Washington food and lodgings, it was testified before the McClellan Committee later, were provided by the Teamsters. Also, ads appeared in the Negro press telling of Hoffa's battles for Negro rights.

Hoffa's aides denied that they had anything to do with Joe Louis' presence in the courtroom, or with the ads in the Negro press. In any case, Hoffa was acquitted.

Soon after, Ed Cheyfitz, Harold Gibbons and Jim Hoffa sat down to ponder a momentous decision. Beck, disgraced and discredited, was on his way out as Teamster president. Now Gibbons and Cheyfitz urged Hoffa not to abandon his aim of becoming Teamster president.

Hoffa hesitated. He had already had more than his share of attention from investigators and prosecutors. The additional heat he'd attract by seeking one of the biggest jobs in American life could dwarf anything that had gone before. Could Hoffa stand the microscopic study to which his past—and present—would be subjected?

On the other hand, if Hoffa didn't gain the presidency, and some other man did, wouldn't that man have to clean Hoffa out of the Teamsters under pressure of the AFL-CIO?

Gibbons and Cheyfitz urged Hoffa to run.

It is a fascinating speculation as to whether Hoffa held another confab on this question with other, less respectable advisers. Gangsters in Detroit, Chicago and elsewhere who needed Teamster power to maintain their jukebox rackets and other business monopolies could wonder, too, whether Hoffa's election as president would attract unwelcome heat. Or whether Hoffa, as president, would assure protection against busybodies who might try to cleanse the union.

Whether Hoffa discussed these matters with underworld friends is not known.

Gibbons flew out to Chicago to organize a meeting "to get the

views of Jimmy's friends on the best course for the union to follow."
The best course, of course, was for Jimmy to run for president. This
Hoffa did in late '57. Thanks to Gibbons' savvy in organizing
Hoffa's campaign, Hoffa dominated the proceedings and was
elected president.

Cheyfitz saved Hoffa again when outraged rank-and-filers went to
court and blocked Hoffa from taking office. This time Cheyfitz came
up with a compromise. If the rank-and-filers would agree to let
Hoffa take office, provisionally, he in turn would agree to submit
to the supervision of a board of monitors.

So Hoffa became provisional president—a qualified office he held
until 1961, when the monitorship was dissolved and Hoffa was re-
elected for a five-year term.

Cheyfitz and Gibbons kept trying to make Hoffa acceptable, but
an old problem persists that even these resourceful eggheads could
not solve.

One day Ed Cheyfitz was holding forth before Gibbons and
several others, in Hoffa's hotel suite in Washington, about the need
for making at least a token clean-up.

If only one ex-criminal were to be kicked out of the Teamsters in
each of a dozen key cities, it would do wonders for Hoffa's name,
Cheyfitz was saying.

At this point, Hoffa entered the room, listened until he got the
drift of Cheyfitz' discourse, then broke into a violent tantrum.

"Who do you think you are, firing guys out of the Teamsters?"
Hoffa raged. It was clear that Hoffa could not or would not take
on the underworld.

Since Hoffa can only stop being controversial by ridding himself
of underworld influence, his tantrum meant that he couldn't stop
being controversial and stay alive.

CHAPTER 8

The Hoffa Phenomenon, Part 2: The Strange Saga of James Hoffa, Banker

The well-set-up, grim-visaged man who had come to borrow $2,400,000 would, in more conservative banking circles, have had trouble getting the money. For one thing, he was a convicted embezzler. For another, police had questioned him about gangster killings and underworld conventions.

But to Teamster President James R. Hoffa, who plays banker with millions in Teamster members' welfare and pension funds, both borrower and proposition were sound. The embezzler got the loan, thus permitting him and an associate, later indicted as a stock manipulator, to retain and bankrupt Georgia's historic General Oglethorpe Hotel. This episode, ironically, was enacted in 1959 when Congress was legislating reforms aimed largely at curbing Hoffa. It is part of a strange drama in which Hoffa has wielded an explosive power: the power to control the lending of big money.

Millions in Teamster funds have poured into the hands of Las Vegas gambling figures, some with old underworld connections, so helping them gain a grip on the business life of the city. From Los Angeles to Miami, from Las Vegas to Detroit, men trekked to Hoffa to win financial support for raceways, beer-distributing companies, funeral parlors, taxicab companies, lavish motels, real-estate developments, apartment houses and even banks. (A Miami bank, whose control was bought with Teamster fund money, now has several Teamster-designated directors on its board and so presumably increases Hoffa's money power still further.)

Many of the pension-fund loans have gone to responsible men for sound ventures: to a bishop in Miami, for example, to build a church. All the deals were secured. Yet some of them have been bizarre. And equally bizarre are the men who, with Hoffa, pass on loans—the union trustees. The fund, supposedly, is administered jointly by union and employer trustees. But Hoffa and his union trustees run the show.

One union trustee, William Presser, long linked with Midwest jukebox racketeers, went to jail for contempt of Congress for refusing to answer whether he had destroyed union records. Two other trustees appear in McClellan Committee testimony as strong-arm men who kept their members in line for Hoffa through terror or who condoned violence against employers. As already noted, Trustee Hoffa, himself, has been found guilty in one federal trial and faces another.

Joint employer-union pension and welfare funds covering union members, as in the Teamsters and other unions, command $5,000,000,000 of assets, and are expanding at the astronomical rate of a billion a year. Funds controlled by employers alone total another $55,000,000,000. Yet pension-fund administrators need tell the Labor Department little more than the names of trustees or summarize the classes of investments. They need not divulge names of borrowers unless they are parties in interest. Only if there is cause to suspect skulduggery can the Labor Department investigate. This power became effective in June, 1962. Prior to 1959 there was no federal regulation at all. Thus the way Hoffa uses his great money power has remained relatively secret.

Let's look briefly at the resources Hoffa commands.

Biggest of the Teamster funds is the Central States, Southeast and Southwest Areas Pension Fund, which covers 180,000 members in 29 states and musters $250,000,000 of assets. This fund is a self-administered one, i.e., run by its sixteen employer and union trustees, in contrast with plans administered by insurance companies. It is the Central States Pension Fund with which Hoffa has been wheeling and dealing from coast to coast. Lawyer for the fund is Stanford Clinton, who also represents the Paul Dorfman family insurance business, facts that were of interest to the McClellan Committee, which probed the huge Dorfman insurance profits.

Several patterns of lending appear. One embraces loans to the business underworld. Consider the Case of the Carpetbag Stuffed with Teamster Gold.

To Savannah, Georgia, several years ago came an entrepreneur from Akron, Ohio, whose moon-round, pleasant face belied the operator beneath. His mission was to buy the famed General Oglethorpe Hotel near Savannah. The town's citizens could not know that the Northern businessman, one Sydney Albert, was at that moment involved in stock deals with racketeer associates which were to result in his indictment as a stock manipulator.

No one paid much attention to the new ownership of the General Oglethorpe until a mortgage filed at the county courthouse disclosed that the Teamster Central States Pension Fund had lent $2,400,000 to the hotel. This aroused the curiosity of Alvah H. Chapman, Jr., publisher of two Savannah papers. Checking on the man who negotiated the loan, he found it was Larry Knohl, who ran the hotel and whose son was president. Yet the elder Knohl's name appeared nowhere. The reason soon became clear.

Knohl had an embezzlement record going back to 1938. Police questioned him in connection with the slaying of Albert Anastasia, onetime chief executioner of Murder, Inc. Even as he was propositioning Hoffa for a loan, federal sleuths were piecing together stock deals—including the alleged sale of unregistered stock in a bankrupt company—that were to lead to Knohl's indictment on stock-fraud charges.

Knohl and company soon failed to meet loan payments. The

Teamster pension fund took over the General Oglethorpe, thus giving Banker Hoffa still another role, that of hotel operator.

Las Vegas, where big-name gangsters hiding behind fronts are deeply entrenched in many gambling casinos, seems to have allure for Hoffa. Here, as far as can be determined, has gone the biggest chunk of Teamster fund money—16 percent of all secured loans. The transactions are spelled out in part in public records involving three chief corporations: Star Investment Company, the 3-0-1 Corporation and A & M Enterprises. The names of officers read like a page from the Kefauver investigation into organized crime.

Key officer is the vinegary-faced Morris "Moe" Dalitz, described in Senate testimony as a onetime bootlegger and gambling-rackets figure who found refuge in Las Vegas. Dalitz, a principal owner of the famed Desert Inn, also shares in the ownership of the Stardust across the way—whose vice president admitted to the Nevada Tax Commission that he had been closely associated with an important member of the Capone gang.

Dalitz, described by a McClellan Committee witness as "a man about the country," once was in the racket-ridden Detroit linen-supply business and knew the man to see to fix a threatened Teamster strike. Dalitz knew the man to see, too, when he and his casino associates needed $3,050,000 for Las Vegas enterprises—to build a golf course, buy a downtown building and expand a privately owned hospital.

Associated with Dalitz in these deals is Israel Alderman, who was one of a group involved in the Flamingo Hotel after its founder, gangster Bugsy Siegel, was murdered. He was also associated in the Riviera Hotel with the ill-fated Gus Greenbaum, who was found, with his wife, trussed up and butchered like a steer. Among these Hoffa borrowers, too, is Allard Roen, a Dalitz associate in the Desert Inn, who pleaded guilty to stock fraud.

With Ed Levinson, who operates the Fremont Hotel and the Horse Shoe Casino—Las Vegas' biggest downtown gambling places—Moe Dalitz and others sought to acquire the Riviera Hotel and weld a giant gambling chain. The Nevada Gaming Commission interceded to block the deal. But Levinson found another way to expand. With a $4,000,000 bank loan later assigned to the Teamster fund, he built a fourteen-story addition to the Fremont Hotel that will make it one of the biggest gambling emporiums in the world.

When a Hoffa crony is the beneficiary of a Teamster fund loan, the reporter must follow a tangled trail to track the borrower down. When search at Las Vegas revealed a $255,000 loan to an Ardmore Leasing Corporation, with the privilege to borrow up to $500,000, an investigator checked on the company's records at the state capital, Carson City. He drew a blank. The officers were obscure, nor was it clear what the company did.

But in Los Angeles the reporter found the missing piece of the puzzle. Had the Los Angeles police who keep tabs on Las Vegas heard of an Ardmore Leasing Corporation? They had. According to Captain James Hamilton, then head of the intelligence unit, Ardmore was the company that had just taken over the Checker Cab business in Las Vegas. Its manager? Homer L. Woxburg. Now the Ardmore Leasing Corporation loan had meaning. For Woxburg once headed a Teamster Los Angeles local. He was Hoffa's spokesman in eleven states and had played a key role in swinging delegates to Hoffa in the Teamster election of 1957. Woxburg was half-owner of the Ardmore Corporation which had received the loan from the Teamster fund, although his name nowhere appeared.

Like a zigzag thread through the Hoffa banking saga runs the career of a go-between, Benjamin Dranow. A chunky man, Dranow was given to natty attire and fast talk, except when he faced the McClellan Committee. Until mail, bankruptcy and tax fraud convictions slowed him up, Dranow's money affairs were so complicated that he required ten bank accounts to handle them. He appeared first as a borrower, winning Hoffa's approval for a $1,200,000 loan for a Minneapolis department store he was running. The department store went bankrupt and Dranow briefly disappeared with more than $100,000, which led to his conviction on bankruptcy fraud charges. Next Dranow popped up as the man who took over the shambles of Hoffa's Sun Valley, Florida, land scheme, serving behind a front as head of the company that acquired the bankrupt project.

Dranow was found behind a front again, according to McClellan Committee testimony, in a scheme to acquire four planes that had been sold as surplus by the government. Certain that they could obtain Teamster fund money to swing the deal, some pals of Hoffa's, including Nunzio "Babe" Triscaro, the convicted robber who is No. 2 Teamster in Ohio, shuttled between Cleveland, Miami and the Caribbean trying to sell the planes to Castro. When several involved in the deal were seized soon after on charges of conspiring to sell arms and a plane illegally to the Dominican Republic, and when McClellan's investigators got hold of the story, the loan authorization from Hoffa and the union trustees was withdrawn "on a legal technicality."

Where were the employer trustees of the Central States Pension Fund when these big sums were going to men in whose hands money could only be the root of more evil?

Two of these trustees were important borrowers from the fund they were helping to administer. Some objected to the kind of loans Hoffa was approving. But an employer who deals with Hoffa at the bargaining table can't afford to cross him. So some trustees just stayed away from meetings, thus assuring Hoffa and union trustees majority control. Others voted against some loans but were in the minority.

It was largely because of the scandals swirling about Hoffa and the Teamsters that Congress passed the Landrum-Griffin Act of 1959, requiring detailed disclosure of union finances. As the full story of Hoffa's pension-fund dealings is unraveled, there may be more pressure for detailed disclosure of pension-fund investments as well.

What's Going to Happen to Hoffa?

Hoffa at fifty-one was a man halfway up a mountain peak. In early 1964 he achieved a nationwide bargaining agreement with truck operators which permitted him to halt truck wheels from coast to coast. Along with this grand design for power there was another, as we've seen: the construction by Hoffa of a towering money edifice which would put in his hands the control of billions of dollars.

But as Hoffa reached for high prizes, a double abyss yawned below. Already convicted of jury tampering (under appeal as this is written), Hoffa, in May, 1964, was on trial again, this time on pension fraud charges. And in the wings, inside Hoffa's own union, powerful adversaries were plotting his destruction.

Some of Hoffa's closest aides, as we've seen, resigned their headquarters jobs, apparently certain that Hoffa ultimately would go to jail—so precipitating a fight for the succession. Other adversaries have moved to block the use of Teamster funds to defend Hoffa. Hoffa's appeal on the jury-tampering conviction may not run its course until late 1965. Should Hoffa go to jail then, an attempt to oust him via a two-thirds majority vote of the Teamsters' Executive Board might not be far behind.

CHAPTER 9

Why They Hate
Walter Reuther

When Walter P. Reuther was a member of a thirteen-man Detroit
Auto Workers' local in 1936, fellow members voted to send him to
the first convention of the United Automobile Workers at South
Bend, Indiana. But how would he get there? The brothers voted to
turn the entire contents of the local treasury over to the twenty-
nine-year-old Reuther.

"Whereupon," as Reuther likes to recall, "the secretary-treasurer, a lady, opened her purse and turned over the money to me. It
was a five-dollar bill."

Today, as president of the United Automobile, Aircraft & Agri-
cultural Implement Workers of America, Walter Reuther commands a union with a net worth of $55,000,000. In the bank, for
strike defense purposes alone, the union has another $37,000,000.
Reuther works out of a $6,000,000 headquarters, Solidarity
House, in Detroit. He approves $4,000,000 loans to build hospital
annexes. And the union has money to spare to build its own college for training union staff people.

All this wealth doesn't make Reuther particularly happy.

"Ideals get tarnished quickly under the corrosion of material
prosperity," he says.

What does make Reuther happy about the UAW is the powerhouse it has become. For the UAW, 1,136,000 strong, is one of

the country's three biggest unions.[1] And a union leader is as strong, usually, as his power base—his membership.

Reuther has cultivated power all his life. He has a surer sense of power and more skill in manipulating it than any other leader. He doesn't want this power in the sordid sense—to line his pockets. McClellan Committee accountants, combing the UAW (at the national headquarters level), found the union belligerently honest. Reuther wants power as a lever of reform and regards his union power base as a launching pad for explosive ideas both at the bargaining table and away from it. For he is a reformer of almost Messianic intensity. He wants to save the country. He wants to save the Labor movement—to give it an ideology, a social mission, a goal. "No one should be in the Labor movement unless he's tied to a cause," Reuther told me.

So, with the mighty Auto Workers at his back, Walter Reuther is forever a man on a beachhead, storming some industrial or political rampart.

Being Walter Reuther, he's a man of many beachheads.

As Walter Reuther, labor leader, he was the first to win paid vacations and pensions for industrial workers in the mass industries —plus what now comes mighty close to being a guaranteed annual wage.

As Walter Reuther, politician, he has been the first to use his union manpower to build a county political machine—so powerful that it helped to revive the Democratic party of his home state, Michigan.

As Walter Reuther, public figure and idea man, he argues before Congressional committees for laws to police corporation prices. He has plans for saving India, for solving inflation, for abolishing unemployment—and for a hundred-billion-dollar scheme to make the planet prosperous—and non-Communist.

With all this, Walter Reuther has created a public image of him-

---

[1] The Labor Department's *Directory of National and International Labor Unions in the U.S.* for 1961 lists the Teamsters with 1,484,000 and the Steelworkers with 1,152,000.

self that is only part union leader. He is one of the few labor leaders who has captured the public imagination.

Being out front, he stirs bitter feelings.

A Day with Walter Reuther

First thing Reuther opens his eyes on in the morning is a view from a picture window of a tumbling stream and a pond. Both the room and the view tell of a man who's improving his world—even in his spare time. For both the room and the pond were built by Reuther.

When police advised him to take security measures after gangsters almost shot his left arm away in an attempt to kill him in 1948, Reuther bought a small house and four acres of land outside Detroit, for which he paid $10,000. When doctors advised him to exercise his injured arm and hand, he took to cabinetmaking, and as a onetime skilled toolmaker was soon filling his house with floor-to-ceiling bookcases, with tables and hi-fi cabinets.[2] But, being Reuther, he went on to build whole rooms as well, getting assists from friends as needed. So the house that started out modestly with living room, kitchen and one bedroom grew into a rambling glass and redwood structure with two additional bedrooms, a sun porch and TV room—all carpentered by Reuther. And on the grounds, with the help of friends, he dug his pond.

As Reuther begins his day, he is likely to have three or four dogs yipping at his heels—among them a canine of indeterminate origin which Reuther's daughter, Linda, brought home and dubbed "Soapy," because on the dog's chest is a mark reminiscent of the bow ties worn by "Soapy" Williams, former Governor of Michigan.

Reuther shares the dogs, and the home, with his wife May, a former schoolteacher, and with their daughters, Linda and Lisa.

An abstemious man who neither drinks nor smokes, Reuther

---

[2] As further therapy Reuther has lately taken to tennis and, at fifty-seven, charges about a court with the same passion he devotes to labor statesmanship.

makes no vice of food either, taking a breakfast of toast, tea and fruit. Later he'll nibble on some fruit or a hamburger at his desk for lunch, dictating or conferring at the same time. So, in effect, he has but one full meal a day.

When the notoriety concerning Dave Beck's high living and $150,000 mansion made all labor leaders self-conscious about the way they live, Reuther invited reporters to visit his home, to scotch rumors that he lived on a luxurious estate. The reporters explored Reuther's "do-it-yourself" home, made small talk with a surprisingly relaxed and warm Reuther, gobbled May Reuther's cooking and were asked only one thing in return. Would they keep a closely guarded secret—the location of Reuther's place? Would they say, merely, that it is thirty-five miles northwest of Detroit?

To get to his car for the hour drive to his Detroit office, Reuther must cross a small bridge across the trout stream that makes an island of his home. "I'm the only union leader who lives behind a moat," he quips.

A path soon brings Reuther to another bridge, and another small island, and from there across a wide expanse of lawn to a small security house at the gate of a ten-foot-high steel fence. Two German shepherd dogs who roam the grounds at night frolic around Reuther as he greets the armed guard at the gate and enters his car.

For a year after the assassination attempt, Reuther was driven to work in an armored limousine at the suggestion of Secret Service experts, who pointed out that the most likely place for another ambush might be Reuther's daily traveled route to his office. But Reuther balked at the idea of a labor leader riding in a limousine even to protect his life and gave up the armored car for the medium-priced autos his union rents for its staff.

Reuther's discomfort in the limousine underlies a rejection of conspicuous consumption so stern as to border on the fanatic. Although Reuther's old salary of $18,000 was but a fraction of the $50,000 and more paid to other union presidents, he stoutly resisted an increase until his vice presidents complained his wage was holding down theirs. He then consented glumly to a $4,000-a-year boost to $22,000. His yearly salary today is $24,040—about one-third that of Jim Hoffa.

Reuther made a public show of his distaste for the AFL-CIO Executive Council's habit of holding its winter meetings at plush Miami Beach, Florida. He'd fly down there in a cut-rate overnight airplane coach flight. He would squeeze his own orange juice for breakfast in his hotel room, then for dinner would take May Reuther and the kids several blocks down the street to a cafeteria that featured a $1.70 special.

This conspicuous underconsumption didn't increase Reuther's popularity with fellow unionists. And when Reuther's constant beefing against meeting at Miami Beach precipitated a full-dress heated Executive Council debate, even Reuther's old friend, David Dubinsky, took after him. Even a laborer's leader is worthy of his hire, Dubinsky remonstrated. But Reuther, ever effective, had his way. (P.S. Reuther or no Reuther, Labor's foxy elders took their 1963 winter meeting to sunny Bal Harbour, Florida.)

Reuther drives to his office with one of three bodyguards. These unsmiling young men are quietly on hand, nearby, wherever Reuther happens to be. If you call on Reuther at his hotel room, a guard will probably open the door. If you walk down the street with Reuther, one or two of the young men will walk along behind. Even when Reuther is locked in secret bargaining sessions with auto executives, a guard is outside—usually playing poker with the waiting reporters, his gun tucked handily inside his pants belt.

As Reuther's car enters the driveway to the United Auto Workers' headquarters on the Detroit River in Detroit, Reuther might muse on the mutability of things. His UAW, which began by meeting secretly in a basement, is now housed in a striking three-story tile and glass structure—with a penthouse for executives' meetings. Called Solidarity House, it rests on land that once was Edsel Ford's estate. In fact, the UAW now uses as a health center the graystone mansion in which Edsel Ford was born.

Reuther enters this businesslike headquarters that houses five hundred executives, technicians and clerical workers who provide the manifold services a giant union gives to its members.

Like a big corporation, the UAW has legal, auditing and purchasing departments, community and public relations staffs. But
Reuther's union has departments that corporations—and many
other unions—don't have. There is the political action department
that turns members into voters and party workers. And, as you
might expect of a union run by Reuther, there is a "special projects" office—a kind of "forward planning" department headed by
a "brain" who could be called a vice president in charge of
thinking.[3]

Reuther's paneled office, the size of a large living room, has a
wall-to-wall picture window, just as his bedroom has. Through it,
from behind the oversized conference table-desk of his own design,
Reuther can look out on a majestic oak on the lawn that once was
Edsel Ford's, and beyond that to the Detroit River and Canada.[4]

Close up, Reuther, now past fifty, has the look and bounce of a
man in his vigorous thirties. That is because time has neither
thinned nor dulled the vivid thatch of hair that won Reuther his
nickname, "the redhead." His slight, trim figure (he's about five
feet seven inches tall) shows no sign of middle-age spread. And his
fine-featured face lights up with youthful excitement when Reuther
talks—which is a good deal of the time.

I saw Reuther soon after he had endured some thirty-eight hours
of almost continuous bargaining with the Ford Motor Company.
Yet, with only a few hours of sleep, his hazel eyes sparkled, and,
when he was carried away by some point he was making, he'd tuck
one foot under him in his chair, like a boy. Reuther's fresh and
youthful appearance is furthered by a meticulous neatness, a her-
itage of orderliness bequeathed by his Teutonic parents.

Reuther may be as "controversial" as John L. Lewis was, but
cartoonists won't have the holiday with him that they did with

---

[3] Nat Weinberg, the economist who holds this post, is no elected vice
president, but a staff man with the title "Director of Special Projects."

[4] Ford family real estate has an odd way of turning up in union hands. In
New York City David Dubinsky of the Garment Workers occupies the office
once used by Edsel Ford.

Lewis' brooding face and bulldog dewlaps. For how can you caricature the perpetual clean-cut all-American boy who didn't miss a Sunday school session in seven years?

For two decades now, Reuther has been called a "young labor leader," and you have a feeling as you watch him that he'll still be called a "youthful union leader" when he's sixty.

Reuther's press aide, Frank Winn, had said, "Walter can give you an hour."

But Walter, launched on talk, forgets his own time strictures. Talk is the vice-free Walter Reuther's one great indulgence, his meat and drink. "Ask Walter what time it is," a friend quipped, "and he'll tell you how to put together a watch."

Although Reuther is a stimulating conversationalist and effective platform performer ("What an amazing, stimulating fellow he is," India's Nehru said of him), his enthusiasm sometimes leads him into punishing verbosity. When he was elected president of the old CIO in 1952, he rewarded his brother delegates with two hours of lofty rhetoric that almost put them to sleep. Neither time nor place can deter Reuther. Although it was 3 A.M., and his own negotiators as well as those of Ford were heavy-lidded and emotionally spent as the end of the 1958 contract negotiations approached, Reuther launched on an hour's sermon concerning "bargaining attitudes."

"I reached them philosophically," Reuther reported happily later. It may have been a coincidence, but right after Reuther's predawn philosophizing the negotiators took a five-hour respite.

Reuther's answers to questions are studded with phrases which, in another man, might seem self-conscious. "The human family without a cause deteriorates," he'll say. Or: "Are the new frontiers more TV sets for people? Or should people have a sense of self-fulfillment?"

Yet Reuther gets these off with such eagerness and warmth that there is nothing ponderous about them. And in his office are reminders to visitors that the talk about causes is backed by deeds. In the bookshelf behind him are plaques and medals. One

honors Reuther's successful fight to open up job opportunities for
Negroes. Imbedded in a bookend, of his own make, is a tear-gas
shell that was fired into the auto plant which Reuther commanded
and held during the sitdown strikes.

Reuther's desk also reminds the visitor that Reuther, who deals
with some of the world's biggest managements, is a manager of
considerable proportions himself. A panel of six push buttons con-
nects him with four executive assistants and two elected subordinates. The latter, elected with Reuther at the union's biennial
conventions, are part of the union hierarchy whom rank-and-filers
half fondly and half suspiciously call "porkchoppers"—union pay-
rollers. In the brawling UAW, the politicking has been so turbulent
that few of the union's early porkchoppers have survived in office.

One exception, besides Reuther, is the union's jolly, round-faced
secretary-treasurer, Emil Mazey. A onetime Hungarian fiddler,
Mazey achieved UAW immortality when he was thrown bodily
from a plant he was trying to organize—and, picking himself up off
his back, shouted, "I'll be back, you sons of bitches. I'll be back
and organize this plant."

Mazey not only kept his word but had the shrewd sense to tie
his union fortunes to those of Reuther, then only a factional leader.

Reuther and Mazey share Solidarity House's executive suite with
the thoughtful, bespectacled Leonard Woodcock. Educated in
England, Woodcock, for years, was Reuther's executive assistant,
a nonelective staff job. Then, he ran for local office and quickly
rose to be vice president in charge of the General Motors Department—the No. 2 spot in the union.

As an executive, Reuther is an "involver." A cautious and
calculating man, despite his glibness, he involves his subordinates
in talk fests that test ideas and plans. Before Reuther took the
stand to answer McClellan Committee questions concerning the
UAW's three-year strike against Kohler of Kohler (Wisconsin),
Reuther's executive assistant, Jack Conway, spent hours digesting
prior committee testimony. Reuther, briefed with this material,
then spent three hours testing ideas and notions on Conway, who

has done graduate work in sociology at two universities, and on his Washington lawyer, Joseph Rauh, who specializes in civil rights cases, and his press man, Frank Winn.

The intellectual candlepower available to Reuther, through staff technicians and elected subordinates, is regarded by union men as among the brightest in Labor.

Concerning Walter Reuther, Politician

Walter Reuther was catapulted into practical politics because of a strange problem of coexistence. He shared the same home base, Detroit, with another great labor power—James R. Hoffa. The inevitable clash took the form of a subterranean struggle which turned the UAW into a county political boss, reshaped the politics of a state and made Walter Reuther an important political figure.

"Candidates for office in this town can't win unless they have the endorsement of the Auto Workers," a Detroit judge told me.

"They'd get down on their knees and kiss Walter Reuther's feet on the steps of the City Hall to get it," the judge said.

This is because Walter Reuther and the Auto Workers have built in Wayne County, which embraces Detroit and suburbs, a political machine at which a professional politician might marvel. A political war between Reuther (and allies) and Hoffa brought it about.

In 1948, Hoffa, contributing Teamster funds, made a power grab for the Democratic party machinery of the state, then in such disrepair that Michigan was virtually a one-party, Republican state. First, Hoffa captured the state Democratic Committee at a stormy meeting. Hoffa's lawyer and partner in deals later probed by the Senate was named National Democratic Committeeman for the state. This was George Fitzgerald. The coup gave Hoffa a voice over federal patronage in Michigan, then valuable because the Democrats were in power in Washington. Another Hoffa lawyer took over as state chairman of the Democratic party.

At this point, Walter Reuther and allies counterattacked. The key to the control of Democratic party machinery in Michigan is the Detroit area—Wayne County. For from it come some 40 percent of the delegates to the state Democratic convention.

Until now, Hoffa had grabbed for political power by manipulating at the top—by making deals that gave him a national committeeman and state chairman. But now, in 1950, he tried to build power at the bottom by going after the precinct delegates, who could make Hoffa the Democratic boss of the state.

It takes a petition with twenty signatures to put a delegate's name on the primary ballot. As filed by Hoffa's cronies, these were interesting for their informality.

"We noticed an astonishing number of petitions filed," a Hoffa critic said later. "Some one thousand out of twenty-three hundred petitions were fraudulent in the wildest way," Neil Staebler, the then state Democratic chairman, told me. "On many petitions, all twenty signatures were in the same handwriting. Even the notary's signature was in the same hand, indicating that one penman had done it all."

Other petitions, it turned out, had been produced by a method known as the "round robin." Groups of Hoffa admirers had sat sociably around a table, signing fictitious names to the petitions, round-robin fashion, in varying handwritings.

Reuther rallied his Auto Workers to enter precinct politics and run for office as delegates. Hoffa was routed, yielding the Democratic party machinery of Wayne County to Reuther and the UAW.

Thus Walter Reuther, ever the man on a beachhead, harnessed his UAW to a unique political operation. By working strictly within the traditional two-party system, Reuther and his members have fashioned a miniature labor government on a local, countywide scale that stands as a pilot plant operation for other labor leaders to copy.

It's true that conditions in Wayne County are unique. For in the area are concentrated some 350,000 members of a disciplined, aggressive union, the UAW. With their wives, these UAW members account for almost half of Wayne County's registered voters. In the county, too, are the union headquarters and officers who can influence these voters.

Walter Reuther probably works harder than any other labor leader at the job of involving members in union work and union decisions—and in selling his point of view to them. Since relatively few members go to meetings, this takes a lot of doing. But Reuther is a pioneer here, too.

"Even if a man doesn't want to come to meetings to listen, you can chase him with your point of view," a Reuther aide said.

The chasing is done with radio programs tailored for the auto workers and beamed at them twice daily as they drive to work for the early shift at 6 A.M. or for the afternoon shift at 3 P.M. A Sunday television program catches the auto worker relaxed in his home.

The "chaser" is a gifted onetime Rhodes Scholar by the name of Guy Nunn. Auto executives say of Guy Nunn and his broadcasts that he is "forever fighting the class struggle." And the Justice Department accused the Auto Workers of violating the Corrupt Practices Act by giving television time to favored political candidates and so making a disguised political contribution contrary to law. The union argued successfully before a jury that the television program was nothing more than a means of keeping in touch with union members. In any case, the Auto Workers spend some $400,-000 yearly in communicating with the members and letting them have the union's view as to where their interests lie.

Naturally, the broadcasts play an important part in shaping members' political thinking. The second step is to get the members to the polls, and this is done through the citizenship and political action department—headed by a full-time director, Walter Reuther's younger brother, Roy.

How all this works out in the practical business of winning elections was spelled out by the UAW's own paper, *Solidarity,* soon after labor support helped sweep Mennen (Soapy) Williams into his sixth term as Governor, and sweep out Republican Senator Charles Potter.

"Here It Is, GOP; Democracy Is our Secret Weapon," a two-page, center-spread headline proclaimed.

"In nearly half the states," an introduction read, "Republicans

ran hard against 'labor bosses' in general and most especially
against Walter Reuther. According to the GOP propaganda, these
'labor bosses' dictated the choice of candidates and herded the
members behind them. Most UAW members know better; and
those who know best are the hundreds, perhaps thousands of rank
and filers who have devoted countless hours to the hard, indispensable routine of politics—without pay. . . ."

The article revealed that candidates seeking the coveted Wayne
County labor endorsement must undergo a grilling by a precinct
committee of union members, then fill out a searching question-
naire, probing personal as well as political matters.

Once the candidate is endorsed, an army of UAW members will
ring doorbells for him, pass out literature, set up shop committees
to register workers and on Election Day bring these workers to the
polls—and serve as poll watchers.

I asked ex-Democratic State Chairman Staebler about Walter
Reuther's role in state politics.

"Reuther gets Labor active. That's his importance," Staebler
said. "Since the Auto Workers muster about one-third of the state
convention delegates, they have a veto power over candidates,"
Staebler added. "But Reuther, himself, doesn't get involved in
choosing candidates."

In Detroit, you inevitably hear that "Walter [Reuther] had
Soapy [Williams] in his pocket."

Concerning this, Staebler said, "If Williams and Reuther had an
argument, Williams would win. If Labor tried to capture the
Democratic party in this state," he went on, "they would wind up
holding only themselves captive. For they'd lose public support."

What Walter Wants

Where Reuther is going and how he is going to get there is a
speculation on which friends and enemies have lavished considerable energy, ingenuity and heat.

Since people look for big things from Reuther, it used to be conjectured about the younger Walter that he had ambitions to be President.

I once heard two reporters speculate approvingly about the kind of job "Walter could do as Secretary of State." And in 1958, critics —less approvingly—insisted in a newspaper advertising campaign that Reuther wanted to grab Congress and rule a Socialist America.

Some of the heat and most of the nonsense have gone from the discussions about Reuther's future. But inside the auto industry, and inside Labor, "what Walter wants" is always good for considerable conversational mileage.

It's true that top auto executives regard Reuther as a leader who holds a disciplined work force together and gives stability to the industry. It's true, too, there have been eras of good feeling. Charles E. Wilson, when president of General Motors, once told Reuther, "I have great respect for you and your leadership."

Too, some of Reuther's most spectacular bargaining successes were actually handed to him on a platter by the industry.

When Reuther first asked for a guaranteed annual wage, the Ford Motor Company, fearful of having to accept an unworkable scheme, set a secret task force to work and surprised Reuther with a counterproposal: Ford would supplement the state unemployment insurance to idle workers. The plan, now prevalent in the auto and other industries, gives an idle worker up to 65 percent of his regular pay for as long as thirty-nine weeks—three-fourths of the year.

General Motors, too, came through with historic voluntary benefits. One is an escalator clause which automatically raises workers' pay when living costs rise. Another is an automatic 2.5 percent yearly pay increase, to let the auto worker share in the continuing increase of productivity due to more efficient machinery.

But for the most part Reuther's relations with the industry have been a mixture of grudging togetherness and hostile coexistence.

Auto executives distrust his aims. The ideological heir of a Socialist grandfather and father, who regarded their Socialism as "practicing Christianity," Reuther was briefly a Socialist himself, but today abjures government ownership. "I'd rather bargain with

General Motors than with the government," he says. "General Motors has no army."

Yet some executives refuse to forget Reuther's early Socialism or his trip as a youth to the Soviet Union, where he worked as a tool and die maker.

"Sure, he hasn't got his hand in the union till, as some leaders have," one company official said. "But he's got his hand in your kid's mind."

Some of the things Walter wants at the bargaining table, but shouldn't ask for, and some of the things he wants outside have helped build the ill feeling.

For example:

Back in 1946, Reuther rushed in where other labor leaders feared to tread. He asked the auto companies to raise wages but hold down auto prices, so making a bargaining issue out of a management prerogative.

"Is the UAW fighting the fight of the whole world?" an exasperated G.M. executive demanded of Reuther.

"Why don't you get down to your size?" the executive went on. "And get down to the type of job you're supposed to be doing as a trade union leader and talk about money you'd like to have for your people, and let the labor statesmanship go to hell for a while?"

Nevertheless, in 1958 Reuther was still concerning himself with auto prices (and still exasperating the industry), this time in Washington. As a witness before the late Senator Estes Kefauver's Anti-Trust Monopoly Subcommittee, early in 1958, Reuther unveiled a new "Reuther Plan," a proposal for a public review board to watch over the prices of the big corporations.[5]

Industry resentment also reflects Reuther's sizable dimensions as an antagonist and his success in winning what he goes after.

"Why do they hate Walter Reuther?" I asked a Reuther admirer, his Washington lawyer.

---

[5] Reuther proposed that corporations that dominate 20 percent of any one market be made to justify proposed price increases in public hearings before a public review board which, however, could not veto price decisions.

"Because he's so effective," the critic said happily.

I asked the same question of a Detroit auto executive. "Because he's so damned effective," the critic answered gloomily.

Yet like two quarreling occupants of the same boat who drop their quarrel to cope with an approaching storm, Reuther and the auto makers are being drawn together in the face of a common problem—automation.

The UAW and the manufacturers have formed joint committees similar to the Human Relations Committee in the steel industry, to develop solutions in advance of contract negotiations.

"They're still suspicious of us," a union man said of the industry, "but acceptance of the joint committee idea shows that some of the old antagonisms are being eroded away."

Within the Labor movement, too, among his own peers, there are mixed feelings about Walter Reuther and diverse views about his aims, and his chances of achieving them.

The old-line building trades leaders who came into the Federation from the old AF of L—pragmatic, primitive exponents of "bread-and-butter unionism"—mistrust Reuther's social unionism. Besides, the scars of the old fights between the CIO industrial unionism and the AF of L craft unionism have not yet healed; new rows keep breaking out as to who should organize whom.

Although Reuther is just another one of the twenty-seven vice presidents of the AFL-CIO, he's recognized informally as the chief vice president—and No. 2 man to George Meany—because he was president of the old CIO. He's the most articulate, to begin with. But he's also the most assertive and the most demanding.

"Let's look at it," he'll say. "Let me give you my opinion. Let's study it." Most of the other vice presidents are too lazy to indulge in this intellectual labor, but they resent Reuther anyway.

As for Meany and Reuther, there is a certain edginess about their relations. There have been a number of confrontations between the two men inside the AFL-CIO Excutive Council—one over the choice of a new vice president, for instance. Reuther wins none of these, partly because there are more old AF of L members on the council than those from the CIO, and partly because of the formidable prestige Meany now enjoys among his colleagues.

For all these reasons, Reuther, the man who knows so well how to handle power, may be denied the power prize he most covets: the presidency of the AFL-CIO.

When Reuther and Meany together banged down a giant gavel as a token of unity at the founding convention of the AFL-CIO in 1955, it was assumed that Reuther would step up when Meany stepped down.

This assumption failed to take into account the fact that the building trades and other of the old AF of L unions muster more convention votes than the old CIO unions, and so would always pose a formidable obstacle to Reuther's hopes.

It also failed to take into account that George Meany, fearing a battle over the succession, would choose to remain on the job for life.

Nevertheless, for some years Reuther disguised his ambitions so little that a fellow vice president, older in years and experience, said to him, "What's your hurry, you S.O.B. Why are you so impatient? George Meany isn't a spring chicken any more.[6] And you have something none of us have, and that's youth."

Reuther seems, in recent years, to be more reconciled to a waiting game, to involve himself less in knockdown and drag-out fights inside the AFL-CIO Executive Council, to concentrate his energies more on building up the Industrial Union Department of the AFL-CIO which he heads. His friends belittle the constant talk that the Federation leadership prize has slipped forever from Reuther's grasp and insist that he is still the most likely to succeed Meany.

"Who else is there?" they want to know.

If Reuther is a frustrated crown prince, waiting for the crown that may never come, he doesn't show it.

Reuther plans keep bubbling. Outside Labor he's busy bolstering the unions' role in Michigan Democratic politics. Inside Labor

[6] Meany was sixty-nine in August, 1963.

he proliferates cloak-and-dagger plans for infiltrating Italy's Communist unions and destroying them. In 1964 he was preparing for further frontier demands on the auto makers.[7]

In other words, Reuther, ever articulate, ever whirring, was continuing to give style and excitement to Labor.

---

[7] A profit sharing plan has already been granted by the American Motor Company. Reuther seeks to obtain similar plans—or "an equivalent in value" —from other manufacturers.

CHAPTER 10

David Dubinsky: He
Bosses 400,000 Women

The International Ladies Garment Workers Union is probably the most famous in the world. Abroad, it's known for the schools and hospitals it built near Paris, at Palermo, Italy, in China and in Israel, and for the rebellion it financed against the Communist bosses of Italy's unions. At home it is celebrated for its workers' homes and summer resorts, for health centers that dot twenty cities, for model arbitration machinery that has made strikes virtually obsolete.

The ILG's president, David Dubinsky, a stooped little tailor of a man in his early seventies, is one of the three or four best-known and respected union leaders.

In all this lies one of the strangest of Labor's strange-as-it-may-seem stories. First, the ILG is a woman's union, and only 20 percent of its members are men. The women flow in and out of the union in great streams—about 200,000, or half of the membership, came and went in the last three years—so that the union has to organize like mad simply to stand still. The members, mostly immigrants, speak so many tongues that the union's paper, *Justice,* has to be published in English, Spanish and Italian.

The soil from which the mighty ILG and Dubinsky sprang adds to the believe-it-or-not flavor of the story, too. It is New York's Garment Center—a murderously competitive commercial jungle where cloak-and-suiters, working on a 1 percent margin, die like flies; where Communists made their first great bid for union power, and nearly won; where gangsters have so woven themselves into the very fabric of the garment industry that neither the full might of the federal government, nor New York County District Attorney Frank Hogan, nor the mighty ILG itself has been able to rip the racketeers out.

In the air the Garment Center breathes are tension, suspicion and struggle. The struggles Dubinsky has seen have been mighty ones. David Dubinsky is forever taking on Goliath. First, there was the Goliath of man's inhumanity to man—symbolized by the sweatshop. First thing that greeted Dubinsky when he arrived at nineteen in New York in 1911 was the horror of the Triangle Company fire, in which 146 garment workers—locked into a sweatshop—lost their lives.

Then there was the Goliath of Communism. The Reds had seized strategic posts in the ILG in the mid-1920's, and plunged the union into a disastrous strike. Only a civil war, in which the then young Dubinsky played a key role, could drive the Reds out. The union emerged so broke it couldn't even pay its telephone bill and could get only incoming calls. Dubinsky, taking over as president in 1932, was called "undertaker"—there was only one thing to do with the union, to bury it.

Goliath No. 3 was and is the gangster. Often, in the Garment Center, the ILG has been able to organize only after pitched battles with hoodlums in which Dubinsky could never know which of his people were loyal and which had infiltrated from the mobs.

Diffident Dictator

A visit with David Dubinsky is likely to be pulse-quickening, if not altogether hair-raising.

The Garment Workers Building in upper Broadway, about a stone's throw from the hubbub of Times Square, once belonged to the Ford Motor Company. But any resemblance between the way the Garment Workers' president, Dubinsky, disports himself

and the decorum that must have prevailed under Ford Motor
Company President Edsel Ford is purely impossible.

Dubinsky doesn't rise from his chair to greet you. He bursts from
it. His diminutive body—he's five feet five—is made even smaller
by a stoop he says he acquired as a boy when he carted his baker-
father's bread on his back to stores in Lodz, Poland. The posture
makes his large head seem even larger.

Dubinsky has the round face of a Herbert Hoover or a Winston
Churchill, but there all similarity ends. As incandescent as an electric bulb, the face lights up at the flick of the slightest emotion. And
the emotion can range from childlike glee accompanied by joyful
cackles to purple rage. So animated by perpetual emotion, his face
has an unlined, youthful look.

The air of youthful vigor is deepened by Dubinsky's constitutional inability to sit still. An uninitiated visitor, new to Dubinsky's
ways, watches with amazement as Dubinsky levitates about the
room, his great head bobbing on his round body, and his voice
raised to a shout. For Dubinsky doesn't talk, he yells—his voice
rising to a falsetto shriek when he really warms to his conversational task.

The volcano flow of words is peppered with earthy S.O.B.'s—
pronounced "sonsapitches"—and, whoever the visitor may be, with
earthy Yiddishisms which Dubinsky doesn't pause to explain. And
should the telephone ring, he'll talk into it, for security reasons, in
Yiddish. Until Dubinsky was forty, when he became the ILG's
president, he spoke more Yiddish than English, because virtually all of the union hierarchy and most of the members then
were of immigrant Jewish origin. Only when Dubinsky's resolute
secretary, Hannah Haskell, locked him in his office with an English
instructor did Dubinsky begin to change his lingual ways. But his
talk is still heavily accented.

Dubinsky's Polish-Jewish childhood and youth helped mold a
complex and often baffling personality. As a persecuted minority,
the Polish Jews sought refuge in a wry humor that mocked their
oppressors and irreverently respected nobody. So Dubinsky, meet-

ing the world's mighty as the head of a great union, takes everybody in stride, with a soupçon of deflating humor.

When the late Albert Einstein pressed Dubinsky to set up a utopian worker's village in New Jersey—and kept on pushing the idea over Dubinsky's repeated no—Dubinsky finally ended the discussion with, "Dr. Einstein, when it comes to physics, you're the professor. When it comes to tailoring, I'm the professor."

As a onetime immigrant boy, too, Dubinsky has absolutely no side. Most labor leaders, except the flashily dressed racketeers, are indistinguishable from their opposite members on the management side. But Dubinsky has the rumpled look of the man who's slept in his clothes. His baggy pants are belted precariously around an ample belly. He wears $7.50 ties, but they're knotted informally beneath a crumpled collar.

Dubinsky pursues informality relentlessly to the point of originality. While other labor giants arrive in style at conferences, Dubinsky is likely to ride up to the meeting place on a bicycle. At a Miami Beach session he made one concession to the vacation resort air of the place. He wore sneakers.

Before food and drink—especially drink—Dubinsky is equally informal, and as a tippler has built a reputation as solid as his other reputation, that of labor leader.

Late for a dinner appointment with Dubinsky, I found him entrenched behind a zombie, a murderous drink composed of a tumblerful of assorted rums. I ordered a daiquiri, which Dubinsky sampled and liked. Dubinsky downed his zombie in several gulps, ordered a daiquiri, then another and another—polishing off four in noisy and gleeful succession. Then, coherently, and with sober shouts—after all, this was an interview—he proceeded to give a lucid exposition of life among the labor leaders at an Executive Council session that day.

Dubinsky talks of his drinking as other men boast of their golf scores and loves to tell of the time when Thomas E. Dewey, then a rising young prosecuting attorney, invited Dubinsky to his apartment to discuss Garment Center rackets.

"He puts out a bottle of brandy," Dubinsky recalls happily. "And I go to work on it, and finish it. He puts out another, and I work on that—and still I'm not saying what I shouldn't."

Despite the two bottles of brandy Dubinsky—as Dewey later put it—was "honest but not frank."

When a man has held union power for twenty-five years, is addressed humbly as "D.D." by understrappers, and hobnobs with other holders of great power, he is likely in time to take himself seriously. Dubinsky, no less egocentric than any other significant leader, does take himself seriously at times and will often refer to himself in the third person—as men conscious of their fame sometimes do.

Still, Dubinsky's Polish immigrant background has saddled him with a diffidence, too, so that he thinks twice about intruding himself openly in the current power politics and power struggle of Big Labor. This doesn't stop Dubinsky from playing a key role. But he's likely to do it through back-of-the-scenes counseling and intrigue rather than open maneuvers and knockdown debate.

Early in 1957, for instance, George Meany startled his fellow elders in the AFL-CIO Executive Council by making a revolutionary proposal. Meany had done his homework, seemingly, was well prepared and had his proposition written out in careful and lucid English. It was the famous proposal that no labor leader henceforth be permitted to take the Fifth Amendment before Congressional committees, courts or government agencies as a means of hiding his union affairs. This was a truly revolutionary move, because it meant that the Federation was butting into the hitherto autonomous and sacred private preserves of the constituent unions.

The twenty-nine members of the AFL-CIO Executive Council swallowed hard and took the historic plunge—away from national union autonomy. And no one at the meeting suspected that the real sparkplug of the move was David Dubinsky, nor that Dubinsky had discussed it with Meany.

Dubinsky had conceived the idea while listening to early Senate committee hearings on union corruption. "If we don't do something about those crooks that are hiding behind the Fifth Amendment, what can we say to the public?" he wanted to know from his lawyer. "We will have to run away and hide our head in shame." So Dubinsky's lawyer prepared a draft of a proposal barring union men from resorting to silence. And it was this proposal, modified by Meany and his lawyer, that Meany read.

Diffident or not, Dubinsky—to use a Garment Center word—is a *Kuechleffel,* a stirring spoon, who mixes in everywhere and knows most everybody's business. At meetings of Big Labor, Dubinsky knows unerringly where the policy winds are blowing, who is doing what to whom, and in what direction some mighty labor cat is likely to jump. Reporters who gain Dubinsky's confidence find him an incomparable guide—and a gold mine.

Once at a San Francisco convention of the old American Federation of Labor, Dubinsky heard John L. Lewis make a seemingly innocuous speech before the local press club. He turned to Victor Riesel, the labor columnist.

"Does the speech tell you anything, Victor?" Dubinsky asked.

"Not much," Riesel said.

"Put a word together here, a word together there, and it still tells you nothing?" Dubinsky pressed.

Then, to the baffled Riesel, Dubinsky explained, "I think he's saying he's going to take a walk; he's going to pull the Miners out of the Federation."

Such a move in 1947 would be page-one, black-headline news. Hesitantly, Riesel flashed the Dubinsky tip to his editors and with misgivings saw the San Francisco papers announce the story in extra editions soon after.

Sure enough, three days later, John L. Lewis strode theatrically to the convention platform, thundered his defiance at the Federation and led the United Mine Workers out of the House of Labor.

Riesel, the trained reporter, had sensed nothing in John L.'s press club speech.

But Dubinsky, "listening with my insides," had "had a hunch."

Papa Knows Best

To his union family of 761 officers and 1,048 staff members, Dubinsky is the jealous father. Or, to be less charitable, the absolute monarch.

When a man's elected to ILG office—whether to a local job or to the International's General Executive Board—first thing he does is to sign an undated resignation. (This is a constitutional requirement initiated by Dubinsky. Resignation follows a two-thirds vote by the ILG board—which Dubinsky controls.) With this ceremonial he hands his official head on a platter to Dubinsky. For the undated resignations hang over official heads like a Damoclean sword. It's as if a United States Senator, elected by the people of his state, were to submit an undated resignation forthwith to the President. ILG apologists say the strange device is needed to combat possible official corruption. If a man is caught cheating, his head can be quickly lopped off, without the need of making out a court case against him—is the way one vice president explained it. But Dubinsky himself signs no such sudden-death device. Nor do the elected officials of any other union, as far as I have been able to ascertain.

Although union members are entitled to elect their own manager-administrators, an election that displeases Dubinsky may bring swift intercession. When the ILG's New York Embroidery Local's manager died not long ago, the local's executive board promptly named a successor—all according to Hoyle, i.e., the local's bylaws. Dubinsky, getting the news while out of town, stormed back and roared his disapproval at the local board's choice. The cowed board reconvened, promptly unfrocked the newly named manager and, hat in hand, asked Dubinsky to name his own man. Which he did, bringing in a manager from another local.

The dictation extends to employers, too. The ILG gives itself the right to check the employer's books. It's to keep him honest in his dealings with the union, says the union—and we'll take a closer look at this when we explore the Garment Center's underworld. But the fact remains the cloak-and-suiters don't like it—and can't do anything about it.

Dubinsky is the acknowledged top dog of Seventh Avenue (as the Garment Center is sometimes known). And a curious rite not long ago underlined this fact.

It was the day on which Dubinsky celebrated his twenty-fifth year as president of ILG. All over the Garment Center, just before noon, the sewing machines whirred to a halt, the steam in the pressing irons cooled. All hands took a half-day off to celebrate Dubinsky's quarter-century reign. Can you imagine General Motors or Chrysler slowing their assembly lines when Walter Reuther marks an anniversary as the Automobile Workers' president?

Union-Made Utopia

For all of his baffling interior and bumptious exterior, Dubinsky is one of the passing breed of great founder-revolutionaries who were to Labor what a Henry Ford, say, was to industry.

Both were world changers. Ford did it by mass merchandising a complicated piece of machinery, the Model T Ford, and so making it possible for the average American to buy it. Dubinsky did it—in the early organizing stages of his union, at least—by merchandising mass discontent. Both were builders and doers. Ford built his car to fit his image of a new world in which the man who labors can afford to buy the product he helps create. Dubinsky built his union in the image of his world, too—a Socialist world.

The story of the ILG really begins with the story of David Dubinsky, teen-age agitator and conspirator. Unions today are businesslike affairs with money to invest, insurance to buy; some worry conservatively about rocking the economic boat. Yet only yesterday the unions were agitational institutions. They organized the discontent of the wage earners in order to build union power and bargain with employers—from strength. So, the great leaders of even the recent past—John L. Lewis and the late Phil Murray, the younger Walter Reuther—were agitators and rebels. In fact, a hero's record of agitation or struggle against the "bosses" or even society, generally, was as vital a piece of equipment to the earlier labor leaders as administrative ability is today.

Dubinsky is the proud owner of what is probably the most picturesque and radical record of them all. He was a conspirator against Czarist oppression at age fifteen. At sixteen, he was languishing in jail as a union ringleader. At seventeen, he was a political exile in Siberia. At nineteen, he was a Socialist agitator, haranguing passers-by from street corners in New York.

Born in Brest-Litovsk, Poland, Dubinsky grew up in Lodz, an industrial town then savoring the miseries of the early industrial revolution compounded by Czarist oppression. Wage earners worked twelve to fifteen hours daily and were barred from organizing or striking by the Czar's secret police. So ugly was Lodz and so barren the life of its 500,000-odd people that two novels were written about it: one, *The Bad City;* another ironically titled *The Promised Land.*

It was the perfect backdrop for a young reformer. So, when Dubinsky went to work in his father's basement bakery at fourteen, he promptly helped form a union and became its secretary. (He was the only baker who could read and write.) He also joined the Jewish Socialist party which was known as the Bund. At fifteen, he was cooling his heels in the Lodz jail for illicit union and political activity.

In jail, young Dubinsky had enemies—and friends. The enemies were the swarms of bedbugs that infested the jailhouse mattresses. Seeking sleep, Dubinsky tried lying on the hard cell floor; to frustrate the bugs he improvised a moat, pouring a ring of water about himself. But war techniques—even in the war between man and insects—are forever advancing. The bugs, as bright as they were ravenous, would climb up the walls, make their way to the spot on the ceiling just above the recumbent prisoner, Dubinsky, then let themselves drop like dive bombers on the unhappy youth. There was nothing for it but to stay up until daylight (when the bugs vanished) and spend the night in long discussions with the politically sophisticated older prisoners or in reading. Books were available, and Dubinsky grounded himself in the Socialist and Marxist texts of the time.

At seventeen, Dubinsky, now old enough for adult treatment, was packed off by the police to Siberia, marching a good part of the way under conditions of near starvation and exhaustion.

This teen-age introduction to tyranny turned many of Dubinsky's radically minded contemporaries to Communism. But with young Dubinsky, curiously, it had an opposite effect. He was fed up with dictatorships of any sort, including the promised dictatorship of the proletariat.

So, when Dubinsky escaped from Siberia and immigrated to New York in 1911, he breathed the air of political freedom and found it good. The government was no longer the enemy. Why seek the overthrow of the government, as the Communist firebrands urged? The real enemy was social injustice: sweatshops, onerous working conditions, poor wages. And this enemy could be fought best under a democracy.

Dubinsky first tried to win reforms through the Socialist party, once a great favorite with New York East Side immigrants. But when the Socialist millennium proved slow in coming, Dubinsky plunged into unionism.

Ten men organized for collective bargaining in a shop could pry more social benefits from the boss than two thousand citizens could pry from a legislature. This was the philosophy of Sam Gompers, father of the AF of L. In time, it was to become the dominant, and saving, philosophy of America's unions.

Dubinsky stopped being an active Socialist about ten years after he came to America. He stopped voting Socialist when Al Smith ran for President in 1928—and he dropped out of the party altogether when the New Deal came. But Dubinsky never stopped building his "union welfare state."

Let's take a panoramic peek at it.

Pins and Needles and Health Clinics on Wheels

The ILG's 450,000 members, spread through 332 cities in 40 states and 5 Canadian provinces, work a thirty-five-hour week.

The union and employers have jointly handled more than a billion dollars of health, welfare, retirement and severance funds for members. These earned $11,000,000 interest in 1962.

The ILG operates health centers in thirteen cities. In New York, the health center occupies six stories of the union's own twenty-two-story skyscraper. In Harrisburg, Pennsylvania, the "health center"—on wheels—brings nurse, technician, doctor and diagnostic instruments to members' homes.

The union has given away $33,000,000 to world-wide good works since 1940, including a $1,000,000 hospital in Israel.

ILG's summer resort for members, Unity House, includes a $1,000,000 summer theater.

The ILG's own "labor college" has trained some three hundred union aides in ten years.

The ILG's "cooperative village" cost $22,000,000 to build, houses 1,660 families on a slum-cleared, thirteen-acre site where sweatshops once flourished.

The union produced a musical comedy, *Pins and Needles,* which packed them in on Broadway for two years, then toured the country in road companies. The ILG's movie, *With These Hands,* has been shown by the State Department abroad.

Most of the above were "firsts" among the unions. The ILG led the pack with the first employer-contributed unemployment compensation plan (1919).

The ILG was first with a Management Engineering Department which helps inefficient employers step up output, cut costs—and stay in business. The union was first to publish its balance sheet and expenses down to paper cups and towels at headquarters. It was the first, too, to build a factory for an employer.

This is the bright side of Seventh Avenue. For the seamier side of the Garment Center you must meet "The Boys."

CHAPTER 11

The Boys from
Seventh Avenue

Gangsters discovered the Garment Center when employers and unions alike hired hoodlums during the bitter organizing wars of the 1920's.

The employers paid off the gangsters in cash. But the International Ladies Garment Workers Union, lacking cash, had to pay off with favors.

The hoodlums who fought the union's battles emerged as owners of dress firms.

And while the mighty ILG made most dress men toe the union line, many hoodlum shops operated nonunion. Or they enjoyed "concessions." They didn't pay the 7 percent—now 8.5 percent—of payroll welfare fund contribution. They enjoyed more "flexible" union regulations.

Dress men say the union was paying off for past favors. The union said the underworld—known in the Garment Center as "the Connections" or simply as "The Boys"—was too tough to handle. If you sent an organizer into a shop owned or protected by The Boys, you signed his death warrant.

Inside the underworld Trojan horse, which the union itself had let into the Garment Center, were some of the country's most lurid cutthroats.

One was the mousy and diminutive Louis "Lepke" Buchalter, who kept eight killers on a weekly payroll and was said to have ordered seventy murders. His loot from garment and trucking extortion alone was a million yearly.

The FBI called Lepke the most dangerous criminal in America. And when he died in the Sing Sing Prison electric chair in 1944—for the murder of a garment trucker—he left the Garment Center an evil legacy: the gang of lieutenants who had filled his murder contracts, collected his extortions and hidden him for two years while state and federal sleuths hunted him.

The men Lepke left behind him were among the Garment Center's biggest businessmen.

As a businessman, Albert Anastasia[1] owned a string of apparel factories in Pennsylvania that produced thousands of dresses yearly for New York jobbers (also called manufacturers). He was secret owner as well of a great fleet of garment trucks. As a gangster, Anastasia was the Lord High Executioner of Murder, Inc., and assigned the killers who filled the orders for assassination from mobs all over the country. Twice jailed as a killer, Anastasia twice walked out when witnesses "disappeared." When Lepke gave himself up, it was Anastasia—the man who hid him—who drove Lepke to the rendezvous with J. Edgar Hoover.

The notorious Johnny Dio got his start in the Garment Center, too. Extortion from Garment Center truckers earned him a seven-year Sing Sing sentence. He came out to become a nonunion dress manufacturer and merchant of "protection" against the union.

Please note that each of the foregoing—Lepke, Anastasia and Dio—was somehow mixed up with Garment Center trucking. This is no coincidence. It's through the garment trucks that the underworld sits in the driver's seat in dressmaking.

To understand why, let's visit the Garment Center.

Go west off Broadway into any of the crosstown streets from Thirty-fifth to Thirty-ninth. In Thirty-fifth Street, known as "Garment Center Chinatown," because the cheapest dresses are found there, you are plunged into a head-reeling world of swarming ac-

---

[1] Albert Anastasia was murdered in 1957, seemingly in a gang war over Cuban gambling.

tivity. Great vans line both curbs, hub to hub, choke the street and permit only a trickle of traffic. On the sidewalks, equally choked, youths push hand trucks laden with dresses and coats. Elderly manufacturers, salesmen, clerks, models battle their way through the tangle. If it's after lunch, salesmen are drifting back from their rounds in the nearby department stores. In knots, they talk wistfully of "clickers"—dresses that click.

As far as the eye can see toward the Hudson stretch the near-skyscraper buildings through whose portals pass 80 percent of all the dresses, coats and suits American women buy.

Now look back at the trucks that choke the streets. These are the jugular vein of the apparel industry. For only a few of the dresses that flow through the Garment Center are produced in it. They are finished by sewing "contractors," in Brooklyn, the Bronx, in New Jersey, Pennsylvania and elsewhere. So into the making of each dress or suit go four truck trips in and out of the Garment Center.

First, a truck fights its way in with the piece goods. Truck trip No. 1.

The manufacturer cuts the piece goods from patterns, loads the "cut work" on trucks and sends them out to the contractor-factory. Truck trip No. 2.

The contractor sews the dress, and it is returned to the manu-facturer's showrooms. Truck trip No. 3.

Store buyers from coast to coast order them, and Truck trip No. 4 hauls the apparel to the store, or to a rail terminal.

"It's a crazy, complex system," said a dress man. "But the store buyers want us all in one place. And we want to be near our com-petitors to smell out what they're doing. Are they making up the A line? Is the H line a dog?"

The wheels of the trucks make the system go around. And it's The Boys who own the big truck firms openly or in the names of close kin. Many of their business partners and ex-crime associates are active in the truckers' trade associations. They have their hooks in the Drivers Union of the ILG that supplies drivers and helpers.

With the trade associations and Drivers Union as "enforcers,"

The Boys run the garment-trucking like an underworld racket. None can cut in without an O.K. from The Boys to "go"—i.e., operate. Territory and customers are parceled out. The customer is stuck with his trucker for life.

This is the picture the United States Justice Department painted in an antimonopoly suit against the Garment Center truckers. The Boys used "violence and threats of violence" to force all truckers into trade associations, charged the government. They "fixed and maintained trucking rates at high and uneconomic levels."

The truckers didn't even dispute the picture the Justice Department painted. They pleaded *"nolo contendere"* (we do not contest) and paid $35,000 in fines. To The Boys, this was peanuts. Trucking is the surest profit maker in the industry. Apparel manufacturing is a fiercely competitive business in which a wrong fashion guess may mean sudden death. One of every five firms folds yearly, and others take their place. But the trucks go rolling on. They haul some $4,500,000,000 of women's apparel yearly. And the trucker gets a sure seven to ten cents per garment hauled.

So the truckers paid their fine cheerfully. That was in 1944. Then many went right on running their trucking like a racket.

To maintain this preserve The Boys gained influence in an ILG local—the Drivers local—and point it like a pistol at the heart of Dubinsky's empire.

Connections in the Drivers local is a life-and-death business necessity for the underworld. Control of the drivers is vitally important to the ILG, too.

The "Edge"

The Boys must control the drivers to safeguard their most profitable traffic—the sale of "protection" against ILG organizing. Such protection gives the protected employer a competitive advantage through substandard costs. This is known in the Garment Center as "the edge."

"The edge" is the garment industry's biggest headache. It hurts the workers, who must work in substandard shops to make it possible. It hurts the ILG, whose agents are corrupted or killed by hoodlums to maintain substandard shops. It hurts the majority of manufacturers, who abide by agreements with the union, then must face unfair competition. It hurts those manufacturers who make deals with hoodlums for an "edge," then fall into gangsters' clutches for life.

But The Boys have made great fortunes from it. In every deal involving an "edge" there are three participants: the sewing contractor who runs a "protected" substandard shop; the manufacturer who uses him; and the trucker. The trucker brings them together and gives "protection" to both.

The payoff is a commission to the trucker—three to ten cents a dress. Or the manufacturer pays the trucker by putting him on his payroll. Or gives him a piece of his business. So, with the "edge," The Boys have pried themselves into scores of companies.

Former United States Attorney Paul Williams of the New York area estimated that some two hundred firms—truckers, contractors, jobbers—are involved in racketeering.

The racketeers are so firmly rooted that one trade association executive despaired, "They're an evil growth on the body of the industry. And I tell you, they'll never be eliminated."

Just ten minutes' subway ride from the Garment Center lies the biggest law-enforcement office in the world, that of District Attorney Frank Hogan. He commands 250 racket busters—sleuths, lawyers, accountants, laboratory technicians. These have kept Garment Center hoodlums under surveillance for years. From time to time Hogan sends some to jail for extortion. But, like the Garment Workers Union, he has achieved no major breakthrough.

There is no crime in operating a nonunion shop. And the bribery or threats that make it possible are hard to detect and harder to prove. Dress men won't give testimony. They're afraid they'll be dead witnesses.

Once District Attorney Hogan's men swooped down on the Garment Center, subpoenaed truckers' and dress men's books, and grilled one hundred manufacturers.

"We suspected the manufacturers were paying tribute to hoodlums for protection against the union," Rackets Bureau chief Al Scotti said.

"But prove it?" he despaired. "That was another thing."

The dress men had rewritten their books to hide payments to The Boys. Some told the District Attorney of tribute payments. But, when asked to testify in court, they became ill. Some collapsed and required hospital treatment.

Hoodlums, facing jail, were just as loath to talk. The District Attorney had found a dress man's canceled check made out to a notorious hoodlum. On it was the telltale notation, "pro." To the racket busters this spelled "protection." Confronted with the check, the recipient, one "Scarface Louie" Lieberman, pleaded guilty to extortion.

When Scarface Louie was pressed to tell with whom he split the protection loot, he blurted, "Put me in jail. Keep me there for life. But I won't talk."

Garment Jungle

Sharing the Garment Center with hoodlums is, for David Dubinsky, an agonizing problem in coexistence.

Hardly a week passes but that some dress man pleads, "The racketeers' competition is driving me out of business." Then the dress men get into a hassle with the union.

"You've got to do something about the racketeers. Or let us get down to their cost levels," they storm.

"Every waking moment," replies some weary union man, "we're devoting to the problem of eliminating the racketeers."

When the union launched an all-out drive in 1949 against the shops The Boys were protecting, a reign of terror ensued. It was the Lepke days all over again.

First, hoodlums invaded the union's office and sent three officials to the hospital. "We'll cut your ears off," they threatened others over the telephone. Roving gangs beat up strike pickets. The union called for help to the Seafarers Union, which sent fifty huskies to the Garment Center to protect the picket lines.

Then the union organizer, William Lurye, was murdered. To this terror was added betrayal. An underworld ally then heading the garment drivers' local permitted his drivers to cross the picket lines—so breaking the strike of their fellow ILG members.

In 1952, when unionized dress manufacturers kicked up another fuss, the Garment Workers Union returned to the attack. This time they brought several dozen protected shops into the union fold. But The Boys continued to offer "protection" to the unionized employers and so encouraged them to chisel on their contracts. This required further knockdown and drag-out fights by the union.

If the ILG controlled the truck drivers' local, it could wipe out the evil of the "edge," since the trucks would no longer haul garments to substandard or nonunion shops.

Yet it's a fascinating measure of gangster staying power, once they've dug in, that the racketeers, not the mighty ILG, have controlled the ILG's own drivers local. The ILG local doesn't even have a written contract with the truck owners.

Until he was indicted on charges of extortion, this local was bossed by one Sam Berger. Tried he was freed, but two union aides were convicted. His office was a hangout for hoodlums from all over the country.

I once asked Dubinsky, "Why don't you fire Berger?"

"Fire him?" Dubinsky screamed in his most excited falsetto. "How would that solve anything? I couldn't ask another man to take his place. He'd be killed."

"If I was twenty years younger, I'd go in there and risk my life and straighten it out," sighs Dubinsky.

Recently Dubinsky has talked of putting an ex-cop or FBI man in charge of the local.

"Could he clean it up?" Dubinsky was asked.

"Don't ask foolish questions," Dubinsky shouted. "The government with the FBI couldn't clean it up. The state with the electric chair couldn't clean it up.

"The only thing that will clean it up," he said, "is when people talk. But people are afraid to talk."

Once the manufacturers refused to give the usual pay raise at contract-signing time.

"Not another penny until you clean up," they said.

Today, the ILG is still struggling with The Boys.

Uneasy Marriage

The ILG is famed for its peaceful relations with employers. Arbitrators kept the Garment Center free of major strikes until the brief walkout of 1958. Yet, because of underworld infiltration, suspicion hangs like a foul cloud over the marriage between the ILG and the employers.

Since some of the dress men are gangsters, or reformed gangsters or grew up with gangsters, the ILG, like a cat at a rat hole, is forever sniffing for evidence that some of its officers and business agents are being bribed by the employer to sell out the union.

The ILG maintains accountant watchdogs who regularly pry into employers' books. They check up on cloak-and-suiters to see whether they're paying their full share of welfare benefit money to the union, whether they're sneaking out cut garments to nonunion, substandard sewing contractors in violation of union agreements.

But in the Garment Center even watchdogs have to be watched.

"Once," a vice president told me, "we heard that some of our accountants had been corrupted. Instead of reporting that a dress man owed, say, ten thousand dollars in welfare contributions, they'd falsify the books to show he owed only five thousand dollars —then split the difference with the manufacturer."

What to do?

The vice president held a secret, after-hours huddle with the head accountant and a handful of trusted aides. They sifted rumors and prepared a list of suspects. When trusted accountants checked up on the untrusted ones, they found four (out of thirty-five) were cheating the union. They were turned over to the District Attorney.

Once Dubinsky hired a former FBI man and instructed him to build a union FBI that would keep the union bunch honest. For two years the ex-FBI man collected dossiers on union officials, snooped in offices and generally scared the hell out of everybody. The cure for corruption seemed more drastic than the ailment—so Dubinsky let the man go.

The Succession

Labor leaders, like southern Senators, tend to hold office for life. Thus Dubinsky, now past seventy-two, gives no sign of stepping down, and a crown prince—designated back in 1956—still waits, although he has passed sixty-two and is but three years from the official retirement age. This is Louis Stulberg, who gave up professional baseball for a union career and rose to be the Garment Workers' executive vice president.

Recently Dubinsky created another putative heir by naming a staff official, Gus Tyler, as assistant president. Tyler, a skilled administrator, headed the ILG's political department and training institute but has held no elective office in the union. Nevertheless, since Dubinsky has unloaded much of the headquarters' administration on him and because Tyler is in his early fifties, some in the ILG family are making book that Tyler will overcome his lack of political following and make the leap to the top.

If he does, the changing of the ILG guard will be a symbolic as well as an actual one. Dubinsky, the class-struggle warrior and organizer, will yield to the new breed of union leader—the administrator.

CHAPTER 12

Wherein a Negro David
Staggers a Union Goliath

The civil rights storm that lashes our country has raised a tidal wave that hammers an ancient wall created by some unions. This is the monopolistic barrier constructed by the building trades and some other skilled craft unions around the jobs in their areas.

By limiting membership and apprentice training openings to friends and kin of members, these unions had virtually excluded the Negro from all but a few of the skilled construction trades. The Negro boy who once aspired to be a plumber, an electrician, a sheet metal worker had to aspire to something else.

By the summer of 1964, pressure from Negro picketers and government officials had forced some scattered but important breaches in the exclusion wall. Despite the fact that apprentice openings had always been limited to members' kinfolk, some unions were agreeing relcutantly to take in Negro apprentices. So the Negro's fight for his rights could have a curious and unexpected result. It could break a practice that goes back to the medieval guilds and weaken the skilled craft unions' stranglehold on the job opportunities in their trades.

To understand what is happening, let's look at a situation that still largely prevails, despite Negro heat.

Of all the battlegrounds on which the Negro fights for an equal shake with the white man, the unions, which control his daily bread, have frustrated him most.

Although union constitutions proclaim liberty, equality and fraternity, many unions—not only in the building trades but in some locals of the Engravers and in the Machinists—have excluded Negroes. This has meant exclusion from a job. For in the industries these craft unions serve, not the employer but the unions control the hiring. The contractor who needs some bricklayers or electricians for several days or weeks will call the union hiring hall for them.

Long after Washington, D.C.'s Negro families could send their children to integrated schools, eat at public restaurants or put up at any hotel they could afford, Negroes could not gain admittance to the Plumbers local there. Nor to the electricians, the steamfitters, the sheet-metal workers, stone cutters and others.

And as late as August 1, 1963—long after Negroes were being served at Southern lunch counters and riding in nonsegregated buses—a New York State Advisory Committee of the U.S. Commission on Civil Rights was reporting that building trades jobs for Negroes were either virtually nonexistent or were available in a few trades only through Jim Crow unions.

"Participation of Negroes in the [building trades] unions," reported the New York committee, "ranged from total exclusion in some trades [structural workers, plumbers] through token participation in others [Plasterers, Operating engineers] to substantial if often segregated, local union membership [Carpenters]."

Nor did the lily-white unions yield easily to outside pressure.

For two years after Negro electrician James Holland left Detroit for Washington, D.C., he couldn't get a construction job. The all-white Washington Electricians Local 26 wouldn't take him in; it wouldn't even give him the routine transfer card that would open the union hiring hall to him. Newspapers, federal officials, Negro organizations and, finally, the embarrassed President George Meany of the AFL-CIO hammered at the local. In vain. Only when the Justice Department threatened to go to court to shut down the construction on which Local 26 members worked, did the local give the Negro a transfer card. But he couldn't get into the local. Even George Meany couldn't get him in.

Since the craft unions that exclude Negroes largely control the apprentice training of the country, it has been virtually impossible for a Negro to get such training. Only after an inquiry begun by the New York State Attorney General's office did the New York plumbers local take in its first Negro apprentice.

For almost thirty years, Victor Daly, Negro executive with the United States Employment Service for the District of Columbia, has tried to place Negro high school graduates as union apprentices. All he could show for his efforts, until recently, was one Negro apprentice with the Washington, D.C., Carpenters local—reluctantly admitted under newspaper pressure.

Once Daly put a Negro youth in his car and made the rounds of federal construction sites. He aimed to get the boy a job as a plumber's learner. With 576 hours of supplementary schoolwork at night, the boy could, in four years, become a full-fledged journeyman plumber. Daly had made such job-seeking rounds before, all fruitless. But this time he offered a Negro boy who had registered a record high score in the USES aptitude test for plumbers and steamfitters.

Yet, on site after site, construction foremen told Daly, "You got to see the union."

The Taft-Hartley Act outlaws the closed union shop under which a man must show a union card before he can work. But this is largely ignored in the building trades. All workers, including apprentices, come from the union hiring hall.

At the Plumbers local office, federal official Daly and his protégé cooled their heels for an hour, waiting to enroll the youth as an apprentice. Then, when the local's president emerged, he saw the dark-skinned applicant and cast a reproachful look at Daly.

"Why, this boy ain't the son of a plumber, is he?"

The Negro boy learned what Daly and others had learned before him. The plumbers, like other skilled craft unions in the building trades, were operating as their ancestors, the closed medieval guilds, did centuries ago. Membership was tightly controlled, as in a fraternal brotherhood, and apprentice openings were the private property of the members.

"It's a family affair," an official of the Washington Electricians local once told me. "From grandfather to son to grandson."

This union-made apartheid has posed a terrifying problem for the Negro. Barred from virtually all but unskilled industrial jobs, he has been the first to be laid off when business slackened or when machines replaced men. Barred from training, he couldn't move into the new jobs that automation creates. Thanks in part to union practices, the Negro was becoming an economic pariah, a reluctant burden on his community.

Galloping automation is wiping out some 200,000 jobs a year in manufacturing alone. Since this is where the Negro has largely been making his living, unemployment figures dramatically reveal his plight.

In the great Northern industrial centers, one of every three Negro wage earners was idle sometime during 1963. His rate of joblessness was two and one-half times that of the whites. In Detroit, for instance, Negroes accounted for more than 60 percent of all unemployed, although they make up but 20 percent of wage earners there. In Philadelphia, Negroes accounted for 52 percent of all unemployment, although they make up but 13 percent of the work force there.

Most idle Negro industrial workers have been without work so long that they have exhausted their unemployment compensation benefits. So the NAACP has warned that the unskilled Negro worker of forty-five who has lost his job "will never again work at productive gainful employment."

As already noted, there have been some significant breaches in the exclusion wall. New York Local No. 3 of the Electricians took in two hundred Negro and Puerto Rican apprentices in one swoop in late 1962. The Washington Plumbers local, once a segregationist stronghold, has allowed in two Negro youths and says it will take in more. Sixteen Washington building trades unions accepted a total of twenty-five Negro apprentices for the

1963-64 indenture year. Similar beginnings are being made else-where in the country.

The barriers began to be lowered—slowly, to be sure—when the late President Kennedy found a way of getting at the discrim-inators—unions as well as employers. This was through the threat of withdrawing defense contracts.

The federal government, the country's biggest employers, spent some $25,000,000,000 with defense contractors during fiscal 1961. The one hundred largest of these, alone, employed ten million persons. Control of defense contracts, then, gives the federal government a powerful weapon. In an early crackdown, the President's Committee on Equal Employment Opportunity swung this weapon against an airplane manufacturer in Georgia. Although the manufacturer operated a government-owned plant and performed government work, he had defied government orders to end discrimination. The International Association of Machinists had gone along with the employer by segregating its local there. Negro college graduates, barred from jobs for which they were trained, worked on assembly line jobs and paid dues to a Jim Crow local. All this was wiped away by the Presidential Commit-tee's intervention. The union integrated its locals and opened its apprentice training to Negroes.

The President's Committee on Equal Employment Opportunity has since moved on to federal construction, using its purse-string power to crack down further.

Negro civil rights groups—which until then had been picketing lunch counters, department stores and hotels—took note of what the government was doing in construction and joined the battle by picketing construction sites, state and locally financed as well as federal. Under this kind of pressure, unions yielded in Phila-delphia and in Brooklyn.

As significant as the crumbling of union opposition to Negroes is the manner in which the building trades unions are beginning, for the first time, to fill apprentice openings.

When Harry Van Arsdale and the New York electricians broke

with past apprentice selection practice, they did it with Van Arsdale's customary dramatic splash.

"You nominate the candidates," he told a panel made up of the National Association for the Advancement of Colored People, the Urban League (also a Negro improvement organization), a former dean at Columbia University and others. Of 1,020 apprentices picked, as already noted, two hundred were Negroes and Puerto Ricans.

When the Washington building trades unions decided to let down the bars, they also gave up their once exclusive right to select apprentices. A committee from the Department of Labor participated in screening apprentice candidates.

These scattered instances may, in time, become general practice —under public pressure. Typical of such pressure was the warning of the New York State Advisory Committee of the U.S. Commission on Civil Rights. If unions continued their old membership practices, this committee warned, they might soon be confronted with a form of civil service selection of members by a government agency.

As in school desegregation, the federal government seems destined to be the prime mover in banishing union discrimination. But in place of court orders, the government here has other weapons. One, as we've seen, is the threat to withhold federal contracts. Another involves the control of training. Through the Health, Education and Welfare Department, the federal government matches state and local funds for vocational training. And the Labor Department registers all apprentice programs. In July, 1963, the Labor Department ordered that apprenticeship programs would not be cleared unless Negroes were given an equal chance at the training.

The federal assault has both long- and short-term effects.

Negro craftsmen who picked up a skill by themselves or learned it in the Army—and were working for nonunion contractors—are getting a crack at union-controlled jobs, and in some instances at union membership.

Negro boys were entering apprentice programs, so that in the long run Negro union membership will steadily increase. It is to this long-range apprentice training that the Negro must look for equal opportunity in skilled craft jobs.

Unlike the walls of Jericho, then, union barriers won't come tumbling down all at once before some government Joshua. As President George Meany of the AFL-CIO told a Congressional committee, more help from federal legal muscle would be needed.

The AFL-CIO conventions have repeatedly thundered against discrimination, and union lobbyists have frequently labored for civil rights laws. But while Labor, at the summit, fights discrimination, some constituent unions of the AFL-CIO have paid little attention. This is because, as Meany testified, the Federation cannot dictate to its constituent union members. Its only effective sanction is to throw them out of the Federation, as it did the Teamsters. But to fire out the offending building trades unions would wreck the AFL-CIO.

So the forthright Meany made an unusual plea to the lawmakers.

"We need the force of law to carry out our own principles," he said.

"We have never at any time tried to gloss over the shortcomings of unions on the subject of equal opportunity. Yes, some of our members take a wrong-headed view. I have said so before, and I repeat it again. . . .

"So, in effect, we need a federal law to help us do what we want to do—mop up those areas of discrimination which still persist in our own ranks."

With the AFL-CIO pushing from the top and the government pushing from the bottom, the venerable craft union monopoly over jobs eventually will have to give.

CHAPTER 13

Journey
to the Underworld

Side by side with the great unions that perform legitimate services for their members, there exists today a nationwide shadow federation of secret labor bosses. Always in the background, they wield power over unions in their own bailiwicks and exchange favors through a subterranean network of influence that spans the country.

Although seldom visible, these phantom wielders of power are real enough. They are the regional overlords of organized crime— the survivors or heirs of the Prohibition era rackets who today are men of substantial business interests, lawful as well as unlawful.

Staking out city and state domains, these men rule cartels of crime that have woven themselves into the very fabric of their communities. In the Midwest, the Chicago Capone mob, bossed chiefly by Sam Giancana, dominates the numbers and policy gambling, the jukebox and pinball racket monopolies and has infiltrated legitimate businesses: laundries, hotels, auto agencies. The gangsters wield great political power and even have their own anticrime lobby at the state capital.

In the East, a New York–New Jersey criminal axis cuts so wide a swathe in business, politics and crime that the names of some of its bosses have become household words: Frank Costello, for instance, and the late Albert Anastasia and Tom (Three-Finger Brown) Luchese. Cleveland has its Babe Triscaro and John T. Scalish.

Stacked about me, as I write this, are the interview notes and documentary materials gathered during a decade of investigative reporting into the underworlds of our big cities. Running like a persistent thread through these annals of crime is the gang boss's back-of-the-scenes influence in unions.

How did bigshot gangsters get into unions?

Why do they stay in them?

How do they use unions in their rackets?

The gangster uses unions to police and protect deeply intrenched, lucrative monopoly rackets.

"Extortion? Shakedowns?" a veteran prosecutor exploded at me one day. "That's not what gangsters are chiefly in unions for. More and more, they are using them as a wedge to pry into legitimate business and turn them into rackets." The prosecutor was Al Scotti, Rackets Bureau Chief in the New York County District Attorney's office who has spent his working life fighting racketeers.

Anatomy of a Racket

Of all the strange dramas that Robert Kennedy pieced together as counsel for the McClellan Committee the "Case of the Golden Garbage" was the strangest, and it spelled out a pattern of underworld enterprise policed by union power.

As portrayed by the testimony, this cast of characters included:

A crime overlord known as "Lord High Executioner" of Murder, Inc., whose union power qualified him for the title of Secret Labor Boss. He was never on stage, but cast a menacing shadow over the action.

A professor with a criminal record who tutored the children of the biggest names in mobdom and served as "watchdog" over the crime overlords' racket interests.

A union man with a wooden leg and a rubber conscience.

A "labor relations adviser" once accused of peddling dope. He used business firms as "whips" and unions as "clubs" to keep racket victims in line.

A corpse—that of an honest union man, "rubbed out" in the line of racket business duty.

Also hoodlums with such names as Joey Surprise, Pasta Fazula (Italian for beans and macaroni), cowed businessmen and cheated union members.

Act I opened in Westchester County, a rich suburban community bordering on New York City. Here, as in other New York suburbs, there flourished a lowly but lucrative service industry: the private collection of waste and garbage from homes, restaurants, stores. Several hundred firms describing themselves as "carting companies"—and sometimes as "sanitation engineers"—operating in New York and its suburbs divided some $50,000,000 of business yearly.

There's gold in those hills of garbage, and the smell of it attracted to genteel Westchester some cold-eyed gents with prison pallor and Lower East Side New York accents. These bought their way into a garbage-carting firm, and this soon brought to garbage collecting an excitement that store owners never expected of it.

First, there came to one store manager the private garbage collector who carted his refuse.

"I want to get out in one piece," he said, giving up the business. "I don't want my trucks burned to the ground."

Next, as was testified, little men in suède shoes and pulled-down hat brims showed up in behalf of the garbage firm.

"You been paying $15 a week for service; now you pay $28," they said.

When the leading stores went out and found themselves a new garbage collector, another new face appeared on the scene. It belonged to a businesslike fellow who walked jerkily because of an artificial leg. This was Bernard Adelstein, one of the two bosses of a Teamster local in East Side Manhattan. The other boss was

Joseph Parisi (now dead), a convicted rapist and underworld figure—whom Adelstein described as "a fine labor leader—may his soul rest in peace."

Adelstein gave the word that the merchants could not use the garbage man they preferred (whose prices, incidentally, were lower); they must use a firm the union dictated. When one chain store company, Safeway Stores, resisted, Adelstein quickly taught the chain store the power of the Teamsters. They coerced the store in Westchester County by refusing to pick up the refuse at Safeway Stores in the Bronx and Manhattan. Attacked on the flank, the Westchester Safeway Store yielded. Its refuse was soon being collected again by a mob-owned carting company.

And death by murder wrote a footnote. When an honest union man who headed the Teamster local in Westchester County disputed the invasion of the underworld union from Manhattan, he was told by its bosses, Adelstein and Joe Parisi, it was testified before the McClellan Committee, "Don't think you are too tough and that we can't take care of you. Tougher guys than you have been taken care of." Adelstein denied making any threats.

Three weeks later, the honest union man was shot twice through the head and killed.

In Act II the scene shifts to another rich New York suburban area, Nassau County. Here in one of the fastest growing communities in America, big and little owners of trucks were peaceably collecting refuse, bidding against each other for business and meeting occasionally in a county trade association.

Into this business paradise there entered a serpent. This was Vincent Squillante, a saturnine man of few words who described himself as "labor relations adviser." "Hire me," he tempted the garbage men, "and your union troubles will be over." As a clincher, he picked up the phone and talked intimately with Bernie Adelstein, whose Manhattan Teamster local also operated in Nassau.

Squillante went to work for the refuse carting companies—on union matters—and soon catapulted himself to executive director

and boss of the cartmen's trade association. He then introduced
some novel business ideas.

First he taught the garbage firms—let's call them cartmen—the
fundamentals of "property rights." Once a cartman had a customer, he always had that customer, and no one could bid against
him or try to take him away. If that customer, a store, say, moved,
the cartman who had served "the stop" would serve whoever
moved in.

Next Squillante taught the cartmen how to bid on business.
Designate one cartman to make the winning bid; then others don't
bid. That way, there'd be no nonsense about competitive prices.

Naturally, there soon sprouted in Nassau County, as there had
in Westchester, new carting companies owned by some of the most
lurid rascals known to the New York police. These were the companies that enjoyed favored treatment from the association, according to the McClellan Committee, and were the ones chosen to bid
on plush business. When some legitimate cartmen refused to go
along with the monopoly association and competed, defiantly, for
business, Squillante, ever resourceful, formed "whip" companies.
Troublemakers who stepped out of line were beaten right back
again by the "whip" companies that raided their customers, under-
selling them when necessary. It was easy to crack the whip, too,
because Squillante worked as a team with union man Adelstein,
and so could deprive the rebel of truck drivers. Whip companies
were permitted by union boss Adelstein to operate nonunion.
Adelstein even loaned the nonunion carters union pickets to coerce
stores into taking his service.

To control the carting firms even more tightly, Squillante—with
an assist from union man Adelstein—forced the businessmen to
take out cards in Adelstein's union, thus creating the phenomenon
of a Teamster local that derived one-third of its revenues from
dues-paying and card-holding employers. The employers might
pull out of the association and make a fight for their business lives.
But if they pulled out of the union—or were booted out—they
were branded "unfair to organized labor" and deprived of drivers.

The narrative up to this point has shown you the pattern of underworld business operation: seize control of a trade association and transform a legitimate business into a monopoly racket controlled by a closed ring of insiders. A captive union, whose resemblance to a legitimate labor organization is purely coincidental, enforces the monopoly by keeping insiders in line and outsiders out through its control of the drivers.

We now come to Act III of our racket drama, the one in which the master criminal and brains of the dirty business is dragged from the shadows and into the light.

When Squillante had established himself as czar of the private garbage collection in Long Island (which embraces Nassau County), he introduced a new trade association activity: "public relations." He brought into the Nassau cartmen's association a little, bespectacled man in his sixties who spoke the English of a college professor. Which was not surprising, for that is what the stranger once was—a college teacher of English. The "professor," C. Don Modica by name, instituted a trade association paper which he dubbed *The Hired Broom*. In it he sometimes ran essays, headed: "Out of garbage grows a rose." It was testified he also lectured the trade association members on the "three E's"—Education, Enforcement and Engineering. (The Enforcement, of course, was the enforcement of the racket monopoly. The Engineering concerned the collection of garbage.)

Nassau cartmen who came to conferences held in Squillante's office on Madison Avenue in New York City found the "professor" engaged in still other activities. As the cartmen talked business, the "professor" quietly busied himself writing mathematical symbols on a blackboard and explaining them to a boy of twelve.

One cartman, who could not contain his curiosity, asked a neighbor, "Who's this fellow?"

"Don't you know? That's Albert's boy," was the reply. "Albert" was the redoubtable Albert Anastasia, probably the most awesome name in the underworld. Anastasia once assigned killers to handle mob underworld executions, and was reputedly responsible for several score slayings. On the side the professor was coaching the boy in his math.

The professor, as the Senate committee later showed, tutored the children of such bigshot gangsters as the deported Joe Adonis and the late Willie Moretti.

The professor, according to the committee, had served time for practicing medicine without a license and for grand larceny and was watchdog over the garbage racket for Anastasia. And Anastasia, not Squillante, was the boss of the racket.

Senate investigators testified that the professor reported regularly to Anastasia by telephone concerning the garbage business. They found that Squillante boasted that he was a "godson of Albert Anastasia." And they found that when one of Squillante's "whip companies" needed capital to expand, an emissary went into New York to see some of "The Boys" with the object of raising $250,-000. One of "The Boys" was Anastasia.

Anastasia is dead. He met the same bitter end—a shot in the head—to which he had consigned so many others.

Mother of Rackets

Underworld access to union power in turn spawns virtually every other labor racket: boodling of welfare funds, making lucrative deals with employers to lock wage earners into substandard wage contracts. And, as long as the underworld dominates some unions, others are in danger of invasion.

The broker who handled the welfare fund insurance for the Distillery Workers Union looked up from his desk one day and into the mugs of two big-name gangsters.

"We control the Distillery Workers' insurance," they said. "Cut us in."

And, as New York County District Attorney Frank Hogan found, they did indeed control it. For, as he also discovered, they were part of a New York–Chicago underworld axis that had got its hooks into the Distillery Workers Union.

One of the gangsters was Little Augie Pisano, a bigshot in the Eastern gangs, now dead. The other was George Scalise, the Chicago Capone mob's labor front. They not only controlled the Distillery Workers but had connections in other unions and so could channel so much business to their captive insurance broker that he set up offices in Newark, New Jersey, Chicago and Los Angeles to handle it.

Please note: the gangsters didn't get into the Distillery Workers Union merely to boodle the welfare funds. They already had influence in the union.

The racketeer with union power can also sell a service to employers.

In Chicago, where the Capone gang has influence in a score of unions, the gang helps fight legitimate unionism in the city's restaurants.

Enter any of Chicago's seven thousand restaurants, and you are likely to find—in that highly unionized town—that your waiter does *not* belong to a union and probably works for subunion pay. As any Chicago newspaper reader knows, there is a union in the field: the Hotel and Restaurant Employees and Bartenders International Union (AFL-CIO). And, as the newspapers have often reported, and as McClellan Committee testimony corroborated, some locals of the union were controlled by gangsters.

Testimony before the McClellan Senate Rackets Committee painted this pattern: On one side of the deal were the owners of 20 to 25 percent of Chicago's restaurants, who belonged to the Chicago Restaurant Association. On the other side were locals of the Restaurant Workers Union, harboring Capone gangsters. The union's "organizers" rarely talked directly to the restaurant workers, the kitchen help and the waiters. Instead, they went directly to the boss. "Put three of your workers into the union," the organizer would tell an employer of, say, twenty workers. The owner would give the union man the names of three employees, who might not even know they'd become union members. For the employer paid the union initiation fees and dues—and kept on paying them for years—even after the workers had left, or had died. The union made no further demands on the boss, nor did it discuss pay or welfare benefits. The employer paid off with dues for several of his employees.

The Senate Rackets Committee heard that as a further, more substantial, regular payoff the Restaurant Association maintained a "voluntary fund" to which employers contributed—and from which came a $125,000 fee for "labor relations" lawyers closely associated with the Capone gang.

The lawyers, testimony strongly hinted, didn't keep the lavish fee but sluiced it to gangster shadow bosses behind the Restaurant Workers locals.

When you hire robbers to serve as cops, you must be prepared to protect yourself against the "cops." The gangster, if opportunity affords, will move in on the employer as well as the worker.

So the voluntary fund, from which the $125,000 "labor relations" fee came, was also a war chest to keep the Capones at a safe distance. When hoodlums demanded that one restaurant chain sign over its employees, the Association's voluntary fund poured out $247,000 to help the restaurant chain resist a ten-week blockade.

The McClellan Committee's exposures forced the retirement of some of the Restaurant Union's more lurid bosses—but there's no assurance that the Capone gang now has no hold on the union.

As long as the underworld dominates some unions, others are under the ever-present danger of invasion. Detroit gangsters shot and almost killed Walter Reuther, president of the United Automobile Workers, because—as one theory has it—they sought to end Reuther's war on a multimillion-dollar numbers gambling racket in the automobile plants.

All for One

The underground network along which the gangs' secret labor bosses interchange favors and union influence is rarely glimpsed by outsiders. Yet sometimes a criminal trial, or a grand jury hearing or a chance wire tap, will expose it to view.

One revealing glimpse was provided when five Capone gang chiefs were tried and convicted of extorting $1,000,000 from Hollywood. Testimony showed that when underworld bosses seek favors from other gangsters around the country, these hasten to "fulfill the contract" with a zeal that points to an unsung solidarity within the underworld.

For instance:

First step in a Chicago gang plot to shake down Hollywood via a racket union was to seize a union. So when Capone gang bosses Frank (the Enforcer) Nitti and Paul (the Waiter) Ricca wanted to install a puppet to run the Movie Projectionists Union, they simply sent word to gangland colleagues around the country to line up convention delegates for their man.

Gang chiefs from the big cities lined up delegates in the locals in their towns, then sent hoodlums down to the convention at Louisville, Kentucky, to make sure the boys voted right. The Capone puppet won hands down.

Hoodlums whose own connections in Labor don't reach far enough have access to a central underworld clearing house of influence: a figure who is a labor power openly, and is the underworld's ambassador or back door to the unions as well.

Two union powerhouses have served in this ambassador's role in recent years: one was Joe Fay of the Operating Engineers. Later, according to McClellan testimony, it was Jim Hoffa of the Teamsters.

Fay, a stocky, hammer-fisted man, was only a fourth vice president of the Operating Engineers Union, but actually bossed that union and so dominated the building trades that he was known in the East as "Mr. Labor."

At conventions of the old American Federation of Labor, Fay made no bones about representing underworld interests. Fay, controlling building trades convention votes, helped raise George Browne, the Capone puppet, to vice president of the AF of L with a seat on its policy-making Executive Council.

Labor boss Fay's best friends included racketeers—such as the late Longy Zwillman of Newark, New Jersey, who spent long evenings at pinochle with him and called himself Fay's "public relations adviser."

So powerful was Fay that, even after he went to jail for extortion in 1948, he continued to run his labor empire from a Sing Sing cell, sending out orders via a lieutenant who visited him regularly. So many big wheels in Labor and politics beat a path to Fay's cell door that it became a public scandal, and Fay was removed to a remote prison upstate.

According to McClellan committee testimony, Fay's successor as "the man to see" when gangsters wanted union favors was Jim Hoffa, then an obscure ninth vice president of the Teamsters.

I first met Hoffa in 1955, long before he had become a household word. And so there began for me a fascinating hunt for clues which, laid end to end, spelled out the significance of Hoffa and the Teamsters to underworld activity.

I spent several afternoons in interview-conversations with Hoffa and watched him at work at a trucker-union conference.

As revealing as the talks was the awesome respect with which those around Hoffa treated him. But most revealing of all was a freckled, redheaded, slight man in his mid-fifties who dogged Hoffa's heels in the hotel lobby, carried his luggage to and from airport cars, waited for him outside conference rooms.

Hoffa introduced the genial redhead.

"Meet Paul Dorfman," he said. Dorfman became president of a waste collectors' local after a predecessor was murdered—then was kicked out by the AFL-CIO as a "corrupt influence." Earlier, I had spent several weeks trying to catch up with Dorfman to ask him about the Dorfman family insurance business, which in three years had collected some $1,000,000 in commissions and fees from Teamster welfare fund insurance. Dorfman had evaded me, just as he evaded questions before Congressional investigators. I had written critically about him in a *Reader's Digest* article on union welfare funds scandals.

But now Dorfman had no hard feelings.

"You should have given me a chance to answer," he said, with no reference to the weeks he spent dodging my calls.

Locked behind that freckled forehead were many answers that Dorfman could give—if he dared.

A Senate committee investigator described Dorfman as "a major figure in the Chicago underworld" and an "associate of most of the leading gangsters in the Chicago area." Then Robert Kennedy, counsel for the McClellan Committee, put Dorfman on the stand. Counsel Kennedy wanted to know whether Hoffa Teamster insurance had been channeled to the Dorfman family insurance agency as part of a deal. Did Dorfman use his influence in Chicago to help Hoffa extend his Teamster power there, in return for the insurance business? Kennedy asked.

"I refuse to answer on the ground that it might tend to incriminate me," said witness Dorfman.

"Weren't you with Mr. Hoffa continuously at the trial in New York [on wire-tapping charges]? And weren't you at the Hoffa trial here in Washington [on bribery charges]?" Bob Kennedy asked Dorfman.

Dorfman pleaded the Fifth Amendment.

"And weren't you in a hotel room in Chicago when Mr. Hoffa and several of his colleagues were selecting those officials who would run on his slate at the Teamster convention in Miami, Florida?" Bob Kennedy asked. Again Dorfman pleaded the Fifth Amendment. "And isn't this one example and probably the most serious of Mr. Hoffa's tie-up with the underworld?" Bob Kennedy asked.

"I refuse to answer on the ground that it might tend to incriminate me," Dorfman said.

Hoffa's relations with the Capones—most powerful crime organization in America—raise fascinating questions. For instance: When Paul (the Waiter) Ricca, elder statesman of the gang, faced deportation and needed quick cash, he got the money—$150,000 —from two Hoffa-controlled locals in Detroit. In a tangled transaction Ricca first gave the Hoffa locals half-title on his Long Beach, Indiana, estate—which meant that Hoffa's locals owned a twenty-room mansion, half of a swimming pool and half of a tennis court. How did the Capone chief come to be selling real estate to Teamster locals? Hoffa explained that Ricca's estate would be used as a "school for Teamster business agents." But why a school at Crown Point, Indiana, for business agents in Detroit?

Was the Capones' elder statesman, Ricca, a secret labor boss with influence in the Teamsters?

Hoffa has played the role of secret back door into legitimate labor.

This is how the back door opens:

When New York extortionist Johnny Dio and other racketeers wanted Teamster charters with which to set up locals in New York, Hoffa helped get the charters for him.

When Samuel (Shorty) Feldman, one of Philadelphia's most notorious criminals, wanted to go into the restaurant union business, Hoffa undertook to help him, too. The Philadelphia District Attorney Victor H. Blanc was tapping Feldman's telephone and overheard Hoffa's promise to deliver a restaurant union charter. But Feldman got his restaurant union charter anyway.

When the Distillery Workers demanded that the big Eastern distillers recognize their union, and the distillers balked, "The Boys" knew just what to do to bring them into line. They telephoned Hoffa in Detroit, who was soon on the phone to New York.

"Sign your salesmen into the union," said Hoffa. Distillery executives, fearing their liquor wouldn't move, signed.

This control of the wheels makes Hoffa the Indispensable Man —to the secret labor bosses from the underworld and to the unions they control. And so around Hoffa and the Teamsters there rotates

an assortment of satellite unions in whose ranks were found the
rascals that gave Congressional investigators their most lurid hearings.

The Mug Who Came to Dinner

The gangsters got into the unions virtually by invitation.

Let's look in on two scenes enacted several decades ago.

The time is 1926. The place is a lavishly appointed office in an
expensive New York midtown hotel.

The actors, left of stage, are a group of taut-faced Garment
Union leaders. To the right is an easy-smiling, handsome gent,
Arnold Rothstein, the then king of New York crime and financier-
overlord of a host of gambling, narcotics and prostitution rackets.

The little tailors had asked an audience with the underworld
monarch—and a boon. Could Rothstein use his underworld influence to call off the gorillas, hired by the employers, to crack
union strike pickets' skulls? To be specific, could Rothstein call off
the notorious Legs Diamond and his gang? Obligingly, Rothstein
picked up the telephone. In a matter of minutes, the dreaded Legs
Diamond and his Boys were shaking the dust of the Garment
Center from their feet. Rothstein said he was glad to do this as a
favor to his aging father, a retired and highly respected dress
manufacturer.

Now came a more delicate problem. The Garment Union
leaders confessed that they, too, had hired gorillas—Augie Orgen's
gang to be exact, to stink-bomb employers' lofts and combat
employers' thugs. Once hired, Augie wouldn't be fired. Could Mr.
Rothstein do something about that, too?

Why not? All that was needed was just another telephone call.

The little union men, watching the suave Rothstein, had a blind-
ing flash of truth. Both gangs of gorillas, those working for the
employers as well as those working for the union, were working for
the same underworld boss, Arnold Rothstein.

Some nine hundred miles away in Chicago, another underworld

chieftain, Scarface Al Capone, also gave an audience to union emissaries. The union men had come, hat in hand, from a high official in the American Federation of Labor, now dead. Would Al Capone work for the unions? Would he supply the troops to fight the employers' mercenaries and help introduce unionism into a number of service industries? Al Capone would—and did.

The men who came to the New York Garment Center as thugs remained to become powers in business and the rackets who defy all efforts to dislodge them. In Chicago, Al Capone gangsters worked for the unions. Later unions worked for them.

If we've learned anything from our journey to the underworld, it's this: the gangster is a deeply rooted fixture of American big-city life. The unions can fight him by refusing to let criminals or known hoodlums hold union office. But more is needed: a war on the gangsters' business rackets. This is essentially a police matter.

Prosecuting the gangster is a back-breaking task. Victims and collaborators won't talk. They'd rather be live collaborators or victims than dead witnesses. Yet New York County District Attorney Frank Hogan and his chief racket buster, Al Scotti, have shown that it can be done. They uncovered the $500,000 welfare fund boodling in the Distillery Workers Union and sent a gang chief and a union puppet to jail. The convictions led to a Senate investigation of union welfare fund frauds and a chain reaction of further exposures. The New York District Attorney also sent Hoffa's friend, Johnny Dio, to jail for income tax evasion.

Frank Hogan's war on racketeers seems to be the exception to local law enforcement rather than the rule. Chicago has witnessed some 976 gangland murders since 1919. There have been only two convictions. Hoodlums who get away with murder get away with much else, too.

Although the McClellan Committee has uncovered scores of instances of thievery and other lawbreaking, local prosecutors have followed through in only a fraction of the cases. This is disinterest bordering on abdication of duty. Or it could be that the gangster has such political influence in his community that he is too hot to handle.

Is the gangster a member of a privileged class? And are his organized rackets the protected evils of a privileged class?

If they are, it's obvious that the war on the hoodlums is one that can't be waged by unions alone.

CHAPTER 14

The Corrupters

One of the country's big industries—just how big no one really knows—is so hush-hush that you won't find its representatives in the yellow pages of your telephone book. And yet there are many who know just where to find it. This is an industry that sells a secret service: the corruption of union leaders. It consists of an underground network of middlemen or union influence peddlers who, for a fee, will get the employer a favorable union deal. This deal may be to keep the union out of the plant or to come in under a "sweetheart" contract.

Everyone now knows about the labor leader who steals from the treasury, or the racketeer who extorts from an employer. But little is known, because he hides in the background, of the man behind the most serious union corruption of all: the collusion between employers and union men.

It is hard to spot this fellow, because he doesn't openly display the wares he sells, i.e., influence with unions. The protective coloration behind which he hides is that of "industrial relations consultant" or "labor relations" lawyer.

Taming unions, through middlemen, is big business. One middleman we'll soon meet collected $2,480,000 in seven years. He had clients in almost every state in the union.

The middleman's influence can reach high, and cost the wage earner much. One labor man, so reached, was Dave Beck. The former Teamster boss was found by the McClellan Committee to have taken, "not borrowed," $370,000 in union funds. But his greater corruption got less attention. Beck connived—the Mc-Clellan Committee also found—with one influence peddler-middleman to permit some employers to have no unions at all, and others to have "sweetheart" deals. To union members, the dues Beck misused were peanuts compared to the loss of pay resulting from substandard contracts. Of all the union problems I've investigated, that of the middleman-influence peddler is most loaded with woe for the worker. For in the deals the go-between arranges, the union's function is perverted. Instead of serving as an instrument to win better wages and working conditions, it becomes a tool for keeping the worker in line. Thus it performs a function similar to that of the unions in Communist Russia.

Good Old Reliable Nathan

One spring day in 1957, an elderly, fast-talking witness before the McClellan Committee chortled and wisecracked his way through a sordid story.

Serving as a "purchasing agent," the witness, according to testimony, had been used by the then Teamster President Dave Beck to drain off $85,000 of union funds—on love seats and roofing for Beck's home, knee drawers for his ample person, on hosiery for his wife, on deep freezes, cameras, guns, garden hose for his son, Junior. And on diapers for his niece's baby.

The witness who could get it for Dave Beck wholesale (Senator John McClellan called Beck's end of it "theft") was Nathan W. Shefferman, who described himsef as a "labor relations consultant." Obviously a big operator, Nathan Shefferman worked chiefly for employers—some four hundred of them from coast to coast. His "Labor Relations Associates of Chicago, Inc." also had offices in Detroit and New York.

The most that Senators could get out of Shefferman was that he "created goodwill" for employers and "made surveys." Try as hard as they could, the Senators could not learn from the sixty-nine-year-old Shefferman precisely what it was that he did.

The Senators had a right to be puzzled. For a man who advised employers, Shefferman led a curious business and personal life. His entertaining was not for employer-clients but for labor leaders. His closest friend was labor man Dave Beck. Shefferman traveled yearly from Chicago to Seattle to spend the Christmas holidays with the Teamster boss, went on European junkets with him, never permitted Beck to pick up a dinner check.

For an employers' man, Shefferman's friendships with other labor leaders while less close were equally impressive. Shefferman was much in demand for speeches before union conventions, where he gave out with catch phrases, Edgar Guest poetry and soporific clichés. Shefferman and his son threw costly dinners for members of the old AF of L Executive Council at their annual meetings. They took the boys sea-fishing or to the races. Shefferman worked hard at making labor friends. His pockets bulged with gadgets: a wristwatch alarm clock, a spring-driven self-powered razor, a miniature camera. A one-man purchasing agency, Shefferman bought some $478,000 of goods at wholesale for 421 persons over a nine-year span, using his connections with employer-clients as supply sources. Among those who benefited—besides Beck—were some ninety labor leaders and labor lawyers.

Shefferman's expenses for new business were equally puzzling. He testified he gave Dave Beck $24,000 "out of friendship," but prudently charged it as a business expense. He gave another Teamster boss $750 for referring an employer client to him.

Why did Shefferman, labor relations consultant to employers, spend so much money and lavish so many favors on union leaders? Where did he get the money? And what could the labor men do for him?

The answer came some months later, in the fall of 1957, when the McClellan Committee paraded a host of witnesses—employers, lawyers, union members and its own investigators—to piece together a startling picture of employer-labor leader conspiracy with middlemen as the catalysts. Disguised as a "human relations" expert, Dave Beck's friend, Nate Shefferman, was a union wrecker straight out of the old world of industrial espionage exposed by the La Follette investigation of the 1930's. With an added service: he could sell his influence with labor powers like Beck and others. Shefferman, who had talked volubly about his purchases for Beck when first questioned by the McClellan Committee, pleaded the Fifth Amendment when recalled for questioning about his middleman role. His testimony about his "labor relations" activities "might tend to incriminate me," he pleaded.

Nevertheless, from Shefferman's own records and other sources, the investigators learned that his Labor Relations Associates of Chicago, Inc. sold $2,480,000 of labor services in seven years. Chief client was the country's leading store chain, Sears, Roebuck & Co. Sears helped put Shefferman in the union-busting business, gave him access to goods at wholesale so that he could do favors for dozens of labor leaders and footed some odd expense bills. (Among these was $96.50 for entertaining Dave Beck on his 1955 trip from Chicago to Indianapolis to attend the funeral of Beck's predecessor, Dan Tobin.)

For the case-hardened Senators who thought they had seen everything in the way of labor rackets, the dramatic hearings on the middleman were a short, short education into the root cause of union corruption. The late Lincoln Steffens once found that for every crooked political boss who gave away a valuable franchise, there was a crooked businessman who bribed him to do it. Now the Senators learned that, where there's union corruption, there are the corrupters as well as the corrupted.

"It has come as a profound shock to see men acting on behalf of American business take the Fifth Amendment before this committee," Senator John McClellan observed.

"Are there sufficient laws to deal with businessmen who knowingly pay off money to union officials to prevent or discourage unionization?" he wanted to know.

How to Tame a Union

As depicted in Senate testimony, Shefferman's methods, employed by other middlemen as well, added up to a blueprint for draining away a union's power or taming the union and turning it against its members.

First and crudest was the "conduit" method. Here, for a fee, Shefferman aides turned themselves into human pipelines through which employers funneled money and gifts—Senator McClellan called them "payoffs"—to union men.

When automobile and electric appliance distributors and other businessmen at Flint, Michigan, faced Teamster unionization, they knew exactly what to do. They testified:

They got in touch with Shefferman's man in Detroit, George Kamenow. "The fee is $100 a month," Kamenow would tell his client-businessman, "and another $2,000 to entertain union officials. I'll need the money to take the boys to the Rose Bowl Game," he'd explain. Once the fee and "entertainment" costs were paid, immediate results followed.

"So you paid $2,000 to have the pickets removed?" committee counsel Bob Kennedy asked an electrical supplier.

"That is correct," the supplier replied.

One Flint car dealer testified he paid labor relations adviser George Kamenow the usual fee and "entertainment-for-the-boys" contribution. Then, when the Teamsters withdrew, he said he went right on paying money to take the union boys fishing in Canada and buy airline tickets for them for union conventions in Seattle and for Christmas presents.

"You were paying to entertain union officials, when they had nothing to do with your plant?" counsel Bob Kennedy asked the employer.

"It looked to me like a good investment," said the employer.

The Senate Rackets Committee transcript here reads:

Bob Kennedy: And this payment was worth while to keep you from being unionized?

Mr. Graff [Max H. Graff, the employer]: Well, you can turn it
around that way.

Some employers stuck to their story that they had hired middleman George Kamenow to give them "labor relations advice." But
others were more forthright.

One builder, fighting a strike of carpenters, knew that he could
win if he could get the local Teamsters to bring supplies through
the Carpenters' picket line. So he called for Shefferman's man,
Kamenow.

"And did he tell you that he wanted $2,000 in cash as well as
a $2,000 check?" asked committee counsel Bob Kennedy.

"That is correct," replied the builder.

"And the $2,000 in cash was to be passed on to certain of the
Teamster Union officials?" asked Bob Kennedy.

"It was told to us that the $2,000 would be passed on to
Teamster officials; that is right," testified the builder.

Senator McClellan summed up the testimony involving the em-
ployer-middleman-union-man triangle:

". . . It looks to me like we are developing a pattern of what
amounts to a payoff to union officials to have them disregard the
rights of the workingmen; to be reluctant, if not to refuse, to press
any drive for unionization."

The Mysterious Strangers

Or, to keep a union out, middleman Nathan Shefferman would
simply copy the methods of the old labor spy agencies. This sort of
union busting is now outlawed by the Taft-Hartley Act. Here,
according to Senate testimony, is how Shefferman turned the clock
back for his chief client, Sears, Roebuck, at its stores in Boston.
We'll call this episode the "case of the mysterious strangers"—a
drama that began to unfold in Sears stores when employees voted
three to one to affiliate their independent union with the Retail
Clerks International.

First, a balding stranger who called himself James T. Guffey arrived from Chicago, put up at a Boston hotel, and from his hotel room began to play an important role in the stores' and employees' affairs.

A National Labor Relations Board examiner pieced together this story:

To Guffey's room, reluctant employees soon began to trek, during working hours, on orders from their superiors. "These meetings are top secret," Guffey hush-hushed his visitors. They were violating the Taft-Hartley law, Guffey told them. So mum was the word. At the same time, new faces began to appear in the Sears, Roebuck stores. About a dozen in all, and scattered through several stores, these newcomers did no selling but described themselves as "public relations" men from Chicago. This "public relations," it soon turned out, consisted in gathering dossiers on employees, spying out their union sentiments, visiting homes and —as the Retail Clerks Union later charged—there trying to brainwash them.

So hidden was Shefferman's hand that nowhere in the subsequent NLRB investigation does his name appear—nor that of his labor relations firm. But Shefferman had left his traces. The man who called himself Jim Guffey or Fred Warren was an old reliable Nathan Shefferman hand. He drew his pay from Shefferman under the name James T. Neilsen—and was a confessed embezzler.

As part of Shefferman's campaign, one employee allowed his car to be damaged. A brick shattered a car window, and the tires were ice-picked. The Retail Clerks were blamed. The car owner got three new tubes—paid for by Sears.

Shefferman's aides stirred up so much confusion that, when a new election was held, the employees reversed themselves and voted against the Retail Clerks Union.

Sears, Roebuck has since dropped and repudiated Shefferman. But the benefits gained from his efforts were substantial. Of 205,-000 employees in Sears, Roebuck, only 14,000 belonged to unions at the time of the McClellan disclosures. Half of these were in the Teamsters.

About Collective Bargaining and Unions at a Bargain

When Nate Shefferman couldn't keep a union out altogether, he'd turn to a second technique: the union-you-can-live-with method.

This brought some strange bedfellows into the factories of Shefferman's clients. Mattress manufacturers usually sign with the Upholsterers Union. But in the Indiana, Illinois, Washington, Texas and Alabama plants Shefferman served, Teamsters stuff the mattresses.

There was method in this strange melange. The collective bargaining of these locals would lead to a bargain for the employer only.

In a New Jersey plant of a Shefferman client, the Englander Company (mattresses), women sewing and stapling machine operators earned (in 1957) an average $1.27 an hour against the $1.88 average of the industry as a whole. At such a bargain, Shefferman's client didn't fight the union. He welcomed the union in. In fact, as the National Labor Relations Board found, the Englander Company assisted the union's leader in organizing the plant. Naturally, the local's boss, one Abe Lew, was a pal of Shefferman. (When Lew died in 1958, it was found that he had looted his local union welfare fund reserves of some $220,000.)

Union leader Lew was entertained lavishly by Shefferman and his son in New York—at Englander Company expense. He'd come running to Chicago and Miami Beach when the Sheffermans beckoned.

In 1955, the Englander Company signed nine of its plants into the Teamsters at one stroke. The contract was signed with Jim Hoffa's Central Conference of Teamsters. The Western Conference of Teamsters, run by other officials, wouldn't have anything to do with it.

The agreement was a top-down contract, i.e., it was signed between the Englander Company and the Teamsters—as Bob

Kennedy put it—"without any consultation with the employees whatsoever."

The Englander Company's labor relations lawyer, Sidney Korshak, explained why the contract was signed, and so let the cat out of the bag:

"The papers were calling attention that the merged [AFL-CIO] federation was going to . . . unionize every unorganized company in the United States. We were fearful of that, and we felt we could live with the Teamsters," Korshak said.

That the Englander Company was right in assuming it "could live with" Jimmy Hoffa's Central Conference of Teamsters emerged from the terms of its contract.

The Teamsters Union is the most powerful in America. Elsewhere it uses its power to win some of the highest wage rates enjoyed by union men anywhere. But in the plants of Shefferman clients, the Teamsters—tamed—were content to accept wages that, in some instances, barely exceeded the dollar-per-hour minimum required by law.

In Michigan City, Indiana, as Pierre Salinger, then a Senate investigator, testified, a porter-janitor was paid $1.27½ per hour in 1955. The contract in Seattle (signed with the Western Conference Teamsters which had refused to go along with the Hoffa contract) paid the porter-janitor thirty cents an hour more.

In the Hoffa contract, female production workers were paid from $1.12½ an hour to $1.42½ an hour. In the Western contract, by contrast, women's wages ranged from border makers at $1.62½ to floor girls at $2.02 an hour.

For his services, it was testified, the Englander Company paid Shefferman $76,400 in a little more than three years. After the company signed its "we-can-live-with-the-Teamsters" contract, Shefferman's job was considered done, and his employment by the company ended.

Tangled Skein

For a fascinating moment, Senate investigators glimpsed the outlines of an interlocking league of labor influence peddlers, some from the underworld, who called on each other when their own connections didn't reach far enough.

This picture emerged when investigators looked into the circumstances under which a Shefferman client "ran away" from one union and into the arms of another.

The unraveling of this episode began routinely enough. A Connecticut bathroom fixture manufacturer who had dealt with a local of the Jewelry Workers faced organization by the United Automobile Workers. He preferred to do business with the Jewelry Workers Union. While the company resisted the UAW for months, it signed a contract with Jewelry Workers on the same day it was approached.

But when the UAW refused to withdraw and went, instead, to the National Labor Relations Board to demand an employee election, curious things began to happen. A varied assortment of influence peddlers materialized who tried to get the Auto Workers to withdraw.

As McClellan Committee testimony showed, a shadowy figure with inexplicable friendships among labor leaders appeared: one Phil Weiss, described by counsel Bob Kennedy of the McClellan Committee as "being foremost in the country . . . as far as selling . . . racket connections." Kennedy also characterized Weiss as having "the most far-reaching effect on labor racketeering of anybody in the United States." To all questions before the McClellan Committee, including the date of his birth, Weiss refused to answer on the ground that it might tend to incriminate him.

Up in Weiss's Room

In early 1956, there trooped to Phil Weiss's suite at the Essex House, in New York City, a number of men. One, according to

McClellan Committee testimony, was Hyman Powell of the Jewelry Workers, who testified that UAW regional director Charles Kerrigan came there, too.

Hymie Powell told the McClellan Committee why.

Counsel Bob Kennedy [questioning Powell]: Did you make arrangements to meet with Mr. [Charles] Kerrigan to see if he would withdraw [his organizing drive]?
Powell: I did.
Bob Kennedy: Where did you meet with him?
Powell: At the Essex House.
Bob Kennedy: Where?
Powell: Phil Weiss's suite.
Bob Kennedy: Why did you meet in Phil Weiss's suite?
Powell: I was going to ask Phil Weiss if he could use his influence with Charles Kerrigan to get him to withdraw.
Bob Kennedy: What does Phil Weiss do?
Powell: I haven't any idea at all.

Powell also went to others who, as he said, had influence.

Bob Kennedy: Did you go out to see Sidney Korshak [a lawyer for one of Shefferman's clients]?
Powell: I did. . . . I made it my business and I especially went out to Chicago . . . and I asked Mr. Korshak whether he could use his influence since he dealt with a lot of . . . people connected in the Labor movement to get the UAW to withdraw.
Bob Kennedy: Whom did you want Mr. Korshak to speak to?
Powell: I wanted him to speak to everybody, but I mentioned to him Phil Weiss's name.

In Hymie Powell's curious union world there's nothing odd about asking an employer's lawyer in Chicago to intercede with a shadowy figure in New York for help against a rival union.

The McClellan Committee then heard Powell testify that up in Phil Weiss's room Weiss spoke to UAW man Charles Kerrigan. Extortionist Johnny Dio also was "interested in getting [the UAW] to withdraw," Powell said.

Senate investigators suspected that Phil Weiss and Johnny Dio were trying to bribe UAW man Charles Kerrigan. This was never proved, and, even if the attempt were made, it didn't succeed. The UAW refused to withdraw and continued to press for an employee election. Four days after the NLRB ordered such an election, the company moved its plant to Chicago. There it signed a contract with the Teamsters to represent employees who make bathroom fixtures.

   The Senate Committee focused, of necessity, on Nathan Shefferman. So it didn't pause to explore the new vistas of investigation opened up by the case of the runaway fixture manufacturer. This was a pity, for many tantalizing questions were left unanswered.

   How wide was Phil Weiss's influence? To what extent were racket figures involved in the union middleman industry? And how widespread and what were the ramifications of the middleman network anyway?

   Still, the investigation was an eye-opener for the Senators and for the country. Union corruption, it turned out, was a two-way street in which some businessmen and labor leaders walk hand in hand and must share equal guilt.

   As was to be expected, the McClellan Committee disclosures led to new labor legislation. But, as we shall see in the next chapter, the far-reaching effect of that legislation was not to be felt until some years had passed.

CHAPTER 15

You Can't Steal a Union
Any More

Of the five toughs who lined up for sentencing before a federal judge in Philadelphia early in 1963, three towered over six feet and weighed more than 225 pounds apiece. All had been at war with the law since their youth; among them, they had forty arrests and ten convictions. Three were employed by local Teamster Union leaders; they specialized in a curious trade: throwing union men out of meetings or roughing them up. Often haled into local courts by their victims, they had just as often got off with a rebuke or a small fine.

But now the muscular defendants faced something new: a federal indictment charging that they had used force to deprive union citizens of their rights. Tried by a jury and convicted, they were sentenced to serve two years each in a federal penitentiary. (The case is being appealed.)

The trial and sentencing marked a historic first for the seventy-five-year-old American Labor movement. It was the first time men had gone to jail for using violence to bar union members from a union meeting. The conviction was made possible by the Landrum-Griffin Act. Although it was passed in 1959, at the end of the McClellan Committee hearings, the law is only now coming into its own as the result of crucial court decisions.

These are cleaning up ancient bastions of union corruption, particularly in the building trades and in trucking, that had defied

Senate committee exposure and the efforts of the Labor movement itself. In the International Brotherhood of Teamsters alone, in the past eighteen months, some twenty officials, from business agents to presidents of locals, have been convicted under the new law.[1] Some of the clean-up has hit close to durable Teamster President James R. Hoffa. In Hoffa's local at Detroit, a business agent is under indictment for embezzlement and falsification of records. And in the nearby Pontiac local, another personal Hoffa preserve, a secretary-treasurer has been sentenced to two years' probation and fined $1,500 on similar charges (he is appealing).

Key to the clean-up is the changed status of the unions in the courts. Only a few years ago, the courts tended to regard unions as private clubs and so kept hands off their internal affairs. Now they have a mandate, in the new law, to view the unions as institutions affecting the public interest. Their bookkeeping, their elections, their meetings and even their officers' pasts are subject to court review and action.

Consider the case of the secret union books. When Labor Department investigators asked late in 1960 to see the books of Detroit Teamster Local 299, of which Hoffa is president, the union refused to honor the subpoena. But now, merely on the suspicion that the Landrum-Griffin Act is being violated, federal lawyers have the power "to enter whatever place and inspect whatever records they deem necessary." The Circuit Court of Appeals upheld the law and ordered Hoffa & Co. to turn over the records.

Curled up with the Teamster books, the federal investigators reached for the law again—that part of it which now makes union treasury embezzlement a federal offense. An indictment emerged that charged business agent Charles "Chuckie" O'Brien, a Hoffa protégé who lives in Hoffa's house in Detroit, with using union money to help buy a car for the brother of a top Detroit underworld figure.

The right to see the books has also let in the sun on curious union officer shenanigans, once relatively free from prying eyes.

[1] During eighteen months prior to June, 1963.

Officers of a Teamster local in Los Angeles set up a fund, without the members' knowledge or consent, to pay themselves severance if and when they left the union payroll. Then they decided to whack up the money (some $35,000) among them, because the money was just sitting there. Sentences (under appeal) of three years each and fines of $24,000 were imposed on one present and one former officer. Two others have been fined.

In Charlotte, North Carolina, a Teamster local president, secretary-treasurer and business agent have been convicted of raiding the treasury of more than $9,000. Each has been sentenced to two years in prison. Thanks to the new access to union records, jail seems to have become an occupational hazard of holding office in some Teamster locals.

The score for embezzlement indictments in all unions through January, 1964, stood at 124. Of these sixty-five resulted in convictions, four in "not guilty" verdicts. The others were awaiting trial.

While the new law fights corruption from the top—by federal prosecution—it also attacks it from the bottom by putting new weapons in union members' hands.

A growing list of rank-and-file victories shows that a union can no longer be stolen the way it once was. Before the new law, the union was about the least protected piece of valuable property lying around. Although a union is a kind of private government, it doesn't have the safeguards of public government—a two-party system, an independent judiciary and press. So there were many ways to steal it. Now there are padlocks.

Suppose, as a union leader, you keep opposition troublemakers off the ballot and just run by yourself, the way the Communists do.

For thirty years James Caesar Petrillo ruled without a contested election of officers in the Chicago Musicians local. When election time came around, Petrillo merely sent out a single slate to the eleven thousand members on the union mailing list—with himself as the head and his son, James Petrillo, Jr., as secretary-treasurer. Aspiring opponents were told that it was not in their interest to run.

But at election time in 1962 Petrillo had to face one of the new padlocks against union stealing: "Every local labor organization shall elect officers not less often than once each three years by secret ballot, and refrain from discrimination against any candidate," says the law. In the first contested election since 1933, the musicians played taps over the rule of Petrillo & Son.

So ended the Chicago musicians' economic as well as political servitude. For Petrillo didn't take musicians into his confidence about the pay and conditions under which they worked. He didn't even negotiate with their employers, the band and orchestra leaders. He simply sent them the new terms by telegram at contract renewal time. Often, the bandleader in sheer frustration would fire a musician or two to make up for the dictated pay increases.

In 1961, rank-and-file members of the Amarillo, Texas, Teamsters local put up a slate in the hope of ousting business agents who, the members charged, were selling them out to employers. Here the "ins" used another venerable union-stealing method: the dues dodge. The "ins" ruled that the "outs" were ineligible to run for office. They had not paid their dues promptly on the first of the month for two years back, as required. True, their employer had withheld their dues as required under the union contract. But for bookkeeping reasons he had got them to the union hall after the first.

The new law, wise to the ways of union stealing, says: "No member whose dues have been withheld by his employer shall be declared ineligible to vote or be a candidate for office by reason of alleged delay or default in the payment of dues." Along with the law, the members had a policeman to report the union theft to the Bureau of Labor Management Reports of the Department of Labor. The cop investigated. The U.S. attorney at Amarillo sued to set the election aside. The federal court in Amarillo ordered a new election.

Biggest padlock of all is the Landrum-Griffin Act's groundbreaking "Bill of Rights" for the union citizen. One provision: "No member shall be suspended or expelled unless he has been afforded a full and fair hearing."

Several months before election time, the "ins" who run Chicago Electricians Local No. 9 of the International Brotherhood of Electrical Workers tried seven members of a dissident group on charges of "slandering" the officers, and suspended them. Suspension also meant loss of work at the union hiring hall.

The suspended electricians appealed to their international union. Failing to win reinstatement, they then sued in federal court. They had not been given a full and fair trial as guaranteed them under the new Bill of Rights. The court agreed. It ordered the men restored to membership and reimbursed for court costs.

A union isn't stolen only at election time. It can be stolen between elections by preventing members from meddling in union affairs.

For nine months, members of Local 18 of the Operating Engineers—drivers of construction equipment—tried to get into their district union hall at Toledo, Ohio, to hold meetings. When union leaders continued to bar the union hall's doors against them, the members used a legal crowbar to pry them open: their Bill of Rights guarantee of free assembly.

Here the judge warned Local 18's leaders: "It is acts such as this, shutting out the membership from any participation in the affairs of their union, that caused Congress to enact the Landrum-Griffin Act. You are going to have to abide by it. The courts will see that you do."

The courts are seeing, too, that the union man is not gagged into submission.

When the sixty-four-year-old financial secretary of a New York City Painters local got up a leaflet accusing the local's president of larceny, he was tried by the union for libel, barred from participating in union affairs for five years and stripped of office.

But in court he had the last word. In a key decision, the Court of Appeals held that union leaders can no longer try members on the charge of libel. The court said:

"It would seem clearly in the interest of honest management of union affairs to permit members to question the manner in which the union's officials handle union funds and how they treat union members.

"Freedom of expression would be stifled if those in power could claim that any charges against them were libelous and then proceed to impose a ban of silence."

The law does not always work automatically to bring relief as in these cases. To get their union back, members often must battle stiff resistance.

This comes chiefly from leaders who use union ownership to ply the cruelest labor racket: collusion with employers to short-change members through sweetheart (soft) contracts. Here the racket stakes are so high that, to hang on to their unions, leaders practice every trick in the book in open defiance of the new law.

Melvin Jackfert, forty-seven, a "cat skinner" (caterpillar tractor driver) by trade, has been involved in a struggle against the leaders of Local 18 of the Operating Engineers, at Cleveland, Ohio. Jackfert has never been able to run for office. His union is divided into a caste system that limits the officeholding privilege to only one-third of the members, and Jackfert is an "untouchable." Local 18 also sprawls over most of Ohio and holds only two statewide meetings a year, which neither Jackfert nor many other rank-and-filers can travel to. True, Jackfert can go to district meetings. But he can do practically nothing there but make recommendations.

Locked into this dictatorship, Jackfert has at times voted against hours-and-pay contracts proposed by union officials, only to find himself overridden. So business agents are free to make soft deals with employers, and sometimes do.

In rebelling against this, Jackfert and others have had to make sacrifices few Americans are called on to make during peacetime. He has had his face crushed in by thugs. He gets virtually no work from the union hiring hall. He and fellow rank-and-filers have had to endure court delays in a struggle against the best lawyers his own union treasury can buy.

Elsewhere, union men, making a similar fight, have put their lives on the line, as the murder of a rebel union member of Teamster Local 560 in New Jersey proved in early 1963. This is the local run by Anthony "Tony Pro" Provenzano, the Hoffa crony whose men voted him a $95,000 yearly salary. A jury found him guilty of extorting $17,000 from an employer.

But the clean-up goes on. Even Hoffa is being subjected to mounting pressures because of the new law. A number of those convicted for embezzlement are Teamsters. This has affected regional Hoffa lieutenants in California, Missouri, Michigan and elsewhere. All this hits Hoffa where it hurts—in his union political power.

The criminal convictions have also made Hoffa's executive board restive. This board has the power, under the Teamster constitution, to remove him. Some members would like to do so. Rumbles along the Teamster grapevine indicate pressure from still another source: the underworld, which relies on the Teamsters to police its jukebox and other monopoly rackets. Ironically, a Teamster vice president who speaks for underworld interests is reported to have suggested to Hoffa recently that he step down. He was attracting too much heat to the union!

But the clean-up in the Teamsters and elsewhere could go faster if gaps in the new law and in its enforcement were closed. For instance:

The law should spell out what a "secret election" is: i.e., permit members to use voting machines, or voting booths if they wish.

The law should prevent the union leader from using the hiring hall to starve out the opposition. As matters stand, a union man's only recourse against hiring-hall discrimination is to file an unfair-labor-practice charge with the National Labor Relations Board, then wait for years before it is acted upon. Union hiring halls should be required to keep records of those who seek work and those who are assigned, and to make these records available to the Labor Department on request. Hiring-hall reprisals would then become as hazardous as union embezzlement is.

Delay in the courts is another cross that rebel union members must bear. Here justice delayed is often justice denied. The federal courts should give priority to union cases that affect a man's livelihood, such as a suit that challenges a member's suspension from his union.

Even so, the new law has already yielded important dividends and will yield more. As decisions continue to be handed down over the country in favor of the union member, the news gets around: The federals are tough. You can't steal a union any more.

CHAPTER 16

How to Get a
$100,000,000 Raise

One day a jaunty redhead walked confidently in to the boss and asked for a $404,000,000 raise. The boss, of course, thought the request high, but he was willing to talk. After eight months of talk, the red-haired fellow walked out with somewhat less than one-fourth of the demand: an estimated $75,000,000 to $100,000,000.

The boss was the world's biggest corporation, General Motors; the raise seeker was Walter P. Reuther, head of the world's second largest industrial union, the United Auto Workers. The raise, granted in 1958, was spread for three years among 365,000 UAW members who work for G.M.

Some 17,500,000 Americans use union negotiators like Reuther to ask for pay boosts. They practice a species of diplomacy that has its own psychological warfare, meetings at the summit, going to the brink and, when all else fails, limited wars, more commonly known as strikes.

When Sam Gompers, father of American unions, was a boy— before the turn of the century—an aggrieved worker simply got up at his bench and shouted, "I'm going on strike. Who's with me?"

Boss and workers then fought it out, sometimes bloodily, until one or the other gave in.

That was because there was no orderly method for asking the boss for a raise. The growth of the unions has brought a business-like relationship between worker and boss. There is a bargaining

143

table to negotiate wages and a business instrument—the union contract—to seal the deal.

The bargaining table is a free society's safety valve against class struggle explosions, providing a place where the free worker may battle for what he regards as justice. But the table's magic works only if both sides have equal strength. If not, one side can bully the other. This can mean, for all of us, price raises without end—or the desperate strikes and riots of preunion days.

What goes on behind the closed doors? What is the secret of getting the boss to say yes or getting the worker to accept a no? What makes a champion bargainer? And is the conference table the only place where bargaining is done?

Strategy

When the giant Auto Workers Union asks for a raise from the giant General Motors Corporation, nationwide interest is so great that the opening day of the bargaining is charged with the electricity of the day of the big game.

Television cameramen and several score reporters strain to catch every facial expression and every word as Walter Reuther, cocky, with hands on hips like a wrestler strutting in the ring, and G.M. Vice President Louis G. Seaton, sober with the burden of dealing with the most dramatic figure in Labor since John L. Lewis, shake hands before the big debate.

With an eye to the gallery—i.e., the whole country—both sides are alert to say something bright, yet make a shrewd bargaining thrust.

"Have you brought a big knife to carve up the goose?" an auto executive once thrust at Reuther.

"It's the only goose I know that the more you slice it, the fatter it grows," Reuther parried.

Yet, although the actual bargaining sessions get the big headlines, the moves that may bring victory begin months and sometimes years before.

As in power struggles between nations, victory depends both on general strategy, or the master plan of action, and on tactics, the specific moves to carry out the plan. So the bargaining sessions sometimes become only a part of the over-all campaign.

Here is the strategy with which Walter Reuther won an historic victory: company payments to idle workers.

In 1952—fully three years before the next bargaining round— Reuther unveiled his next grand demand: the famous Guaranteed Annual Wage proposal. He gave no details as to how this radical plan could work—indeed his thinkers hadn't yet figured any out. Reuther said merely, in the press and on the radio, that employers should pay blue-collar workers a year-round wage whether they worked or not. Reuther asked a panel of leading economists to air their views on the Guaranteed Annual Wage (let's call it GAW), and soon had virtually every magazine, newspaper and luncheon club in America taking sides on it.

Reuther's strategy was matched by the employers' counter-strategy. There were two ways to resist Reuther's scheme. One was to seek to convince public opinion that the plan was unworkable, then take a strike, if necessary, to fight it. General Motors, deciding on this strategy, announced it would not yield and spent $100,000 secretly on an anti-GAW movie (which it decided at the last minute not to show). The Ford Company took a different strategic course. As matters stood, the company had two choices —both bad. One was to fight it out in a crippling strike; the other was to accept Reuther's GAW, which might be equally crippling. So the company took a third way out. Behind closed doors, the Ford Company set a task force to work to develop a practical plan of its own for paying workers during layoffs.

At bargaining time, the Ford Company surprised Reuther with its own, closely guarded plan: to supplement an idle worker's state unemployment insurance with company payments and so build up his income to 65 percent of his regular pay. Reuther leads a double life as a bargainer. Outside, before the public, he's a terror, scaring the daylights out of the other side with extreme demands; or he infuriates his adversaries by sounding off on matters that aren't properly a matter for collective bargaining: car prices, for instance. But inside the conference room, Reuther, courteous although loquacious, drops the radical demands and concentrates on the possible. So, although the Ford plan was not a guaranteed annual wage in any sense of the term, Reuther grabbed it up. He said it was his guaranteed wage in principle.

Reuther's strategy in whooping it up for an extreme demand, and Ford's counterstrategy of developing a workable scheme, achieved an ideal bargaining result: both sides were happy.[1]

To counter Reuther's strategic fight for public opinion in advance of bargaining, General Motors has abandoned its orthodox policy of confining the bargaining to the conference table and slugs it out in the press with Reuther.

"If Walter throws a rock, we'll throw it right back," a company man vowed.

So one year G.M. manned the corporate ramparts with a lookout task force whose mission was to anticipate and retaliate.

Researchers went back over eighteen years of life with Walter, following his well-marked trail through millions of words of newsprint, magazine articles, Congressional testimony, UAW convention reports. From this was boiled down a fifty-two-page manual of excerpts which, added up, gave a blueprint of Reuther bargaining strategy and tactics.

G.M.'s anticipators knew that Reuther would invite a committee of influential citizens—clergymen, probably—to hear him argue his demands; that he would appeal to the company's dealers, to the president of the corporation, to the President of the United States—and even, possibly, to the heads of other governments. That's what Reuther once did when he appealed to the British government to intervene in his negotiations with G.M. Clement Attlee, then His Majesty's Prime Minister, although a solid Labour party man, politely declined.

---

[1] General Motors went along with the Ford plan reluctantly. In the automobile industry, what one company gives all give, or suffer costly quickie strikes.

G.M.'s counterstrategic fight for public opinion paid off. Reuther dropped his two chief demands—a short work week and a cut of profits.

Tactics

Some sixty days before a contract expires, both sides meet at the bargaining table, and strategy gives way to tactics. Here the adversaries are no longer trying to convince the public; they're trying to convince each other. The responsibility is sobering. For General Motors, for instance, a penny per hour saved at the bargaining table is $7,000,000 earned that year.

A quick brain and a ready tongue are weapons. Here, the union leaders, used to the rough and tumble of union hall debates, sometimes have the edge.

Once, during bargaining, a Ladies Garment Worker leader demanded that employers be more efficient. Even with high piece rates, the ILG man argued, a worker could starve if his boss didn't keep the machines in order or slowed production with slovenly methods. When the employers, fearing a trap, wouldn't promise to be efficient, the union negotiator, a veteran of forty years of bargaining, whirled on the employer spokesman.

"What do you know about fatigue?" the union man bellowed. "Have you ever read a book on fatigue?"

The employers' man didn't even know there was such a book. Crushed, the poor fellow subsided into silence. The union got its efficiency promise.

Cyrus S. Ching, who negotiated for U.S. Rubber Corporation for twenty-eight years, then headed the last War Mediation Board, says two assets are more prized than all others at the bargaining table. One is to be prepared: to know the other fellow's problem as well as or better than he does. The other is to be so honest the other side trusts you implicitly.

As the all-time bargaining-table great, expert Cy Ching nominated John L. Lewis of the United Mine Workers. First, he had the force of personality. An autocrat at the bargaining table, Lewis would say, "Gentlemen, I have the miners in the palm of my hand. What am I bid?" Then he'd sit still and imponderable until the fretting and talking coal operators came around to his way. Equally important, according to expert Ching, is that "Lewis knew as much or more about the economics of coal than anybody in the industry. He knew what the industry could pay without hurt." Because he knew the industry, Lewis departed radically from the usual labor practice of several decades ago and let the coal operators mechanize. Half of Lewis' miners lost their jobs, but those who remained got twice as much pay and the finest medical and pension protection of any workers.

"The best union negotiator in recent years," in the opinion of mediator Ching, "was the man who bargained for the United Steelworkers, Arthur J. Goldberg, now a Supreme Court Justice. When Goldberg reported on a condition among workers or a situation in a plant, executives believed him. Goldberg boned up on industry conditions with great care and pressed the union's demands with the courteous decorum of the courtroom and with a gifted lawyer's disciplined skill."

Courtesy goes a long way in asking for more pay—or in convincing the other side to take a no.

Louis G. Seaton of General Motors talks in a deliberately low voice to the UAW bargainers three feet across the table. Soft speech, he finds, keeps tempers down and makes the other side listen more attentively. In the Niagara of talk that pours over the participants, it's sometimes hard to keep awake, let alone attentive. So Seaton introduced the coffee break. G.M. provided the coffee for both sides until Reuther, objecting to the fraternization, insisted that the union men pay for their own and have it by themselves.

So eager are both sides of the rubber industry to avoid bad blood that might delay an agreement that union leaders and company executives, alike, "mister" each other decorously, and weeks of talk go by without anyone ever raising his voice in anger. This gentle dealing comes easy to the rubber company bargaining, because the United Rubber Workers' president emeritus, Leland

Stanford Buckmaster, is a former schoolteacher and tended to turn the conference room into a classroom. "He's always trying to teach you something," a company man said.

Yet the bargaining sessions can get rough. A bitter strike against the Westinghouse Electric Corporation by the International Union of Electrical Workers was prolonged because personal feelings between union leaders and executives became so strained that negotiations were broken off and weren't resumed for weeks. At General Electric negotiations, when tempers flared, General Electric's chief bargainer, urbane Virgil Day, would say, "We'll take a ten-minute recess, gentlemen, so that you can compose yourselves."

Since the modern union contract is as big as a fat, pocket-sized book—and spells out hundreds of items ranging from management rights to toilet facilities—the bargaining moves forward in several stages. In the first or "once over lightly" stage, the union makes its demands, and both sides look for words, facial expressions and signals which will telegraph what the other side will fight for. In the second stage, the bargainers talk out technical details: how the contract will be administered, how to settle "beefs" under the contract. Then comes the sticky stage: the argument over money.

Here the poker game really begins. Because boss and union men have dealt with each other for many years, the executives may know whether a union man is bluffing or means business by familiar personal mannerisms. One union man pounds the table when he's not sure of his ground. Another rises and walks nervously about the room, because the talks have gotten down to the cents-per-hour line on which the union man will fight—all summer if necessary. Union men, knowing that their mannerisms telegraph their intentions, sometimes try to change them or to show no emotions at all. The ultimate in this kind of poker-face negotiation was reached several years ago in a session between the International Typographical Union (the printers) and employers in New York. Both sides just sat there for days, with arms crossed, without uttering one word. They feared that such a word would give away their true bargaining position.

When tongues and attitudes get knotted this way, the union makes its power play. The leader takes a strike vote and sets a deadline. "Collective bargaining gets down to this," a veteran mediator said. "How much will a company pay to avoid a strike? How much will a union take without having to strike?" Often, then, the bargaining doesn't enter its final stages until the union unsheathes the sword.

"Why don't you fellows set a strike date, so that we can get down to business?" an auto company negotiator asked an Auto Union man in the 1958 bargaining.

Secret Diplomacy

Once the strike date is set, the official bargaining sessions may become mere shadow play for public consumption, while the real bargaining goes on elsewhere. Often bargainers can't reach an agreement at the bargaining table, because the union spokesman must always remember his audience—the rank-and-file members back home; the company spokesman, on the other hand, can't reveal his innermost, candid thoughts, because he has executive brass above him to consider. So two or three men from company and union get together at the summit—away from the bargaining table —for closely guarded exploratory talks.

"You don't have the boys in the bleachers," a company man will say to a union leader. "What do you really want?" Talks like these the public rarely hears about.

Confidential soundings at the summit require long friendship and absolute trust between participants. Once, after a U.S. Steel vice president and the late Phil Murray of the United Steelworkers had secretly explored each other's bargaining demands, the two men met for a further talk a week later. At this discussion, during luncheon at the swank Duquesne Club in Pittsburgh, the steel executive protested to Murray, "But you agreed to this last week."

"How do you remember what I said last week?" Phil Murray wanted to know.

"I wrote it down," the executive replied.

Murray was so incensed at the idea that the executive had recorded their confidential, off-the-record conversations that he rose in anger and stalked from the club. The executive, in turn, was so dismayed at innocently risking a valuable, lifetime relationship that he followed Murray outdoors. It was raining, and the steel executive presented an odd appearance, running along beside the stalking union leader, holding an umbrella solicitously over him and calling, "Mr. Murray! Mr. Murray!"

A similar friendship between Phil Murray and a Bethlehem Steel executive led to negotiations at the summit that paved the way for one of the Steelworkers' most important gains. When Murray asked for pensions for steel workers, and the companies balked, Murray made a tour of the steel towns to arouse the workers to fighting pitch. Arriving in Bethlehem, Pennsylvania, Murray asked for a suite at the town's only hotel. He found that the hotel's only suite was permanently reserved for a vice president of Bethlehem Steel.

But, said the hotel clerk, the steel executive had left orders that that suite be made available to Mr. Murray, who had come to town to denounce the executive's company. It was the first tipoff to Murray that the executive was willing to talk. Soon after, the two men reached the understanding that broke the industry-wide front against worker pensions.

When union leader and management man reach a secret understanding in an off-the-record talk, a famous New York mediator told me, "They may even write the script"—agree on the way they'll "bargain out" the already agreed-on result. The "script" may call for a fake break in negotiations or belligerent statements or even an all-night final bargaining session to make believe that hard bargaining is going on. With this kind of shadow play, bargainers convince the people they represent that they've fought as hard as they could for the best possible bargain.

"Unless you write about the off-the-record deal," one veteran negotiator said, "you won't give a true picture of collective bargaining."

Perhaps the most curious secret summit role played in any bargaining, anywhere, was that of David Dubinsky of the International Ladies Garment Workers (ILG).

Since the dress business is probably the most competitive in America, and a penny an hour may break an employer's back, getting a raise in the New York Garment Center involves the wily trading of an Oriental bazaar—plus every trick in the book, besides.

One year, as usual, the dress industry's periodic asking and resisting match opened with a public show. Some three hundred union people, representing locals in New York, New Jersey and Pennsylvania, met in a hotel ballroom with two hundred-odd representatives from the five trade associations that bargain for twenty-five hundred employers in the region. For the benefit of television cameras and reporters, a union man solemnly read the union's demand. An employer's man just as solemnly said, "We'll think it over."

Then the several armies of union and trade association committeemen dispersed to their home towns, and two teams of ten key spokesmen each squared off across a table in New York City. At neither of these two bargaining places, the hotel ballroom or the small conference room, did Dave Dubinsky appear. He sat back in his office on upper Broadway and awaited events.

Within a week or so, the bargainers disposed of most of the contract details and got down to cases: the wage demand. Here the union asked for a 15 percent boost and held its ground; the dress men offered 4 percent and wouldn't budge. When the adversaries couldn't stand the ordeal of hearing each other's arguments repeated any more, both sides started sending emissaries quietly to Dubinsky.

Union boss Dubinsky commands respect in the Garment Center because he's the biggest man in it, and because he scrupulously observes a basic bargaining rule: know what the other side can afford. Although a word from him can shut down the dress factories, his union had asked for no pay increase since 1953.

Now, in 1958, when his own bargainers came to him, Dubinsky

wanted to know, "What do you fellas really need? What are you ready to trade away?" Some of the union men, facing members' revolts in their locals, told Dubinsky heatedly they couldn't trade anything, and the bargaining between Dubinsky and his own aides became as excited as any with "the bosses."

To the emissaries from the employers, Dubinsky said, "How far do you think your people will go? Look, you don't have to give me a commitment. I'm not holding you to anything. I'm just sounding you out." With this sort of maneuvering, Dubinsky narrowed down the bargaining. His own people went down to an 11 percent demand. The employers went up to an 8 percent offer. At this point they wouldn't budge unless the union showed it meant business by calling a strike, something the Garment Workers had not done since 1933.

With the dress factories shut down and both sides standing firm, only mediation could break the deadlock. But here came a problem. If Dubinsky asked for mediation, it meant his union was willing to come down. If the employers asked for mediation, it meant they were ready to go up. Secretly, Dubinsky sent a message to New York City's Mayor Robert Wagner, which said in effect, "This is your own idea, but don't you think that a man like ex-Senator Herbert Lehman would be a fine mediator for this strike crisis?"

Soon, with the eighty-year-old Lehman mediating the dispute, and with a bargaining session that began early one day and lasted until 4:30 A.M. the next morning, an agreement was reached. It gave Garment Workers an 11 percent pay increase plus benefits including severance pay for discharged workers.

Build-up

Union leaders and management men know that theirs is a marriage—for better or for worse. They know that there will always be another bargaining table, just as in marriage there's always a breakfast table in the cold light of the next morning. So union man and executive try to do nothing during bargaining that will humiliate or embitter the other. If the marriage is a happy one, one partner will even try to build up the other.

When Phil Murray died, some steel industry executives believed that his successor, David McDonald, would be a force for stability —a man who could hold a disciplined work force together and give the boss a full day's work for a full day's pay. So the steel industry gave McDonald concessions to build him up with his followers. As a result (and thanks to the skill of McDonald's former lawyer, Arthur J. Goldberg), the steel worker is one of the highest paid wage earners in industry.

When Charles E. Wilson was president of General Motors, he liked to exchange ideas with Walter Reuther. There'd be small meetings between the two men and their top aides. Wilson would get on the telephone and chat with Reuther—sometimes for a half-hour. From this warm relationship came General Motors' historic voluntary offer of automatic wage increases to cover rising living costs—and give workers a share in improved productivity.

Even when executives don't get along openly with the union leader, they respect his position as spokesman for their employees. They seek to avoid acts that will hurt him with his people and so drive him to irresponsible retaliatory acts.

When General Electric developed a savings and security plan for its employees, the company kept the plan under wraps until executives had a chance to explain it to union leader Jim Carey and his aides. Even during the most heated bargaining table tiffs, G.E. bargainers respect Carey's good faith and integrity. After such sessions Carey would sometimes go off to a social dinner with G.E. executive Virgil Day, where Carey—the Mr. Hyde of the bargaining table—would become the witty and engaging Dr. Jekyll of the dinner table.

Company people have long been restive about the dog-in-the-manager role that the bargaining process imposes on them. An employer who wants to give his people a ten-cent raise won't dare to make this his first offer, for fear he'll be bargained up to, say, fifteen cents, by the union. So he starts with two cents, makes a shadow fight and yields the ten cents he wanted to give in the first place—under the seeming pressure of the union. The union gets the credit, and the employer emerges as a churlish fellow who must be forced to do the right thing.

Today, automation is forcing historic changes in the collective bargaining process. For at today's bargaining tables two forces collide head on. One is the unions' dread of automation and determination to save members' livelihoods. The other is the employers' need to operate more efficiently, i.e., to install payroll-cutting machinery.

Labor Secretary W. Willard Wirtz has summed it up in this way:

"When employers and unions bargained over bread-and-butter issues, when a few cents divided them, compromises could be negotiated. But now jobs are at stake, and industry survival is at stake, too. And these put strains on employer-union relations we've never had before."

These strains were dramatized in early 1963 when New York City printers shut down the big city's newspapers for 114 days and the East Coast dockers immobilized shipping for thirty-four days.

One result of these union-employer confrontations over automation has been to lengthen the bargaining period. The lesson taught in recent strikes is that employers and unions can no longer meet, say, thirty days before the expiration of a contract and find ways to let the boss have his new machine yet protect the workers' jobs.

It took Harry Bridges and his West Coast longshoremen and the Pacific Maritime Association five months to hammer out an agreement that gave shipping men a free hand to introduce labor-saving machinery. And, as we've already seen, it took the United Steelworkers and the Kaiser Company several years to reach a long-range plan to cope with automation.

As we've seen, too, employers and unions have set up machinery in some industries that permits a virtual year-round, perpetual dialogue, aimed at threshing out problems that will arise at the next contract negotiation.

CHAPTER 17

Labor U.S.A.
vs. the Kremlin

Of all the unions' wide-ranging activities, their war against U.S.S.R. aims to export Communism makes one of their most glorious chapters.

American union men and dues payers' money prevented the Communists from seizing Western Germany's unions at the war's end, which would have created chaos and blocked recovery. America's unions dug up the evidence on Russia's slave labor camps and fashioned it into a major international scandal.

Union researchers in New York ferreted out the ammunition that blasted open the deadlock truce negotiations at Panmunjom in Korea. American unions provided an estimated $1,000,000 and leg men to smash a Communist monopoly over the unions of Italy, France and Japan. Not long ago, the unions took the lead in forming The American Institute for Free Labor Development. With employer support, the Institute teaches young Latin Americans how to promote free unions as a means of combating Communism. And today, the AFL-CIO pours some $1,000,000 yearly of American unionists' dues money into a world fight against Communist imperialism. The unions thus are one of the major unofficial forces in American life waging war on Communist expansion.

The late Sam Gompers first turned Labor's eyes overseas in 1910 by taking the old AF of L into the International Federation of Trade Unions. Housed in London, it had two modest aims: to collect union membership figures and to press for laws to bar the importing of strikebreakers.

Until World War I, international affairs were the concern almost exclusively of the striped-pants set. But the rise, after the war, of a nation that called itself a "workers state" yet introduced a new type of state slavery turned American union leaders' eyes abroad. As leaders of a pragmatic union movement, free from dogma, American union men were the first among the Western labor leaders to awaken to the challenge of Communism.

Today, the AFL-CIO has its own "State Department," the Department of International Affairs, headed by Jay Lovestone. It has a "Secretary of State," George Harrison, who counsels on foreign policy with a cabinet committee (the Executive Council's committee on International Affairs). And there is even a union "Voice of America," that is beamed to foreign readers: the *Free Trade Union News,* published monthly in English, German, French and Italian.

Behind George Meany, who was a member of the American delegation to the United Nations in 1957 and is a foreign affairs authority in his own right, is a little-known figure who has sparked ideas and often spearheaded major union campaigns against Communist intrigue abroad.

He is Jay Lovestone. Inside the Federation he holds two jobs: director of the International Department and director of international publications. But as we shall see he's much more, and at one time was so controversial a figure that explosions over him rocked the Federation.

Until 1957, Lovestone played an independent role, working outside the Federation with a Free Trade Union Committee financed voluntarily by half a dozen unions. He directed the anti-Communist cloak-and-dagger activities of field workers in Western Europe and North Africa, had his own anti-Red intelligence network, published an anti-Communist paper for foreign consumption and lobbied mightily before the United Nations.

All this stirred varying emotions in high union places. Walter

Reuther demanded that Lovestone's free-wheeling, lone wolf work abroad be curbed; that he be brought into and supervised by the Federation; and that the AFL-CIO itself stop going it alone abroad and channel its work through the international trade association of national labor movements—the International Confederation of Free Trade Unions (the ICFTU).

George Meany insisted that the AFL-CIO, as the biggest workers' federation in the world, couldn't simply content itself with paying dues to the ICFTU, but could make the most of its great influence abroad through independent projects. Reuther won the battle; Lovestone was brought into the Federation as a staff man. But Meany seems to have won the war. As months passed, and tempers cooled, the AFL-CIO worked more closely with the ICFTU, to be sure. But American unions, sparked by Lovestone ideas and the Lovestone information-gathering network, continued to push their own independent fight against Kremlin activity abroad.

To Catch a Red

George Meany regards Lovestone as the "most effective anti-Communist in America." He has lectured before the U.S. and Canadian War Colleges. For all that, only a handful of men inside the labor movement—and hardly anyone outside it—know the dimensions of the job that Lovestone, backed by union funds, has done.

This is a tribute to Lovestone's self-effacement, which borders on invisibility. He even has a phrase to describe it: "Technological anonymity." Lovestone has worked out a science or technique for remaining in the shadows.

One reason for the withdrawal is that it is no easy matter to bear the burden of having once been a Communist; even if it was long ago and one has atoned with a quarter-century of zealous fighting against Communism.

A reporter's first meeting with Lovestone takes on a sparring and cloak-and-daggerish quality. After an initial interview in Lovestone's book- and pamphlet-cluttered office in the Garment Workers Building—which yielded little information—I left him and walked down the corridor to the elevator. He dashed after me.

"You have violated the first rule in undercover work," he said. "You have left telltale documents behind." He handed me my notebook.

At nineteen, Lovestone was already secretary of the American Communist party. This was in 1917, when it was underground. He journeyed often to Moscow (he made eighteen pilgrimages in all) to meet with the bigwigs of the Communist world. An unregenerate name-dropper, Lovestone engages in the sport with a subtlety that goes beyond the mere mention of the mighty. Lovestone drops only the first name of the great man, leaving the listener to infer the depth of the intimacy.

"Joe would send for me, most every time I was in Moscow," Lovestone will say casually. "Joe had a wicked sense of humor," Lovestone will go on, "but mostly at other people's expense."

"Joe," of course, was Joseph Stalin. And the most exasperating part of the business is that Lovestone seems to have earned the right to drop "Joe's" name. He not only saw him at the Kremlin but chatted with him over a glass of tea at Stalin's home.

Conversation with Lovestone is likely to be a fascinating business. Out come stories of the time that "Tito stood up in a meeting of the Comintern and defended me and shouted everybody down, and yelled, 'Let the comrade from America speak!' "

Or Lovestone tells of his last talk with the old Bolshevik Nikolai Bukharin in Paris, who, facing certain death at the hands of his old partner, Stalin, nevertheless chose "to return to my homeland and die."

Lovestone even knew the mightiest Bolshevik of them all, V. I. Lenin, the architect of the Russian Communist Revolution.

"He was a master of dirty politics," Lovestone will recall.

Lovestone's palship with the Russian Communists ended in 1929 when he came to Moscow to resist Stalin's efforts to take over the American Communist party. No less a figure than Vyacheslav

Molotov was named by Stalin to look into Lovestone's "deviationism," and to boot him from the party.

The disgraced Lovestone—to his former Comrades he was now a leper—lingered long enough in Moscow to get an audience with his onetime pal, Joe, and complain about the rough treatment.

"A Bolshevik must know how to take a horse brush through his hair," Joe Stalin said.

Lovestone, penniless in Moscow, sold his underwear and his typewriter to get fare home. Back in America, he tried for a while to create an "American Communist party" free of Kremlin control, (the Lovestonites), then broke with Communism altogether in the mid-thirties. Today, he forms a unique human bridge to the minds, the methods and the drives of the conspiratorial Communist world. To this savvy, he adds further attributes.

Jay Lovestone is a medium-sized man with the look of an owl and the telltale facial pallor and softish body lines of the intellectual who spends too much time in libraries.

The birdlike cast of features is heightened by a strong nose, surmounted by heavy-lensed glasses.

These are honestly come by, for Lovestone has condemned his eyes to hard labor all his life. None of the usual adjectives that describe excessive reading can convey what goes on between Lovestone and the written word. In his modest two-room flat in midtown Manhattan, the four walls of the living room are lined with books from floor to ceiling. Additional thousands of volumes have spilled over into a warehouse nearby. These contain, Lovestone says, virtually everything published on the Russian Revolution, on the early Nazi movement and much on American history.

To his bookish aerie, Lovestone nightly lugs a briefcase or two plus a supplemental manila envelope crammed with periodicals, newspapers, field reports and monitored radio programs. Some forty-seven newspapers and magazines flow to Lovestone's office weekly from the four corners of the earth. About fifty correspondents—scattered from Reykjavik in Iceland to Delhi in India and from Warsaw in Poland to Melbourne in Australia—add periodic field reports to the flood of political and economic information.

Pencil and notebook in hand, Lovestone curls up for a night's study with a *Far Eastern Economic Review* (published in Hong Kong) or the *China News Analysis,* a compilation of news from Communist Chinese newspapers, or the Manchester *Guardian,* or the *Armenian Review.*

Even Russian novels—relaxation for others—are read with pencil and notebook.

"Novels are a social force," says Lovestone. "Very important. Give me a Russian novel and I'll give you a rundown on what the Russian people are told to like, what they hate, what they are doing."

The information gathering and monumental sifting and ingestion of counter-Communist intelligence are part of his own private war with the Communist enemy. This occupies almost every waking hour of his day.

He takes no vacations, and, until friends presented him with one, he didn't have a television set. Unencumbered by family—he never married—Lovestone battles Communism with the zeal of one who has seen the enemy up close. His influence is felt in the most unlikely places.

Lovestone has been listened to in the State Department. And on occasion he would canvass the world Communist situation in a talk with the then Secretary of State John Foster Dulles.

He helped convince the Eisenhower administration to name a labor man to the United States delegation to the UN.

To understand Lovestone's influence, it is necessary to go for a moment to Lovestone's shield and power source, George Meany.

Back in 1933, when George Meany was president of the New York State Federation of Labor, he attended a meeting at which labor men discussed Hitler's rise to power and formed the Anti-Nazi Non-Sectarian League.

"I learned there," Meany says, "that under any dictatorship, whether Fascist or Communist, no unions can survive. Nor can any other kind of voluntary organizations where people can meet and express themselves.

"For the first time, I realized how the impact of events in other areas of the world could affect the unions."

When Meany became secretary-treasurer of the old AF of L in 1934, there was virtually nothing for him to do because William Green, then president, jealously tended to everything. So, with the encouragement of his friend, David Dubinsky—already head over heels in foreign relief work—Meany turned to international affairs.

As is his tenacious custom, Meany read widely, boning up on events abroad, and so became the logical choice for delegate to the UN when the late Secretary of State Dulles looked around for a labor man for the job. Meany was assigned to the Third or "Human Rights" Committee. Long dominated by the Russians, it was known as the Lullaby Committee, because Soviet filibusters there put other delegates to sleep.

Meany changed this. As the voice of the American toilers, Meany became something of a puzzle to the Russians, who had been in the habit of assaulting American UN delegates as spokesmen for the "capitalist exploiters." Meany's resourcefulness in debate, particularly his boundless erudition and information, confounded the Soviet delegates even more. And this brings us back to Jay Lovestone.

Once Meany found himself up against a woman Soviet delegate who thundered—with glares at Meany—that "American unions belong to the ruling classes."

After the recess, Meany showed up with a copy of the Soviet Constitution (in English) and read that part of it that declares that the unions in the Soviet belong to and must take their guidance from the Communist party that rules Russia. It was a stopper.

None in the committee knew that Meany had hastened to the phone during the recess and posed his debating problem to Lovestone, a human Univac for storing information.

"You can murder them with their own constitution," said Lovestone, and from his memory dredged up chapter and verse.

One nonadmirer has described Lovestone as "Meany's intellectual valet," implying that Lovestone helps lay out Meany's pronouncements. Meany, as everyone in Labor knows, has a tough mind of his own. Still it is Lovestone who digs up ammunition for the policy decisions that Meany threshes out with his Executive Council.

The ammunition Lovestone culls from his researches sometimes explodes with historic results.

For months, truce negotiations in Korea were stymied by Communist insistence that prisoners in Allied hands be turned over to them—and to certain death as defectors. The Allies held out for "voluntary repatriation," the right of prisoners to choose the lands they'd return to. Agreement seemed impossible.

Then, as the *New York Times* reported on July 21, 1952, "A stunning blow [was struck] against Communist opposition to voluntary repatriation."

The chief United Nations truce negotiator dumfounded the Communist negotiators with documented evidence that the Soviet Union itself had applied the principle of voluntary repatriation during World War II. The evidence, said the *Times,* "was produced by historians of the AF of L."

Lovestone and a team of researchers had learned from Russian lawbooks and from propaganda in Russian newspapers that Stalin had broadcast a promise to enemy soldiers besieging Stalingrad. If they laid down their arms, they would be granted the right of voluntary repatriation after the war. The findings blew up the log jam at Panmunjom.

Monthly, there flow through Lovestone's office some three thousand pieces of mail, most of it from abroad and much of it bearing reports from correspondents.

Many of these reports are not entrusted to the mails and are brought in secretly, by hand. The correspondents, some of them disillusioned ex-Communists, sniff the wind of possible Communist intrigue and penetration.

To Lovestone's sensitive nostrils, once, came a field report from Iceland concerning fish, but smelling of much more. The news was that the British were cutting their fish purchases from the Icelanders. Lovestone caught the next plane to Washington and buttonholed friends in the State Department.

"Let's buy the damned fish ourselves, if we have to," Lovestone urged. "If we don't, the Russians will. It will be a Red foot in the door. And how about our bases in Iceland?"

We didn't "buy the damned fish ourselves," and soon—sure enough—the Russians were buying it. Commerce was followed by culture, and next the Russians were sending their ballet to Iceland. Before long, Icelandic voices began to protest against the American bases.

The protests and the Russians vanished from Iceland when the British resumed buying fish. But the incident gave point to one observer's comment about Lovestone's information. "Can't you get some of that information for us?" a high government official asked.

The Silent War

It was immediately after the war, in the subterranean struggles with the Communists in Western Europe, that American Labor played its most important role.

In 1944, David Dubinsky of the Garment Workers, the late Matthew Woll, an AF of L vice president, and George Meany formed the Free Trade Union Committee to help rebuild Europe's unions after the war.

Dubinsky suggested that Jay Lovestone head the Free Trade Union Committee.

As a man who had once known Lenin, Lovestone never forgot that Communists are guided by Lenin's advice.

"It is necessary to agree to any sacrifice," Lenin taught, "to resort to all sorts of devices, maneuvers and illegal methods, to evasion and subterfuge, in order to penetrate the trade unions, to remain in them and to carry out Communist work in them at all costs."[1]

If the Kremlin could "penetrate and remain in" Western Europe's unions after the war, the Communists could sabotage reconstruction, prevent the movement of coal to industrial plants, foster unemployment, hunger and chaos—and ring down the Iron Curtain on democracy.

The assault on the West's unions began on the day Russian troops marched into Berlin. The generals in charge of our military governments, knowing little or nothing about unionism, were little prepared for it. To this innocence was added betrayal. For the manpower departments of our military governments were crammed with American Communists.

The Russians urged the Allies to adopt Russian-proposed rules for regulating the unions. Union "experts" arriving with the Russian troops had these rules ready.

The Russians proposed as a chief regulation that no man could hold union office unless he was a worker in a plant.

Fair enough? Yet had this rule been imposed, the West German unions would have been lost to the West.

Western labor leaders had had a cruel time. The Nazis in Germany and the Fascists in Italy had herded them into concentration camps or simply slaughtered them. A similar fate awaited labor leaders under the Nazi occupation. Even those union men who evaded the Nazis and joined the underground resistance movements couldn't be sure of their lives. Communists fighting at their side, their own countrymen, murdered key democratic unionists to remove opposition to postwar Communist control.

Now, liberated from concentration camps and returning to rebuild their old unions, the union freedom fighters found themselves barred from union office by Russian regulations.

It was as if George Meany and Walter Reuther, having been jailed by an occupying power, could not return to their union offices because they weren't plant workers.

Nevertheless, the Russian union blueprint had the support of

[1] *Left Communism, an Infantile Disease,* by V. I. Lenin.

American Communists within the military government—including one who later renounced his American citizenship to live in Czechoslovakia.

At this point, from the trade unions of the New World came help to the unions of the Old.

The AF of L sent Irving Brown, a onetime associate of Lovestone in his youthful radical political adventures (but never a Communist) and later a union organizer and then adviser to the War Production Board. Brown, at fifty-two, is an intense, darkish, bespectacled man with fierce energy—and a mission.

Brown bombarded our military government with public harangue. And, at the risk of life and limb, he started to help reorganize free West German unions. Back home, the AF of L raised a clamor before the War and State Departments against the American Communists in the military government. These were cleared out, and the West German unions were rebuilt as anti-Communist labor organizations.

During the era of good feeling in 1944 toward "our gallant allies, the Russians," the powerful British Trades Union Congress and our CIO joined hands with the Soviet's labor organizations to form the new World Federation of Trade Unions (WFTU).

The CIO had been blocked out of world affairs, because the older AF of L would threaten to withdraw if the rival CIO were invited into any world federation of which the AF of L was a member. Now, with the AF of L refusing to have anything to do with the Russians, the way was clear for the CIO. Sparked by the ambitious Sidney Hillman, head of the Amalgamated Clothing Workers, the CIO was eager to play a world role and to make a go of the partnership with the Russians. As for Britain's unions, they had joined up reluctantly, largely under pressure from the British Foreign Office.

The new World Federation had noble aims—on paper: to improve the conditions of working people everywhere; to help build unions everywhere; to oppose war.

But to the AF of L, and to Lovestone, in the wings, the new

federation was a classic Communist united front. Behind it the Communists would pursue Kremlin policy. But how do you wage war on a worldwide federation claiming 70,000,000 members in fifty-three countries?

American politics teaches: if you can't lick 'em, join 'em. But Communist politics teaches: if you can't lick 'em, split 'em. Lovestone had learned how. You raised questions and issues on which those inside the enemy camp could not agree. To be specific, you raised questions which would make it impossible for the CIO and Britain's unions to remain in the Communist-dominated world federation.

The AF of L's top command gave the green light to Lovestone to polish up two wedges.

One wedge: the Soviet union is using slave labor. Hundreds of thousands, perhaps millions, of workers are herded into forced labor camps, both in the Soviet union and in the satellite countries.

From outposts behind the Iron Curtain, there was dug up the slave labor evidence, the first to be gathered. A pamphleteer with a dagger for a pen, Lovestone broadcast the evidence as far as the printed word could reach. Before AF of L conventions and the United Nations, and through Irving Brown in Europe, the slave labor disclosures were turned into an international issue and into prickly thorns for the free unions inside the Communist-controlled World Federation. Unable to convince the Communist majority to take a stand against slave labor, the CIO and the British unions began to wonder what they were doing inside the Red-controlled World Federation.

Another wedge was available: the Marshall Plan for economic recovery abroad. To West Europe's unions, the Marshall Plan meant jobs and food. The AF of L needled these unions to force their world federation to support the Marshall Plan. This brought out the World Federation's true color—Red. In its *Information Bulletin* the World Federation branded AF of L field man Irving Brown as a "propagandist of American Capitalist Monopolies." It published the captive Iron Curtain unions' attacks on the Marshall

Plan, but permitted *no* space *for* the plan.

In vain, the CIO sent its secretary-treasurer, James Carey, to Europe to demand that the World Federation support the Marshall Plan. When Carey failed, the West's unions withdrew. The World Federation was split. Only the Communist unions remained. The World Federation's potential for mischief was blunted, for it could no longer pose as anything but a Kremlin puppet.

This big split was followed by lesser splitting operations of Red-controlled unions in France, Italy and Japan.[2]

Soon after, the AF of L and the CIO buried the hatchet to help form a new world labor organization, the International Confederation of Free Trade Unions, limited to the bona fide unions of the free world.

Now, in 1950, there was in the field the largest federation of unions in history. The International Confederation of Free Trade Unions could draw on the resources of 53,000,000 members in eighty-three countries to pursue its chief aims: to build unions, particularly in underdeveloped countries, and to fight Communism on all fronts.[3]

Lovestone is much in evidence around the United Nations and is probably the most zealous lobbyist there. His acquaintance among delegates, like his researches, is impressive.

These UN friendships and lobbying bore dramatic fruit during the Hungarian revolt. Lovestone's aim, as an instrument of AFL-CIO policy, was to hang the Hungarian revolt and suppression like a bloody albatross around the Soviet's neck. Here is how it was done:

A distinguished Hungarian refugee, Anna Kethly, Minister of State in the democratic Nagy government, who had started to

[2] In Italy, with American help, dissidents were split away from the Communist Italian General Confederation of Labor to form the democratic Italian Confederation of Workers Unions (CISL—pronounced Chisel). In France, the Red Confédération Général du Travail was pried open to let out anti-Communists who formed the Force Ouvrière.

[3] One example: The International Confederation of Free Trade Unions raised $854,000 among its 117 affiliates to provide Hungarian relief and help labor leaders flee during the revolt of 1956.

America as her country's representative to the UN, arrived to find her government suppressed and herself without friends or funds. The AFL-CIO supplied both, and won friends for her among the United Nations delegates.

Lovestone worked for the idea of a "watchdog committee" to investigate and report on the Hungarian revolt. The watchdog committee evolved into the Special United Nations Committee that unearthed and reported the now famous UN findings on Hungary.

In the fall of 1957, Lovestone had a quiet dinner in New York with a friend whose occupation is as secret as his own: the "king's taster" and security chief for King Sidi Mohammed Ben Youssef of Morocco. The King himself, by his own royal request to our State Department, had met, on arriving in America, with George Meany. The King visited the AFL-CIO's headquarters, a stone's throw from the White House. There the King passed the time of day with high and low labor bureaucrats.

It was the first time that visiting royalty had paid this homage to the American Labor movement.

It was the King's way of thanking the unions for a significant piece of dungaree diplomacy: the role the unions had played in making Moroccan independence an international issue.

Capitalism with a Union Label

Dungaree diplomacy is yielding an unexpected dividend. Contact with American unions, plus agitation by visiting American firemen, is causing foreign unions to break with dogmas of the past. Before Mussolini, Italian unions, for instance, were organized on religious and political lines. There were the Christian unions (Catholic), the Socialist unions and the Anarcho-Syndicalist unions. The Italians have begun to take a leaf from the book of the American workers who organize simply on economic lines and shun domestic political and religious entanglements.

The American union example of bargaining for more now rather than waiting for a worker-government millennium is even having an influence in England, where the unions have long been the back-bone of the Labour party. English unions are having second thoughts about nationalization of industries as a cure-all and are turning to more aggressive bargaining instead. There is a diminishing faith in the concept of the state as a hander-outer.

The American union label, it turns out, is doing a giant job of selling the idea of a free economy abroad.

CHAPTER 18

Samuel Gompers:
Father with Labor Pains

A country, an institution or a movement usually has but one father. The American union movement had two. In fact, the union child was born in two stages—one set of birth pangs lasting fifty years. The baby nearly died. The second father took over with a new idea for its survival. Revived and regenerated, the union child shot up like a beanstalk to its present giant size.

The two fathers were Samuel Gompers and John L. Lewis.[1] The two men had many similarities. But they also had one great difference. Gompers passionately believed in organizing skilled workers of the same craft, to build unions of plumbers, or carpenters or cigarmakers. If the wages of the skilled were raised, the wages of the unskilled would take care of themselves, Gompers felt. With the craft union instrument, Gompers established a Labor movement beachhead against incredible opposition. But it was only a beachhead. It remained for Lewis, who passionately believed in another method of labor organization, the industrial union which embraces everybody in a plant or industry, to make the breakthrough—organizing the mass industries—that transformed the unions. From a minority, tolerated movement, they became a major participant in American life.

[1] A good case might be made for including a third father—Franklin Delano Roosevelt, whose Wagner Act broke the mass industries' resistance to unions.

Still, Gompers had to come first and make the one great contribution that would make possible John L. Lewis' vast organizing drives of the late thirties.

Gompers' contribution was to divorce the American unions from the class struggle. He forged a "pure and simple" unionism: "pure" of any revolutionary isms, and "simple" in that the union concerned itself solely with "more now" rather than with social panaceas and politicking for pie in the sky later. Gompers made the American unions a middle-class movement unlike any other in the world, a partner rather than a deadly enemy of the growing young American capitalist giant. He therefore made unions respectable to a people who had always regarded labor organizations with suspicion.

When Gompers died after wandering for thirty-eight years in the wilderness of hostile public opinion, he was buried with military honors. A postage stamp was struck off in his honor. A monument was erected to his memory at Washington, D.C., and dedicated by the President of the United States.

New York's East Side, where Gompers grew up toward the end of the last century, was an intellectual melting pot that stewed with every ism of protest then known to man. Socialism, anarchism, Communism—imported by refugees from European oppression— were in the air that Gompers breathed.

The sweatshops, the killing dawn-to-darkness workday, the poverty and hunger imposed on wage earners by early factory owners provoked agitation for social panaceas. Under these conditions, the Labor movements overseas had cast their lot with the politicians of protest and sought the better life through class "solidarity" and government by and for the proletariat. Yet here Gompers threw in his lot with a free economic system on the ground that a free union movement could survive only under free capitalism.

How did Gompers get this way?

In the answer lies the fascinating story of the growth of a trade union idea that fitted America. But, first, let's get acquainted with Gompers.

"But I'm President of the AF of L"

In aspect as in ideas, Sam Gompers was an original. He was, in fact, on first acquaintance—as his own secretary put it—"startling." Depending on how you felt about him, Gompers could be described either as a squat frog or as a pouter pigeon. His great chest and torso, those of a big man, moved on a little man's legs. He had the rough, boulder-like head of a peasant, but the knowing blue eyes and face of a man of great sensitivity. His long arms reached almost to his knees, but his hands were as finely shaped as those of an artist. And, to top this list of incongruities, there was the Gompers voice: rich, sonorous as a pipe organ and quite up to filling a Madison Square Garden or a cathedral.

The great chest and the greater voice gave Gompers an importance he took no trouble to dispel. Like many a small-sized man who makes a splash in the world, he bristled with humorless dignity and self-assertion. His two-volume autobiography has hardly one light word in it. It is stiff and formal and with perfectly straight face will picture Gompers attending an early union conference at which "practically every man [including Gompers—then as poor as a church mouse] wore a silk hat and a Prince Albert coat."

Gompers didn't unbend even in his most intimate letters to his family. The stiffness was due in part to Gompers' lifetime love affair with the English language, which he courted with the passion of a stranger who goes on discovering new resources in it all his life. Gompers seldom used a colloquial word where a "prose" word would do. Even his conversation had the rolling, elegant quality of a sentence from Gibbon.

At a time when every man's hand was raised against the unions and against the union leader, Gompers' humorless dignity was armor against a hostile world. Once when the then President Theodore Roosevelt tried to cut short an argument with Gompers with the assertion, "But, Mr. Gompers, I'm President of the United States," Gompers shot back, "But I'm president of the American Federation of Labor." When Teddy Roosevelt roared with laughter, Gompers didn't know what the other President was laughing about.

Gompers' rounded, fancy prose was highly effective on a platform. Once Gompers so shook up a Madison Square audience that the crowd started breaking up chairs. Gompers was thundering out against unemployment. Alarmed at what he had wrought, Gompers called on other oratorical powers to calm down the frenzied crowd. "Never again," Gompers vowed in his autobiography, "would I give such free rein to my emotions."

This oratorical talent, coupled with the showmanship and quick presence of mind of a carnival barker, helped Gompers through many an AF of L crisis. Once, during a convention, an exasperated Socialist foe leaped to the rostrum and thrust a pistol into Gompers' ample belly. A man with less self-importance might have panicked. But Sam owed it to his audience not to. With several hundred eyes fixed on him, Gompers placed his left arm on the pistol-packer's shoulder. Then in a stage voice he intoned, "Sir, hand me that pistol." The sonorous demand, repeated with increasing volume and dignity, was too much for the gun-toting wretch. He handed the pistol over. This, of course, brought down the house.

Another time, when radical foes heckled Gompers from the convention floor for patronizing a nonunion barber, Gompers challenged one detractor to rise and state his grievance.

"Who shaves you?" the critic demanded.

"Who shaves me?" Gompers intoned in his cathedral-organ voice.

"Yes, who shaves you?" the man wanted to know.

"Sam Gompers shaves me," said Gompers with dignity. Gompers, as usual, was dead serious. But he broke up the house anyway.

Since much about Gompers had a touch of the unexpected, it was logical that his private life should provide the greatest contradiction of all. For here Sam was the playboy of the union world.

The corner saloon, when Gompers was building the AF of L, played an important role in a worker's life. The bartender cashed his checks and had the latest news on jobs. During strikes there was the free lunch. Since the fledgling unions had no meeting halls, the saloon's back room served as a meeting place. Here in the dear dead days of the nickel schooner of beer, the boys nursed their drinks and talked union business. If the bartender complained about the beer nursing, the union meeting adjourned to another saloon.

To succeed as a union leader, then, a man had to develop the belly and kidneys of a brewery dray horse. Sam Gompers was equal to the challenge. In fact, Gompers' drinking exploits in time became a public matter that got into the newspapers and were aired before an AF of L convention.

"I love life and enjoy living," Gompers once admitted in a rare lapse into candor. "I have always rebelled at conventions that merely repress . . . and have hated hypocrisy."

"On any night," as one biographer painted the picture, Sam— lover of life—"might be found leading a crowd of men into a saloon where, far into the night, they would make merry with foaming beer and sometimes with more potent liquor."

Gompers was a man who hated to be alone. Solitude, as he put it, "had no joy or comfort for me. A companion with the love of life added pleasure to the day's work."

So when Sam was in some strange city on a union mission and evening fell, he'd become restless. "Let's take a walk and get some fresh air," he'd say.

Then, with the instinct of a homing pigeon, he'd set a course for some side street lined with workmen's saloons. There he'd find the "fresh air" he sought: the yeasty, sometimes miasmic, air of the saloon's back room.

"Many a time over a mug of beer or a drink of whiskey," Sam Gompers recalled, "I won men for the cause of trade unionism when I would fail in every other way."

In his early days of grinding poverty, Gompers could make a meal of soup created from flour, salt, pepper and water. Gompers

and his burgeoning family (he had eight children in all) knew
hunger even after Gompers became AF of L president and had a
hard time collecting his twenty-two-dollars-a-week pay. But when
the AF of L became stabilized and per capita revenues poured in
from the constituent unions, Gompers turned to good living with
gusto.

Gompers got to be so well known as a night-life figure that
comedians in New York's old burlesque or girlie shows would
signal his arrival by patting their bellies affectionately and calling
them "my Sam Gompers." After the show, he'd play the role of
jolly host at supper and, flanked by pretty girls—as one biographer
relates it—he'd consume endless drinks and cigars.

Naturally this lust for life was not lost on Gompers' enemies. The
Knights of Labor, a bitter rival of the AF of L in the 1890's, broadcast a pamphlet which declared: "The General Executive Board [of
the Knights of Labor] has never had the pleasure of seeing Mr.
Gompers sober."

Gompers' anguished protests never did catch up with this canard.

Hard work—Gompers sometimes got by with one hour's sleep at
night—harder play and even harder knocks from a bitterly antiunion world showed on Gompers toward the end of his life. At
seventy-four he was almost blind; his hair had come out in great
patches, accentuating the ill-health and homeliness of his rugged
face. His body was racked with diabetes.

"I have been tried and seared as few men have," Gompers wrote
at the time. "I have almost had my soul burned in the trial of life."

Being no angel contributed to the searing. The times in which
Gompers built his union contributed even more.

It was Gompers' fate to arrive in America as a thirteen-year-old
immigrant boy when the Civil War was ending and the curtain was
going up on America's explosive rise toward world industrial leadership. The new age of invention was creating great industries and

turning millions of farmer boys and small-town Americans into industrial workers and potential union recruits. The machines also brought social chaos and unrest. The times were tailor-made for the labor organizer role Gompers was to play. But they also held obstacles that were to limit this role.

Between young Gompers' arrival in 1863 and his founding of the American Federation of Labor in 1886 (when he was thirty-six), some 400,000 new patents poured forth. The Westinghouse air brake, interlocking block signals and George Pullman's palace car had revolutionized rail travel and freight hauling by 1870. The refrigerator car, making its debut in 1875, created a new meat-packing industry.

By 1900 Edison's incandescent lamp, Alexander Graham Bell's telephone, Hoe's rotary press that could print and fold 240,000 eight-page newspapers in an hour and Christopher Shole's typewriter had changed the lives of city dwellers and businessmen.

By 1900, too, thanks to the Bessemer open hearth process, electricity and chemistry, America's great ironmasters were producing as much steel as Great Britain and Germany.

So by 1910—when Sam Gompers was a vigorous sixty—more than 50 percent of Americans lived in towns and cities. And the United States had become the leading manufacturing and industrial power in the world. Factory workers had swelled to an army of 9,000,000.

No other country offered such a market for the union organizer's services. Although machinery in time made the American worker the envied home- and gadget-owning aristocrat of the Western world, few of machinery's early benefits went to the worker. Floods of immigrants—18,000,000 poured in between 1880 and 1910—competed for jobs and depressed wages everywhere. In the basic industries workers were idle 20 percent of the time.

"A large part of our industrial population," a Presidential Commission reported at the turn of the century, "are living in a condition of actual poverty." With indignation seldom found in a government document, the Commission report went on: "Between one-fourth and one-third of male factory and mine workers 18 years and over earn less than $10 a week; from two-thirds to three-fourths earn less than $15 weekly." This was less than was needed to keep body and soul together. The difference was made up by hunger or by the labor of women and children.

Nearly half of women workers in factories, shops and laundries worked at less than six dollars a week, the President's Commission found.

"Last of all are the children," the report continued, "for whose petty addition to the stream of production the nation pays a heavy toll in ignorance, deformity of body or mind and premature old age. The competitive effect of the employment of women and children on men's wages can scarcely be overestimated."

It wouldn't occur to anybody today to pay a fireman only when he goes out to a fire, and to keep him unpaid as he waits in the firehouse. Yet when streetcars first appeared on New York streets, motormen and conductors reported at dawn at the car barns, then waited their turn to take a car out. "Often," as Gompers told it, "days passed without their obtaining more than one round trip."

As late as 1923, the year before Gompers died, steel mills operated on a twelve-hour day and a seven-day week. Trainmen worked seventy hours a week, and textile mill operatives, most of them girls and women, worked sixty to seventy hours.

When Gompers set out to organize worker discontent, he found he had a lifetime war on his hands.

The union curbs the owner's absolute control over his producing property through the "work rules," wages and working conditions it bargains out. To the early industrial giants, the idea that the worker could exercise this power was a revolutionary one to be resisted at all cost.

"You are willing to let . . . killings take place rather than settle conditions?" John D. Rockefeller, Jr., was asked during the Ludlow, Colorado, mine strike of 1913.

"We believe so sincerely . . . that the [mining] camps shall be open [nonunion], that we expect to stand by our officers at any cost," Rockefeller replied. The cost was the lives of seventeen miners, their wives and children.

Some employers, like railroad man George F. Baer, had a divine-right explanation for it.

"The rights and interests of the laboring man will be protected and cared for, not by the labor agitators, but by the Christian men to whom God, in his infinite wisdom, has given control of the property interests of the country," said Baer.

So the struggle for a voice over the conditions of one's work, i.e., industrial freedom, plunged America into a half-century of violent industrial war which at times flared into something akin to revolutionary class struggle.

The difference was that in the class struggles of older countries an oppressive government was the target. Here the target was the employer. The worker's weapon was the strike and the boycott. The employer resisted with the lockout, the black list, with private armies, detective agency spies and with compliant police and state militia.

The history of the unions, then, is largely a fighting history with its own Bunker Hills, Gettysburgs and Waterloos.

One battle had for its battlefield virtually the entire continent. This was the railroad workers' revolt, now known simply as "the Great Strike of 1877." It started when Eastern railroad executives ordered firemen then working for five dollars and six dollars a week to take another 10 percent cut. The men struck and were soon joined by mobs of unemployed who blocked rail traffic and destroyed rail property. Riots and pitched battles with militia spread from New York to San Francisco. More than one hundred rail workers were killed. Several hundred were wounded. For the first time during peace, federal troops were called out to suppress a strike.

At Homestead, Pennsylvania, in 1892, strikers fought it out with an army of rifle-bearing Pinkerton detectives imported by the Carnegie Steel Company. The strikers suffered three dead and won that battle from the Pinkertons, who lost seven men. But the strikers lost the war. They couldn't cope with continued use of force. The pattern of armed suppression (to break picket lines) introduced at Homestead helped bar unions from the steel mills for forty years.

The names of the industrial war's battles are as gory as those in any military history. "Bloody Ludlow" describes the fight between the Colorado Fuel and Iron Company and its miners. "The Herrin Massacre" is the name by which Illlinois disorders, bordering on civil war, are remembered. "Bleeding Harlan" described similar struggles between miners and owners in Kentucky.

The industrial war even included a "children's strike."

When textile millowners at Lawrence, Massachusetts, precipitated a strike with a wage cut in 1912, they faced professionals in the class struggle. These were strategists sent by the radical Industrial Workers of the World, who took over the strike and welded the twenty thousand untutored immigrant strikers into a disciplined resistance group.

Chief problem was to feed the strikers' families—some fifty thousand mouths. To meet it, the strike leaders appealed to families all over America to take in the strikers' children. Soon, trainloads of children were pouring out of Lawrence to eager foster parents in Boston, New York, Philadelphia and other cities. Each trainload removed hundreds of mouths that needed feeding. And wherever the children went, they aroused public indignation against employers who had forced the separation of mothers and babies. The employers tried to stop the exodus by force, obtaining court injunctions against the removal of the children. When the migration persisted, state militia men invaded the trains, clubbed mothers and children and hauled them to detention centers. This, of course, fanned public indignation further, and the millowners had to settle on the strikers' terms.

In twenty-five turbulent years—from 1881 to 1906—the country was rocked by 38,000 strikes and lockouts in which some 9,500,000 wage earners battled for union recognition or better conditions against 200,000 resisting employers.

If Sam Gompers were to build an enduring union movement where none had survived before, he had the triple job of overcoming resistance from employers on the right, radicals from the left—taking care meanwhile not to scare the living daylights out of the fearful middle class in the middle.

Rope Trick

Into a bare, brick-floored shed near New York's East River docks one day in 1886, Sam Gompers and his schoolboy son, Henry, lugged a kitchen table borrowed from their home. From the grocer across the street they brought some tomato crates. From a school nearby they borrowed ink. Gompers and son were furnishing the first "headquarters" of the American Federation of Labor.

The shed, eight by ten feet—the size of a dentist's anteroom— had been donated by Gompers' Cigar Makers Local 144. It had a door and a small window. Gompers looked about him with pride. At thirty-six, he had just been elected president of the newly founded AF of L. Gompers balanced his chunky body on an upended crate, dipped his pen into the borrowed ink and thoughtfully composed a letter—so transacting the AF of L's first piece of business.

At the AF of L founding convention at Columbus, Ohio, several weeks before, Gompers had presented a blueprint.

This blueprint Gompers had drawn by studying the rise and fall of prior attempts to unite workingmen.

Led by intellectual reformers, some of these early "unions" had been curious catch-alls. One, the National Labor Union, had not only embraced local and national unions but women's suffrage leagues and farmers' groups as well. Another, the Knights of Labor, was open to all workers, skilled and unskilled, as well as to farmers, merchants, capitalists. Only "professional gamblers, bankers, liquor dealers and lawyers" need not apply.

Then there were the Sons of Vulcan, the Knights of Industry, the Followers of Lafayette, the Washington Guards, the Lincoln Leaguers—all with secret passwords and rituals, boyish hand-shakes, and vague, political reform goals.

Into these, workers in quest of better conditions poured, in and out as through great sieves.

Gompers introduced two simple, but then novel, ideas: The first was "autonomy." He convinced fellow unionists that the AF of L should be patterned on the federal principle of the United States government. National unions could join and (unlike the states) withdraw voluntarily. The unions could elect their own officers, make their own deals with employers and call their own strikes without interference from the Federation government at the top.

The second principle was that only trade unions working for economic goals—more pay, shorter hours, better working conditions—could belong.

The AF of L founding convention voted its president a thousand-dollar yearly salary. For a staff, Gompers had a treasurer at $100 a year and an office boy, his son Henry, who worked after school and summers at $3 a week. The AF of L started with 25 affiliated unions embracing some 317,000 members, who, it was figured, would bring the AF of L some $5,000 operating money the first year.[2]

Since there was no president's salary until the AF of L constitution became effective several months after the convention, Gompers, his wife Sophie and their six children had a hard time of it to eat and pay the rent. But Gompers had a solution. He asked his family to make believe he was on strike.

When Gompers took to the road to organize unions, he became even poorer. In contrast to the $128-a-day luxury hotel suite Dave

---

[2] In 1963, the AFL-CIO collected $8,440,698 per capita dues from 131 international and national unions, plus another $928,471 from directly chartered federal locals.

Beck of the Teamsters was to lavish on himself later, union provision for traveling expenses was sketchy in Gompers' day. From
one cross-country trip Gompers returned "$90 out of pocket." A
trip through New England left him "$35 short."

Gompers had as little power and authority as he had money.

He could advise or persuade; he could arbitrate. But he couldn't
order or compel. This was done by the officers of the autonomous,
constituent unions.

The public couldn't understand that the leader of all of America's unions had no direct power. So Gompers spent a good deal
of time explaining to the public he was no "labor generalissimo,"
as some newspapers described him.

"I have never ordered a strike, I have never decreed a strike,
and I have never had the power to call off a strike after it is
called," he once said.[3]

Gompers' job was to give the AF of L permanence, make it a
force in the industrial life of the country, and to win for it the
loyalty of American workmen.

Gompers coined a slogan, "Organize the unorganized." As the
AF of L's treasury grew, he built an army of recruiting sergeants
(union organizers). He helped organize twenty-eight new international unions, among them such future giants as the Garment
Workers and the Carpenters. The army of union organizers also
became Gompers' eyes and ears around the country, and was the
foundation on which he built a political machine which kept him
in power for thirty-eight successive years.[4]

Gompers showed how a Federation could endure. But, to make
the lesson stick, he had to develop a type of unionism that fitted

[3] The Federation president's role is still so little understood that, in the
fall of 1957, George Meany was still explaining to Senators Barry Goldwater
and Carl Mundt that the Federation had no power to negotiate contracts or
settle strikes.

[4] With the exception of 1895, when the Socialists and Single Taxers ganged
up on Gompers and sidelined him until the next annual convention.

the America of his time. And to win a bitter, eighteen-year civil war in which the Socialists, boring from within the Federation, tried to take the unions away from him.

Antiradical Radical

The man who was to build a middle-class, conservative Labor movement in America was born into a world in which everything cried for change. The time was 1850, the place was London's East Side. Gompers' home was a single tenement room where his Dutch-Jewish immigrant parents and their five children ate, slept, bathed and pursued such family life as was possible.

In the neighborhood lived silk weavers then losing their jobs to new machinery. They tramped the narrow streets, wringing their hands and filling the air with a cry that was burned into young Gompers' mind.

"God, I've no work to do," the men wailed. "Lord, strike me dead; my wife, my kids want bread, and I've no work to do."

Sam was taken out of a Jewish religious school at ten and apprenticed to a shoemaker, promptly begged off, because he couldn't stand the noise, and asked his father to apprentice him to the quieter cigarmaking trade instead.

When the Gompers brood migrated to New York and Sam found jobs at his trade, the shops were so quiet that the cigar-makers would choose one among them to read out loud or spend the time debating the problems of the day. The reading and debating naturally turned to schemes for social change. Much of the talk concerned unions, then little more than social clubs.

Young Gompers, then approaching twenty, was a sight for startled eyes. Eager to get on with the job of being a man, he had cultivated a walrus mustache. This, on a face lighted by dancing blue eyes, gave Gompers a half-bumptious, half-prankish air. Eager to get on, too, Gompers had married at seventeen when a friend had imprudently entrusted his best girl to Gompers for a summer. So, emerging from his teens, Gompers was already a paterfamilias with four mouths to feed.

He was also an assertive figure among his cigarmaking shop-mates. He learned to think on his feet, to use every trick of show-manship and timing and so become one of the most effective orators of his time. From the worktime discussion searches for the millennium, Gompers graduated to an inner circle of workmen-thinkers who called themselves the "Ten Philosophers." Out of their orgies of talk into the early morning hours, according to Gompers, "came the purpose and the initiative that finally resulted in the [modern] labor movement."

Two of the "Ten Philosophers"—older men than Gompers—be-came his mentors, helping him pick his way through the forest of Socialism, anarchism, greenbackism, single taxism, toward the idea that in the trade union lay the workers' best hope for a better deal. One was Ferdinand Laurel, a big and powerful Swede, known for his practical longheadedness as *Ferdkopf,* horse head. The other, a taciturn, blunt man and Jewish immigrant like Gompers, was Adolph Strasser. All about Gompers on New York's Lower East Side were rebels and revolutionaries. When everybody's a leftist, it's radical not to be one. That's the kind of radical Gompers be-came.

Laurel had an insider's knowledge of Europe's revolutionary movements—and an insider's disillusion. This had turned him from politics to unionism.

Strasser, also a disillusioned radical like Laurel, helped distill the slogan for which Gompers is perhaps best remembered: "More, now."

Testifying before a Senate committee in 1873, Strasser, then president of the Cigar Makers Union, was asked, "What are your ultimate ends?"

"We have no ultimate ends," Strasser replied. "We are going on from day to day. We are fighting only for immediate objects—ob-jects that can be realized in a few years."

Question: You want something better to eat and to wear and better homes to live in?

Strasser: Yes, we want to dress better, and to live better, and become citizens generally.

Gompers boiled all this down to one sentence: "It takes no philosopher to see that $3.00 a day is better than $2.50 a day." Then, to one phrase: "More, now."

The first task that practical men Gompers, Strasser and Laurel set themselves was to turn their local Cigar Makers Union—the famous Local 144—into a guinea pig.

Strange as it may seem, the pre-Gompers unions had no formal method or machinery for making demands on the employer.

Sam Gompers introduced the union contract and so put the union's relations with the employer on a stable and continuing basis. The discovery of the union contract was to modern unionism what the discovery of the wheel was to civilization. It made unionism go by solving problems raised by two central actors in the union drama: the boss and his worker.

The boss's dilemma was this: how do you accept and live with a union which, after all, is a device for curbing your control over your own property? The contract made possible a working partnership. The boss continued as property owner, risk taker and profit taker. The union, through the contract, became the administrator of the job. The contract set wages, conditions for overtime, for seniority (priority to the job). The contract stipulated who could become an apprentice and how he'd be trained; it even set the conditions for introducing new machinery. While the union didn't own the job, it established control over it.

The wage earner's dilemma was this: in older countries, where a man was born into a class and remained there, it made sense to fight for improvement through "class solidarity," i.e., by allying one's self with others in the same boat. But in the land of the American Dream, where a man could strike it rich, move out of his class through education or energy, class solidarity and the class struggle held little luster. What could a class organization like a union do for you that you couldn't do for yourself? The answer, as Gompers worked it out through the union contract, was that a union protected your rights to the job. The American worker who wouldn't buy "class solidarity" would buy "job solidarity." He would band together with others to protect his job.

So the union contract became the taproot from which a Labor movement could flourish in free enterprise soil.

Soon, full-time officials and staff men arose to serve the contract: to study the market for the labor of union members so that it could be sold, in a businesslike way, for the highest price; to police or enforce the contract; to settle disputes arising from it. With the contract as the local's backbone, the union became the business agent for the workers. This was pure and simple unionism, business or fundamentalist unionism, built around the contract.

On Guinea Pig Local 144 of the Cigar Makers, Gompers tried other ideas. One was the payment of regular, substantial dues. A man who gave little to his union would have little interest in it, he felt. Nor could he expect anything from the union in time of need, because it had no treasury. Gompers also pioneered with out-of-work benefits, union death and sickness insurance. He wanted the worker to rely on his union for the security he might otherwise seek from the government. A Jeffersonian Democrat with a distrust of government, Gompers felt so strongly that the worker should make his own security through his own unions that he helped kill Social Security legislation when it was first introduced in 1916.

Gompers' pure and simple unionism was tested in the depression year of 1877 when cigar manufacturers dismissed many of their workers and cut the wages of those who remained, bringing on a strike. Gompers and his practical philosophers led a disciplined strike in which, for the first time, the united strength of the strikers approached the solid front of resisting employers.

The times were against the strikers. Unions were not popular or even respectable. Gompers' cigar strike ultimately collapsed when the employers—who knew a thing or two about organizing, too—joined hands to lock out those workers whose earnings were sup-

porting the strikers. Unions used to blossom forth during strikes
to die when the strike was over or succumb during depressions. But
Gompers' Local 144 survived the strike and the depression.

Gompers thought through a union fundamental to which he
adhered with the religious fervor of a true believer. It was this:
Americans are essentially conservative and property-conscious,
and labor unions can't afford to arouse public opinion by threats
to private property.

Gompers learned this precept at first hand in 1874 when he
narrowly escaped death under the hoofs of mounted police who
were suppressing a New York workers' demonstration that had
been captured by leftist fire-eaters.

"I saw how professions of radicalism and sensationalism concentrated all the forces of organized society against the labor
movement," he wrote. It was a lesson he never forgot.

The Socialists, who battled Gompers for AF of L control for
almost two decades, regarded the unions as mere palliatives and
useful only as spearheads in a war for social change. So, to Gompers, everything they stood for was a threat to his fledgling unions.

The first big battle came over the Socialists' notion that sections
or cells of the party had a right to affiliate with the AF of L as a
party. It was as if Tammany Hall, the Democratic organization in
Manhattan, wanted to affiliate today with the AFL-CIO.

The showdown came about when unions in New York asked
Gompers for a charter to form a city-wide "Central Trades Federation." On the list of petitioning "unions" was the New York section
of the Socialist party.

Gompers gave an indignant no to the charter petition; then beat
the Socialists three to one in a test at the next convention.

Year after year, the Socialists would propose at conventions
that the AF of L harness itself to drives for the collective ownership
of industry—or the "cooperative commonwealth."

To this Gompers once replied, "I want to tell you Socialists that I've studied your philosophy and read your works. I declare to you: economically you are unsound, socially you are wrong, industrially you are impossible."

About Rewards and Punishments

Sam Gompers drew about him a hard-drinking and hard-fighting group of Irish huskies. The Irish took as naturally to union politics as they took to big-city politics, soon built union machines that kept them in office for years and were Gompers' solid underpinning in the Federation.

By 1905, only two decades after the founding of the AF of L, Sam Gompers, still beleaguered by enemies, could nevertheless look about him with some satisfaction. His pure and simple unionism dominated the union field with 1,500,000 members, by far the largest agglomeration of union power ever assembled.

Politics, in Sam Gompers' union book, was something to be scorned altogether—or used sparingly. It could be used, for instance, to pressure state legislatures to help those workers who could not help themselves, say women and children.

Then, suddenly, Gompers plunged head over heels into politics.

The enemy, the employer, had wheeled up weapons which had turned Sam Gompers' economic artillery of boycott, strike and picket line into peashooters. One employer weapon was the court injunction which could spike a strike—the union's ultimate weapon—by banishing the picket line or barring the boycott. The union man who dared defy the injunction went to jail for contempt of court, without jury trial. If the union appealed, it faced years of treasury-draining lawsuits.

Another weapon was the Sherman Anti-Trust Act. Passed by Congress in 1890 to curb business monopolies, the famous law had gathered dust until the government turned it against unions—a use that must have surprised many of the Congressmen who voted for it.

For instance: When hatmakers struck against a Danbury, Connecticut, employer in 1903 and urged a boycott against his products, the Hatters Union was prosecuted as a monopoly in restraint of trade. The punishment was a $250,000 fine which cost the hatters their homes and their life savings. The famous Danbury Hatters Case—upheld by the U.S. Supreme Court—exposed the unions to widespread suits and impotence in the battle with anti-union employers.

When St. Louis metalworkers struck the Bucks Stove Company, Gompers put the company on the "unfair list" published in the AF of L magazine. This meant that good unionists would boycott its products. The stove manufacturer obtained an injunction which not only forbade the strikers to boycott the company but also barred published comment on the dispute. Gompers defied the order, was held in contempt of court and ordered to jail for a year.

The judge belabored Gompers as "a leader of the rabble who would unlaw the land, bring hideous pestilence and . . . subordinate the law to anarchy and riot."

Gompers took this with controlled rage. Then in tones that Patrick Henry might have used, Gompers orated, "If I cannot discuss grave problems in which the people of our country are interested . . . I shall have to bear the consequences. . . ."

Gompers never went to jail, because the Supreme Court held, seven years later, that the issue was moot, i.e., the strike was over.

For ten years Gompers battled to win laws that would curb the use of the injunction and exempt the unions from the Sherman Act. But, being Gompers, he devised his own kind of politicking: Don't get married to any one party. Don't give birth to a Labor party of your own. Play the field. Reward your friends and punish your enemies, whether they are Republicans or Democrats or whatever. Gompers launched campaigns to unseat hostile Congressmen and stumped Maine in a drive against a Republican officeholder. The campaigns had mixed results, but they did scare some hostile Congressmen into a more cautious attitude toward Labor. In time Woodrow Wilson helped Gompers win the Sherman Act curb he wanted, which the courts promptly emasculated; and it remained for the New Deal to bring the relief that Gompers had sought.[5]

But Gompers had laid down a principle which the unions still religiously follow: No matter what the provocation, don't be drawn into Labor party or other third-party adventures.[6]

The Summing Up

The time was the fall of 1924; the place was El Paso, Texas. The chief actor: Sam Gompers. Now, seventy-four, ravaged by disease and incredibly hard work (and play), and almost blind, he sat huddled on the rostrum while the Labor movement bade its "Grand Old Man" good-bye. Men who rise to the leadership of the Plumbers, or the Miners, or the Stone Cutters don't burst into tears easily. But on that day, the last of the AF of L convention, there wasn't a dry eye in the house.

Delegate after delegate rose to pay homage to Gompers' forty years of service to the unions. For the last time, friends and critics alike cast a unanimous ballot for Sam Gompers for president. With tears rolling down his cheeks, Gompers said his last words of farewell.

This tearful praise for Gompers' lifework, coming in 1924, had an ironic twist. For here was the state of the unions at that moment:

In five years, after hitting a membership peak after the First World War, the unions had lost more than a million members. Now, although the AF of L still mustered 2,800,000 dues payers, it was relatively worse off than in 1910. Then it commanded 10 percent of the country's workers. Now it had only 5 percent.

Not only that. The AF of L also seemed permanently barred

[5] The Norris–La Guardia Act.

[6] At least not on a national scale. David Dubinsky of the ILGWU and Alex Rose of the Hatters Union helped form and run a Labor party, later renamed a Liberal party, that plays a balance-of-power role in New York City and State politics.

from the one great reservoir of workers that could make it a significant movement—the mass industries: autos, steel, rubber, cement. In a great industrial nation, the AF of L mustered virtually no industrial workers, drawing its members from the building trades, clothing manufacture, printing, mining.

The unions couldn't even retain the minority position to which their impotence doomed them. They faced disintegration through a new counterattack from antiunion employers. At the very moment that Gompers was receiving the tearful kudos of his followers, employers were wooing away union members through the "American Plan," i.e., through company unions.

The unions were crumbling, and resisting industries seemed impregnable.

Had Sam Gompers failed?

No one could give the answer in 1924 when Sam Gompers "went out into the silence." The answer—that he had not failed—came a decade later when the Labor movement's other father, John L. Lewis, backed by the New Deal sentiments of a depression-battered people, picked up where Gompers had left off and forced the mass industries to accept unions.

CHAPTER 19

John L. Lewis:
Labor's Rogue Elephant

One day in 1955, the elders of the AFL-CIO Executive Council, whose ponderings cover lots of territory, had an argument over oil paintings. At the entrance to their oak-paneled conference room atop the new AFL-CIO Washington headquarters building, they had already enshrined on canvas four Labor greats: Samuel Gompers, William Green, Philip Murray and George Meany. Now the debate swirled around a painting that wasn't there, that of John L. Lewis, boss of the miners, father of the mighty auto, steel and other mass-industry unions, and, all in all, the most resplendent figure the unions have yet sprung.

Bouncy David Dubinsky, who has a forthright New York Garment Center English all his own, rose to ask, "Are you fellas trying to rewrite the history books just like the Russians? Trotsky is kicked out of Russia, so you don't find him in the Communist encyclopedias. Lewis kicks himself out of the Federation. So are you going to treat him like Stalin treated Trotsky?"

The "fellas" on the Executive Council nevertheless decided against sanctifying Lewis with a painting. They declared, in effect, "To hell with him. He ain't one of us."

The incident of the missing painting points up Labor's grandest enigma, the life and works of John Llewellyn Lewis. It was Lewis who broke the mass-industry barrier to unionism, recruited millions and so transformed a dead-end, minority Labor movement into a major factor in American life. Lewis, in the late thirties, was a popular leader who swayed multitudes of men, gave Churchillian phrases to their aspirations and bent foes outside of Labor—and inside—to his will. For a brief moment, Lewis gave the unions excitement, drama and purpose. Men pinned their hopes on him, and in millions of homes his picture hung side by side with that of the Virgin Mary or Franklin D. Roosevelt. Then, on a caprice, Lewis dropped the reins of the CIO he had founded.

Lewis said farewell with "I have done my work." That was in 1940 when Lewis was sixty, at the height of his powers, and with the union-organizing job by no means finished. Since then, the man who has done so much for the unions has been outside the pale of Labor's councils. President emeritus of the Miners since 1960, he played the role of a great rogue elephant, using his declining strength to harass the labor world he once dominated.

Man on a Mountain Peak

Few men, dubbed great within their own lifetimes, have accepted their own grandeur as unquestioningly as John L. Lewis.

He could couch it in sublime terms:

"The heights are cold," Lewis confided in his farewell speech of 1940. "Who ascends to the mountaintop finds the loftiest peaks encased in mist and snow."

Or go to the ridiculous:

"Even the posterior of a great man is of interest," he said, after stooping over to tie a shoelace and straightening up to find a busload of Washington rubberneckers watching him.

Such is the awe that Lewis cast upon his office family that a visitor to the United Mine Workers Building in Washington was likely to feel he was in the hushed temple of some feared tribal deity.

Toward the rear of the spacious entry hall, an elevator operator sat silently, like a guard.

"Mr. Lewis," he would repeat with seeming incredulity. "You

mean you want to see Mr. John L. Lewis?"

On the second floor the visitor would pass through two ante-rooms, each easily the size of a Washington Cabinet member's office. In the first, two stenographers worked silently beneath a John L. Lewis who scowled down upon them from a portrait in oils on the wall. There was tension and a damn-your-eyes look about Lewis—from the gray mane of hair to the turned-down, firm mouth, the broad, outthrust chin and the dewlaps. This was the face that launched a thousand jibes when Lewis was the symbol of massed union power. It was the face of an angry man and of one who was playing a part in the grand manner.

Does Lewis ever smile in public, you wondered as you looked up at the famous dark cliffs of eyebrows that overhung and recessed the steel-gray eyes.

Through a second anteroom you went, where a union functionary sat silently behind a bare desk and outstretched newspaper.

Now you entered the lair—or shrine—of the great man and began the trek, dubbed the "last mile," to the outsized desk in the farthest reaches of the depot-like room. The office, some forty by forty feet, was weighted down with overstuffed leather furniture once favored in corporate executive suites and men's clubs. The ceiling was vaulted like that of a small church, and from it hung a magnificent crystal chandelier. Behind a giant desk that has been described as "the throne" sat John L. Lewis, massive, silent and portentous like a great Buddha.

The first time this writer walked the "last mile" to Lewis' desk was on the delicate business of asking questions about the "provisional" system with which Lewis abolished elections for key posts in the UMW and ran the show with appointees.

The brief interview yielded more insight into John L. Lewis than it did into autocracy in his union.

After a few questions, Lewis said, "If you want to paint John L. Lewis as a tyrant, go ahead and paint him as a tyrant. You aren't going to get any help from Lewis."

He referred to himself in the third person with the same lack of self-consciousness that Charles de Gaulle does.

But, as a subsequent interview proved, Lewis could be charming too, and again in the grand manner.

When the Lewis scowl unfreezes, the Lewis smile can warm the visitor all over. He can perform virtuoso feats of conversation, clothing his speech with so picturesque and literary a quality that the visitor feels Lewis is putting on a show especially for him. An ordinary labor man says, "If you raise the wages of the lowest paid, the wages of the higher paid will take care of themselves." Lewis said, "If you raise the valleys, the peaks will take care of themselves."

Face to face, Lewis could melt the most determined critics. Columnist Westbrook Pegler was so warmed over by a Lewis tête-à-tête that he wrote a laudatory report, confessing later—when distance had lent disenchantment—that he had been taken in. Even labor leaders important in their own right were awed. David Dubinsky once sat down with Lewis for a two-hour talk right after F.D.R. had honored Dubinsky with an hour's White House audience—during wartime.

"Nothing that has ever happened to me," vows Dubinsky, "not even that hour's interview with the President, has ever given me as much pride as the two-hour talk with Lewis."

This was the Lewis power over acquaintances. Over those closely associated with him, the effect was likely to be that of a Svengali over Trilby. Associates (even the closest couldn't be called friends in the sense of a shared relationship) who broke with Lewis suffered emotional torments and couldn't leave him without looking back on him as the most memorable experience of their lives.

Although Philip Murray achieved distinction in his own right, his break with Lewis after twenty-five years of association was like that of a baby who has to cut its own umbilical cord from its mother. First, when Murray got out from under Lewis' shadow and accepted the presidency of the CIO, he told himself as much as he told the CIO convention.

"I think I am a man. I think I have convictions. I think I have a soul, and a heart and a mind. With the exception of course of my soul, they all belong to me. Every one of them."

And when Lewis tried Murray before a United Mine Workers board and ousted him as vice president, Murray broke down and cried like a child.

"I don't wish to go," he sobbed.

"When John L. came into a room, you knew it," men said of Lewis. And when occasion required he could wring the ultimate drama from even the most prosaic incident.

Once, when Lewis wanted to embarrass the AF of L's leaders before their own convention, he asked permission to present two resolutions. Delegates usually don't interrupt their chatter and socializing while a brother drones off a motion. But as Lewis edged his 240-pound bulk out of the Miners' delegation and into the aisle, the chattering lessened. Then a hush fell as Lewis, head down, seemingly lost in thought, moved ponderously toward the platform, bearing, to all appearance, a most fateful message. The distance to the platform was but fifty feet, one witness recalls, but Lewis moved with such deliberation that it seemed to the hushed hall that he would never get there.

Arrived, he took little more than a minute to intone two resolutions which together added up to twenty-six words—one barring antiunion employers from advertising in the Federation journal, another barring labor leaders from associating with such employers.

Lewis so dominated his own UMW conventions that for years he performed near miracles in bulling down open revolts.

Once, when Lewis had turned the convention over to the then vice president Phil Murray, a delegation of rebellious miners set up a clamorous demand to be heard and wouldn't stop.

"You couldn't hear yourself think," one witness recalls. "It sounded like a riot, like a bunch of madmen." Lewis meanwhile sat silently toward the rear of the platform with his head down, looking up now and then to stare some of his critics in the eye—or draw reflectively on his cigar, then blow out the smoke contemptuously as if he were blowing the smoke into the face of the howling delegates.

Then, as the observer tells it,[1] John L. Lewis, who was some twenty-two feet away from the lectern and the gavel-wielding Murray, suddenly seemed to leap from his chair and face the convention with one bound.

"Of course, it was an impossible thing to do," one witness reported, "and we didn't know how he did it."

"This beating of breasts like savages in Africa pounding on their tomtoms must cease, you understand?" Lewis shouted. And it did.

"I am something of a man," Lewis liked to say of himself. Which nobody could deny.

John Llewellyn Lewis was born in Lucas, Iowa, on Lincoln's Birthday in 1880, the son of an immigrant Welsh coal miner. As a boy and young man, he suffered injustices at the hands of mine owners, so creating a reservoir of emotion which he could tap as mine leader for the rest of his life. Young John's father, a brawling scrapper of a man, was blacklisted for leading a strike. This barred him from work in his home town and followed him like the mark of Cain from minehead to minehead, bringing hunger and insecurity to Lewis' family. Too restive to remain in school beyond the eighth grade, young Lewis was digging coal at fifteen—putting in agonizing ten- and eleven-hour days in air so "thin" (lacking in oxygen), that often he had to give up and go home.

It was obvious, not only to Lewis, but to those around him, that he was destined for bigger things. So in his early twenties Lewis began to calculate his chances and make those lunges for power which he was to repeat time and again until he reached old age.

Here Lewis had the help of the only person he probably ever respected and lastingly loved—his wife.

Myrta Bell Lewis, whom John L. Lewis married at age twenty-

[1] In Saul Alinsky's *John L. Lewis, an Unauthorized Biography*.

five, was a doctor's daughter and schoolteacher with resources of will that led family friends to describe her as stronger, even, than her redoubtable husband. The young wife took her young spouse in tow in the manner of the schoolteacher in *How Green Was My Valley*. She taught Lewis to read Dickens and Shakespeare and the classics. *Time* magazine remarked wryly that later she tried to stop Lewis from quoting them. The young wife also served as audience and critic as Lewis practiced his oratory.

So armed, Lewis took his first fling at power. He ran for Mayor of his home town of Lucas, Iowa, and was licked because his father-in-law, the doctor, persuaded the townsfolk to give their votes to another.

Lewis and his wife decided his career lay in labor leadership. So the Lewises moved to the mining country around Panama, Illinois. Conscious of his Lincoln's Day birthday, Lewis might have felt that John L. Lewis of Illinois had a finer ring to it than John L. Lewis of Iowa.

Within a year, Lewis was the president of the Panama, Illinois, UMW local. Soon after, the regional or district organization of the UMW sent young Lewis to the state capital at Springfield as a lobbyist, where he gave the first hint of the Lewis powerhouse to come by winning a State Workmen's Compensation Law and mine safety legislation.

Now, through a curious twist of fate, came the most significant event in Lewis' life. Sam Gompers, the AF of L's founder and president, spotted Lewis and took him under his wing as lobbyist and organizer. So, unwittingly, Gompers prepared Lewis for his later revolt against Gompers' own cherished craft unionism and for his role as reviver and second father of a greater Labor movement.

Lewis, thirty-one, vigorous and on the make, fawned on Gompers and studied the Grand Old Man, thirty years his senior, as a student might study a textbook. He mimicked Gompers' grand manner, deliberate speech and oratorical flourishes. Lewis watched Gompers at work as Labor's ambassador to the public, and learned that "labor leadership is 90 percent showmanship." But the most important lesson Lewis learned stemmed from his assignment as organizer in the steel, glass and rubber industries.

"I got the measure of that problem," Lewis later told this writer.

Lewis found that these great industries, hostile to unions, could not be organized with the tools of the time, the craft unions of skilled workers.

After nine years of apprenticeship with the master, Sam Gompers, Lewis performed a masterful stroke of his own. With lightning speed, and without the benefit of an election, he rose in 1920 to the presidency of the Miners, then the country's most powerful union.

Lewis helped the then Miners' president to get a government post, and in turn was rewarded with a job as statistician and UMW journal editor at headquarters. When the president resigned and was succeeded automatically by the vice president, Lewis moved up, by appointment, to the vacated vice-presidency. The new president soon dropped out of the picture, and Vice President John L. Lewis automatically became President John L. Lewis.

At forty, Lewis was the youngest leader of a big international union. He had an oaklike body and the driving energy of a bull. "See this desk?" he told a visitor. With one bound, the 250-pound Lewis was atop his desk looking down triumphantly on his startled guest.

Hardly had Lewis made his somewhat similar leap atop the UMW than he tried again for greater power. Sam Gompers had ruled the AF of L for thirty-four years. Lewis ran against Gompers and was trounced two to one.

Worse defeats followed. As coal lost its dominance after World War I, the coal operators fought each other fiercely for business, squeezing wages to the lowest levels since 1878. Thousands of miners quit the union that could no longer protect them, and the UMW—500,000 strong when Lewis took over—tobogganed to 75,000 by the early thirties.

To hold power during this descent into the economic maelstrom,

Lewis waged war against self-rule in his union—winning victories against his own people that he couldn't win outside, so setting a pattern of union autocracy later copied by less imaginative men.

Lewis destroyed self-rule through a species of union martial law. UMW locals are usually small, sometimes numbering little more than several dozen miners. The effective unit of union representation, then, is a district union government—embracing the locals within a region and having its own president. As district officers got into money or negotiating difficulties, Lewis replaced them with appointees. Most international union presidents have the power to name "trustees" to take over locals for the duration of an emergency. Lewis called his appointees "provisional" officers, but kept them on for years.

Outraged miners fought Lewis' "provisional" officers in the union hall, in the courts and, as in Illinois, on bloody local battlefields.

UMW conventions were wild and turbulent, but Lewis and his machine rode down the opposition.

In answer to one near riot, Lewis roared, "May the chair state that you may shout until you meet each other in hell, and he will not change his ruling."

For years, eloquent pleas for self-rule have been laughed down by delegates much in the manner that Mussolini's followers once shouted, "We spit on freedom."

Let's listen as one unsung Patrick Henry pleads for union liberty. The time is October, 1956; the place is the UMW convention at Cincinnati, Ohio.

"Delegate Komchak: 'This may be amusing to some of you. I came here as a representative of my local that sent me here to do a job, and I'm going to do it. They sent me here for the fourth time to try to convince the members and our officers that we want democracy in our union. Do you believe in democracy? If you do, I am not a laughing subject.

" 'I want to say whether or not some officers in some districts have mulcted the funds twenty years ago is no reason why their members today shouldn't have democracy in our union. If any member doesn't want democracy, does that deprive me of it? Everyone knows that men who are appointed are there on sufferance of those who appoint them. I am pleading with the delegates. . . . Give the districts the right to elect their own officers.' "

To which a pro-Lewis delegate replied that this reminded him of "Gabriel trying to run the heavens better than God could."

"If there is one way to get Communism in the Mine Workers it is to have elections," the delegate said.

Another delegate once summed it up, "Mr. Lewis don't want it [autonomy]. So why fool around with it?"

Man at the End of a Lifeline

By 1933, when Lewis was fifty-three—an age when men are usually resigned to whatever life has brought—Lewis seemingly was headed for oblivion. The coal industry and its union, sick even during the 1920 boom, seemed at a dead end. Worse, the entire Labor movement—the greater stage on which Lewis once hoped to play a part—seemed at a dead end, too.

The unions in the AF of L, which could boast a World War I peak membership of 4,500,000 dues payers, had lost more than half of their members by 1933. Worse, industrialists had unleashed a counteroffensive against unionism that threatened to grind all unions out of existence.

Few realized the Labor movement's precarious position in 1933, except the scared labor leaders themselves. At this juncture of the unions' sinking fortunes, a lifeline was thrown them by the federal government.

This was the famous Section 7A of the National Recovery Act (NRA) with which Franklin D. Roosevelt's New Deal set up codes to regulate and revive industries. It stated that employers must bargain with unions of their employees' choosing.

Lewis pounced on Section 7A, calling it "Labor's Magna Charta," and said later that he conceived it and "it was written right here in the Mine Workers' offices." Professor Philip Taft, the labor historian, says he has proof that the AF of L Executive Council insisted on such a provision as a condition of supporting NRA.[2]

Still, Lewis was the first to seize the lifeline.

He scraped $75,000 from the bottom of the UMW barrel, hired organizers and deployed them in the mining towns with the fighting slogan: "The President [Franklin Delano Roosevelt] wants you to join the union."

Miners sang a jingle:

> *In nineteen hundred and thirty-three*
> *When Mr. Roosevelt took his seat,*
> *He said to President John L. Lewis*
> *In union we must be.*

Thousands who had dropped out of the UMW poured back in. Membership rocketed to 400,000 in a matter of weeks. A union was reborn. So was Lewis' power inside Labor. He looked about for new fields to conquer, and chose the antiunion mass industries and their millions of unorganized workers as his target.

When Lewis tried to harness the AF of L to his organizing dream, he collided with two obstacles deeply imbedded in the Labor movement: craft unionism and union imperialism.

Sam Gompers had built a lasting union movement with skilled workers organized in craft unions. But assembly lines had reduced skilled workers to a splinter of the labor force, and no modern Labor movement could carry weight unless it embraced the new millions of partly skilled or totally unskilled industrial workers. For the new assembly line plants, the craft union of Gompers' day was obsolete. If you organized a five-thousand-man Ford plant on a craft union basis, you'd have thirty to forty trade unions bargain-

[2] The Railway Labor Act already contained such a provision affecting railroad employees, but for industry generally, the stricture was revolutionary.

ing for men working on the same assembly line. In a word, chaos.

A different organizing idea was needed: industrial unionism. In an industrial union, all the skilled electricians, carpenters, sheet metal workers as well as all the unskilled assembly-line tenders and plant sweepers belong to one big union, and bargain as a unit.

But here is where union imperialism came in. The heads of the craft unions—Big Bill Hutcheson of the Carpenters, John Possehl of the Operating Engineers, Dan Tobin of the Teamsters—had staked out empires of dues payers based on craft jurisdictions.

Anybody who handled wood, be he a woodsman felling a tree or a carpenter installing a window frame, belonged to Bill Hutcheson by right of a charter granted by the AF of L. With jurisdictions like these, Hutcheson and other craft union barons had job patronage to dispense, deals with employers to fatten on. And, although Hutcheson, for instance, had virtually no members in the auto, or steel, or rubber plants, he didn't want someone like Lewis to organize them into an industrial union. They belonged to him, said Hutcheson—and the AF of L backed him.

Besides, the craft union lords of the AF of L had another fear. If new millions poured into great new industrial unions, these would outnumber and outvote the dominant craft union politicians and shift labor power and emoluments to a new, upstart breed of unionists.

Lewis had none of these fears. For one thing, his UMW was an industrial union embracing all crafts employed in the mine and at the minehead. Besides, Lewis had urgent fears of his own.

Unless the steel industry was unionized, Lewis' own United Mine Workers was in mortal danger. The United States Steel Corporation had kept the UMW out of its own "captive" coal mines —and so menaced UMW's position in all mines.

So Lewis pleaded with the AF of L's president, onetime coal miner William Green, to put men and money into the field to "organize the unorganized." When Green and his high command temporized, Lewis plunged the Labor movement into a civil war. His Fort Sumter was the 1935 AF of L convention at Atlantic City.

Lewis' oratorical effort in 1935 has come down as a classic, and no story of the rise of the unions is complete without it. He was the popular leader rallying his people.

Lewis said, "The Labor movement is organized upon the principle that the strong should help the weak. Isn't it right that we should contribute something of our own strength, our own knowledge, our own influence toward those less fortunately situated, in the knowledge that if we help them and they grow strong, in turn we will be the beneficiaries of the changed status and their strength?"

Lewis warned of the unions' precarious position.

"The strength of a strong man is a prideful thing, but the unfortunate thing in life is that strong men do not remain strong. And that is just as true of unions and labor organizations. And whereas the craft unions may be able to stand upon their own feet and, like mighty oaks before the gale, defy the lightning . . . the day may come when these organizations will not be able to withstand the lightning and the gale.

"Prepare yourselves by making a contribution to your less fortunate brethren. Heed this cry . . . that comes from the hearts of men. Organize the unorganized."

Inaction would encourage the enemies of Labor, Lewis said, and "high wassail will prevail at the banquet tables of the mighty."

To the oratorical punch, Lewis added a blow that landed the unions' family row on page one of the newspapers. In a brawl on the convention floor, he knocked down and bloodied up the human symbol of intrenched opposition to fresh union ideas: Big Bill Hutcheson of the Carpenters.

But neither Lewis the orator nor Lewis the pugilist prevailed.

John L. Stirs the Multitudes

On the day after the convention, Lewis called a council of war in an Atlantic City hotel lobby. Surrounded by Sidney Hillman and Dave Dubinsky of the needle trades, and Charles P. Howard of the Printers, Lewis pledged money and men from the UMW for an organizing drive. So was born the Committee for Industrial Organization which later became the Congress of Industrial Organizations (CIO). In four tidal years, some 5,000,000 men washed into the new Federation.

First targets were the two chief citadels of antiunionism, U.S. Steel and General Motors.

General Motors fell in forty-two days, and U.S. Steel signed up with Lewis two weeks later.

Some four hundred-odd organizers, led by Lewis' aide, Phil Murray, and paid almost wholly by UMW cash, poured into the steel towns. When steel companies took $500,000 worth of advertising space to warn of "CIO coercion," Lewis thundered back on the radio, "Let him who will, be he economic tyrant or sordid mercenary, pit his strength against this mighty surge of human sentiment now being crystallized in the hearts of thirty million workers who clamor for . . . industrial democracy. He is a madman or a fool who believes that this river of human sentiment can be dammed by the erection of arbitrary barriers of restraint."

Lewis was, at long last, playing the massive role for which, he felt, his talents and energy had cast him. He was a leader stirring masses of men. He was a man to whom a nation listened. He was a giant who would grapple with other giants—the lords of industry, for instance.

Before Lewis' army could come to grips with "Big Steel," the war shifted unexpectedly to the automobile industry.

Without consulting their generalissimo, Lewis, the buck private auto workers launched an offensive of their own. They locked themselves into their plants and vowed they'd sit there until General Motors recognized a union.

The plant seizures were not part of Lewis' master plan. They burdened him with unexpected anxieties and doubts. The key to the mass-industry drives was the hands-off policy of a newly benevolent government. But could the New Deal withhold troops if men forcibly seized other people's property? Besides, how could Lewis square these acts with his rock-ribbed Republicanism and his orthodox views on property rights? The property problem Lewis put to the leftist professionals who had flocked to his organizing standard—who knew their way around in the class war, in union organizing and in slogans. The leftist brains whirred, and came up with a rationale to answer the capitalists. The sitdown strikers have property rights in their jobs, was the slogan.

The threatened use of bayonet-wielding troops to evict the strikers, Lewis blocked with his finest moments—as a ham actor.

"All right, you've got the National Guard," he told Michigan Governor Frank Murphy as the Governor agonized over public pressure to use troops. "What kind of bayonets do you think that you'll use? You know, if they use the flat, sharp kind, they can push them in a long way, but they can't twist them. . . . On the other hand, if you use the square kind, they can twist them around and make a big hole, but they can't push them in so far."

When Murphy felt he could no longer stay the troops, Lewis told him, "Tomorrow morning, I shall personally enter G.M. Plant Chevrolet No. 4. I shall order the men to disregard your order and to stand fast. I shall then walk up to the largest window in the plant, open it, divest myself of my outer raiment, remove my shirt and bare my bosom. Then, when you order your troops to fire, mine will be the first breast that those bullets will strike."

The troops remained outside the plants. Instead, Roosevelt secretly intervened to persuade G.M. to meet with Lewis.

With the solemnity of a President embarking for a Summit Conference, Lewis entrained for Detroit accompanied by a carload of reporters who wired hourly bulletins on the journey. At Detroit, the combination of a scowling Lewis plus the realization that you can't fight City Hall (i.e., the federal government) brought the General Motors executives around.

Victory in the steel industry came almost as an anticlimax soon after. The human key to Lewis' success here was Myron Taylor, Big Steel's chairman of the board. Lewis met Taylor, so one story goes, when Mrs. Taylor spotted Lewis in a restaurant and said, "What an interesting man. I'd like to meet him."

In any case, Lewis and Taylor closeted themselves in Lewis' Washington hotel suite and, after ten days of generous breakfasts and lavish lunches (one menu included oysters Rockefeller and pheasants under glass), ate their way to agreement.

"Within one year we organized 5,000,000 men in the basic industries," Lewis told this writer. "They had contracts, were paying dues and their unions were going concerns. . . ."

It took Sam Gompers forty laborious years to build an AF of L of 4,000,000 members. Lewis bettered this in one roaring year. The difference, of course, was that Lewis had the government with him while Gompers had the government against him—something Lewis won't concede to this day.

A Niagara Falls of fame washed over Lewis. At one time the *New York Times* devoted 5 percent of its space—roughly sixteen columns or two pages per day—to activities in which Lewis was involved. All heads turned when the well-caricatured figure of Lewis entered a restaurant. When he addressed a Labor Day meeting at Pittsburgh, some 200,000 wildly cheering unionists turned out for him. Men scrawled his name on fences as an act of defiance against antiunion employers. And Lewis' Washington office rivaled the press room in the White House nearby as a journalists' hangout.

"Remember you are in the center," Lewis is reported to have told an aide at the time. "The world will come to this office."

Not long after, the world was going elsewhere. Lewis' office was an Elba, and Lewis was an embittered spectator to great events rather than an actor in them.

Lewis' Biggest Mistake

In a conversational post-mortem over his career, Lewis once confided to David Dubinsky his biggest mistake. It was the mistake, he felt, of surrounding himself with Communists during the early CIO days. These caused him to exaggerate his own political strength, plunged him into the fatal break with F.D.R. and led to Lewis' self-exile from national Labor leadership.

John L. Lewis' "biggest mistake," however, was to be born with —or acquire along the way—a fatal flaw: inordinate vanity and pride.

Arguing with Lewis once, Labor Secretary Perkins exclaimed, "But that's the sin of pride!"

"That's my pride," Lewis bristled. "It's as good as the pride of the Vanderbilts."

This pride led Lewis to make an initial mistake in 1940.

As Roosevelt later told the story (with relish), Lewis came to the White House and asked for a place with Roosevelt on the third-term Democratic presidential ticket.

"We are the two most prominent men in the nation," Lewis is supposed to have said. "It will be an invincible combination."

"Which place will you take, John?" Roosevelt replied. Roosevelt and Lewis had needed each other. Now Lewis, miffed, broke the alliance. He threw in his fortunes with the extreme isolationist groups that fought American aid to the Western Allies. On the eve of the third-term election, Lewis went on a radio network that reached an estimated 60,000,000 Americans and urged his labor following to vote for Roosevelt's opponent, Wendell Willkie. If Roosevelt was elected, Lewis vowed, he'd step down as president of the CIO.

Thirteen days after Roosevelt was elected for his third term, on November 5, 1940, Lewis went before the CIO convention at Atlantic City and redeemed his pledge to step down as leader. Neither Lewis nor the delegates expected this abrupt ending of his CIO career. Lewis had watched with tear-filled eyes as the delegates opened the convention with an hour-long ovation and floor demonstration for him. He felt this would inevitably be followed by an insistent and unanimous draft to remain.

Yet the hoped-for draft never came. The men who hadn't followed Lewis in his crusade against Roosevelt wouldn't get down on their knees to Lewis now. They chose, instead, to follow Sidney Hillman, who blocked the Lewis draft and brought Phil Murray to power.

As many hard-bitten labor men cried unashamedly in a stilled, vast auditorium, Lewis recited his own funeral oration over his career as CIO president—and finished himself off as leader.

Until this capricious resignation as president of the CIO—Lewis had moved with sureness and grandeur toward the greatest prizes of fame and power America could offer. *Time* magazine wondered in the late thirties whether "this vast and glowering Welshman would wind up in the White House." Instead, it now seemed, in 1940, as if the tidal forces that had created Lewis cast him aside when the need for him was over. The CIO which he had founded no longer needed an imperious leader to summon the working host and battle the lords of industry. That battle won, the CIO needed a Phil Murray to conciliate the brawling elements within it and hold the CIO together.

Lewis, the ex-CIO president, was still president of the United Mine Workers and so held strategic control over the nation's coal pile. At sixty, he was in the full pride of his manhood; he had achieved much, and he had dreams of doing more. This was not a man who could bottle up his explosive power within the confines of one union.

So Lewis, who had been running with the grain of events when he led the CIO, began in 1940 to rub history the wrong way. Like a gambler who tries to retrieve his fortunes with reckless tosses of the dice, Lewis made lunge after lunge for grand prizes of his own devising. Being Lewis, his flounderings made a great splash. He even managed, from time to time, to scare the country—and the unions—out of their wits. But he never regained the glory that was his during the three brief years from 1937 to 1940.

In his new role as national gadfly, Lewis' first adventure was to try and organize the nation's 3,000,000 milk farmers in the midst of war in 1942. The drive was a bust, and the catch-all union Lewis formed for the purpose—District 50 of the UMW—remains like a tombstone today to mark the grave of a $3,000,000 Lewis folly.

Next, disregarding the wartime need for coal and the freeze on wages and prices, Lewis shut down the coal mines with demands for pay boosts and kept shutting them down every spring in leonine defiance of the President, the Army, the Congress, the Justice Department, the courts, the press and the people.

Lewis succeeded in prying higher pay for his coal diggers, and, as a scholar of the classics, had a glorious time playing the role of Titan battling the gods of Olympus. As soon as Congress could get around to it after the war, it passed a law to cut leaders like Lewis down to size. This was the Taft-Hartley Act.

Ironically, the man whom Congress chiefly had in mind when it passed the Taft-Hartley Act over Harry Truman's veto was already a spent locomotive, shunted off the main track of union events.

Lewis still sat atop the nation's coal pile, but it was a shrinking pile as oil, gas and electric power provided an increasing share of the nation's energy. From a union 750,000-strong in 1920, the United Mine Workers had shrunk to 200,000 by the mid-fifties. Lewis, without power of his own, could only fish in troubled labor waters to annoy those who held power.

When George Meany forced the gangster-ridden International Longshoremen's Association out of the American Federation of Labor and then spent $1,000,000 of Federation funds in a drive to woo the ILA's members away, Lewis lent the beleaguered dockers' union $300,000 and so helped it survive.

When David McDonald toyed with the idea of pulling his 1,000,000-man Steelworkers out of the CIO and so wrecking it, Lewis met portentously with McDonald and Dave Beck of the Teamsters and encouraged reports that a new Federation was being born. Nothing came of it.

In between these sorties, Lewis used the ample time on his hands to win a model welfare plan and build a chain of modern hospitals in coal country which had few doctors and fewer facilities. He used UMW money to buy control for the union of the second biggest bank in Washington, D.C. He put the UMW into the shipping business.

The hold that Lewis has on union men's imagination won't die.

I asked the president of a world-famous union recently what the unions could do about their gravest problem: that of recruiting new members.

The labor man shook his head.

"What we need today," he said, "is another John L. Lewis."

CHAPTER 20

Six Days That Shook
the Union World

Sam Gompers founded the American Labor movement. John L. Lewis gave it size and power. George Meany and Walter Reuther welded two warring labor federations, the AF of L and the CIO into the giant AFL-CIO. Then it was Meany's fateful task to cast out the merged federation's biggest and most powerful union member—the Teamsters.

The time is December, 1957.

The place is Atlantic City, and the action takes place in the five-thousand-seat Convention Auditorium, on the boardwalk and in hotel rooms.

A Federation convention is the greatest union show on earth, and the supreme authority of the Labor movement. Every other year, the unions in the AFL-CIO perform as if under a big tent. In many rings, some open to view in the Convention Hall, others hidden in smoke-filled hotel rooms, the unions make laws, hold court and set the course which the Federation will follow.

All who come want something. Suspended union bosses come to fight for their union lives, treasuries and power; rank-and-file members come for help to redress wrongs. Union emissaries from overseas come to seek American union cash. These had sent convention currents swirling around Federation President George Meany as he struggled with the central problem of corruption.

Now, on the eve of the convention's key act—the vote to expel

213

the Teamsters—Meany's hotel suite resembled a state governor's office in the final hours before an execution.

Communication lines were kept open between AFL-CIO President Meany and go-betweens for the condemned man, James R. Hoffa, president-elect of the Teamsters. On trial on federal wiretapping charges ninety miles away in New York City, Hoffa was trying to get court permission to dash to Atlantic City for a last-minute plea—or surrender. Meany waited as the hours slipped by and midnight approached.

For Meany, as for Hoffa, it had been a difficult day.

In a sense, it was not Hoffa alone but all of Labor that was on trial. The corruption disclosures had so outraged public opinion that Congress threatened to strike back with anti-Labor laws.

Meany had to find a way out of Labor's dilemma.

"Are we going to turn the McClellan Committee into a permanent investigating committee? Or are we going to show we can police ourselves?"

But for unions to police themselves, it would require revolutionary changes in the unions' over-all government. As a Federation, the AFL-CIO had no power of its own except the power to expel; it was a union of unions—a loose confederation of union states. A strong, central union government with police powers would have to be fashioned to do the clean-up job. The Federation presidency would have to be changed, too. From being merely Labor's ambassador to the public, Meany would have to transform himself into Labor's chief executive.

In six fateful days of the AFL-CIO convention he put his rugged strength to the hardest labor known to man—the job of making other men accept change.

The expulsion of Hoffa and the Teamsters would be the test demonstration of a necessary change, that the Federation was now greater than any of its parts.

Hoffa was fighting desperately to stay in the Federation. To be in meant respectability: the AFL-CIO with its six ethical practice codes was now a shield and a cover. To be out was to be branded.

When a Senate committee exposed you, that hurt. But when your own people, the Labor movement, threw you out, you were a marked man—even if you headed a 1,500,000-man union.

Hoffa couldn't understand that the union world he had grown up in was no longer acceptable. Senate testimony showed that only a few years ago he could, with impunity, put his wife secretly on union payrolls, let his union enforce jukebox rackets, accept favors from employers, give charters to gangsters—and regard all this as strictly his own union's affair. What he couldn't understand was that this was now the affair of all Labor—and the American public's affair, too. Unions were now affected with the public interest and could no longer be permitted to hurt their own members or the public.

Hoffa could think of his troubles only in personal terms. "Somebody don't like us," he felt. Somebody like Walter Reuther of the Automobile Workers.

So Hoffa waged a contest of wills with Meany. He pressed secret negotiations, offered to step down for a caretaker successor that he would name. He even volunteered to submit to supervision by a watchdog committee of public men.

Meany steadfastly said no. A Federation vice president put it this way: "We talk about corrupt influence. We don't spell it out. We don't want to spell it out. But we're drawing the line at the underworld." As an underworld associate in the Labor movement, Hoffa could not remain in the Federation, nor could anyone he named or dominated be accepted.

Now, in his hotel suite, Meany waited for word from the Teamsters. The telephone rang.

"We have Jimmy [Hoffa] on the phone," the voice on the line said. A car was ready, and Jimmy would hurry down from New York. Could Meany wait up for a predawn conference?

Meany glanced at his watch—10:40 P.M. It would be 3 A.M. before Hoffa could arrive.

"Why don't you get a commitment from him [Hoffa] and bring it to the convention?" Meany suggested.

"No," said the voice on the phone. "We can't try that, because he might repudiate it. We don't trust him."

Meany refused to wait up for Hoffa. The die was cast.

The wind that swept in from the ocean, spattering a chilling rain on the bent backs of the delegates, was no bleaker than their spirits as they trudged the boardwalk to the convention's second-day session.

A subdued lot, they had shown little stomach for the usual convention horseplay. They had gone to bed early the night before, and the hotel corridors were strangely still.

I picked up a conversation with the seventy-two-year-old ex-president of the Bakers, Herman Winter. He was a member of Labor's house of elders, the Executive Council, and his own union was under suspension.

"I've seen fifty-six years of the Labor movement," the aged man said gloomily, "and I'm glad I won't be around to see the next fifty-six."

At the Convention Hall entrance, a veteran labor reporter studied the delegates' faces.

"Have you ever seen such a scared and bewildered bunch?" he said.

The delegates had a right to be scared. Most unions can hurt the public—if they go on strike. But the Teamsters control the movement of goods and so can hurt other unions: those who voted against them, for instance.

Inside the hall, George Meany, limping heavily from an old heel injury, crossed the dais and signaled the opening of the debate.

An aged, lean and dour man arose: the $50,000-a-year secretary-treasurer of the Teamsters, John F. English.

He had achieved fleeting fame by refusing to O.K. some of Dave Beck's spending. When Beck was booted from the Executive Council, Meany replaced him with English, in the hope that English would clean up the Teamsters from the inside. The hope had turned into deep embarrassment. English, true enough, was anti-Beck. But he was also violently pro-Hoffa.

The aging English, proud and straight under the klieg lights on the convention floor, was a symbol of the Teamsters' resistance to change in a changing union world. He was spokesman for an era that was passing—the era of "union autonomy"—in which the union regarded itself as a private affair, such as an Elks Lodge. Like a mastodon caught in the ice, English struggled against forces that had trapped him, and that he didn't understand.

"I am nearing the end of my days," the old teamster began in the high-pitched twang of his native New England. With deep emotion that visibly shook his listeners, he pleaded for his union in the primitive terms that his hero, Jimmy Hoffa, might have employed.

First, there was the flick of the dragon's tail—the Teamsters' defiance.

"How many times in your lives," English asked, "if it hadn't been for the Teamsters, would you have lost strikes and maybe you would not be here?"

Then there was the bewilderment of the mastodon from the union ice age. Why, despite all their power and despite all they'd done for other unions, were the Teamsters now being punished?

"Some people don't like us, because we are a big organization, and they are afraid we are going to be overpowerful." English pointed a finger at the dais where "some people" like Walter Reuther of the Auto Workers and James Carey of the Electrical Workers, fire-eating foes of Hoffa, stared back, unperturbed.

There was the call on old friendships, and the demand for repayment of old debts.

"Don't forget, Mr. Meany, you never had a better friend than Dan Tobin [when he was head of the Teamsters] and you never had a better friend than the Teamsters. The Teamsters stood by you. What are you going to do for us?"

Finally, there was the plea for compassion.

"My friends, the penalty is too severe. It is too severe.

"We ask for one year. After giving you fifty years, giving you all our time and money, we ask for one year to clean up our house.

"If Dan Tobin and Big Bill Hutcheson were alive today," the

old teamster finished, "this never would have happened. Oh, it makes my blood run cold. I never thought I would live to see this." (Tobin of the Teamsters and Hutcheson of the Carpenters, between them, had long dominated the old AF of L.)

A convention is usually a noisy affair, and the clattering of delegates' tongues can add up to a roar like that of a subway train. But as English spoke, the great hall with its two thousand-odd delegates and spectators was quiet.

On the floor, delegations from 131 unions leaned forward. These ranged from the Horse Shoers "International" with its 266 members and the Wire Weavers with 430, to the Automobile Workers and the Steelworkers with more than a million members each. In the gallery, several hundred rank-and-filers who had come at their own expense to pour tales of persecution by racketeers into official ears strained to catch every word. Some two hundred reporters, about as many as cover a championship fight, shifted in their ringside seats near the dais. Television crews played their cameras and brilliant lights on the speaker and on the dais with its burden of dignitaries, as a reminder that the outside world was looking in.

The debate revealed deep misgivings about the Federation's emerging great power.

One of the most respected and democratic unions in the Federation, the Typographers,[1] fought the expulsion of the Teamsters. Every union had the right to order its own affairs, the Typographers' president, Woodruff Randolph, argued. Autonomy was the rock on which the Federation had been founded. Now it was being eroded. By dictating to the Teamsters, the Federation itself would become a dictatorship of "twenty-nine old men" (Meany's Executive Council).

A further eloquent argument for the Teamsters came from the head of another respected union, Sal B. Hoffmann, president of the Upholsterers.

As the debate rolled on, it was clear that two men dominated the convention. One was the solid man visible on the dais, George

---

[1] International Typographical Union.

Meany. The other wasn't even at the convention, but was on everyone's mind and tongue, the junior Senator from Arkansas and chairman of the Senate Rackets Committee, John L. McClellan.

The judge and lord high executioner of the convention, Alex Rose of the Hatters Union, who had the job of turning down union appeals, then asking the convention to lop off union heads, summed it up:

"Labor cannot stand alone," union judge Rose said. "It must look outside itself. It must have the support of the middle class, of the white-collar workers and professional people. Or punishing laws will follow."

Not one delegate rose from the convention floor to speak against the Teamsters. The powerful AFL-CIO vice presidents on the dais remained silent, too. No one would bell the cat. Meany, pale and visibly moved, walked heavily to the dais lectern to do the job himself.

Two years before, when the AF of L had merged with the CIO, Meany had vowed in his inaugural address, "I will never surrender principle for expediency. . . . Decisions will be made without regard to how big or how little a union is. . . ."

Meany could still grant the Teamsters a face-saving year to clean up. The convention would support him with cheers. Instead, his gravelly voice punched out the plain, short, infighting sentences that gave no quarter and sought no compromise.

Meany reminded his audience that the Teamsters had made no effort to investigate their officers' "crimes against the Labor movement."

With angry sarcasm, he pictured the recent Teamster meeting at Miami Beach. "They went through a performance, and they read the Ethical Practices Committee Report in an atmosphere of hilarity. They had quite a nice time doing it."

One Teamster vice president had been convicted of the worst crime in the union book—taking bribes from an employer to break a strike. He was still vice president, Meany said.

"We have to free the membership from these men, from this

dictatorship," Meany finished. "The secretary will call the roll. You vote yes or no."

The voting, like the debate, revealed the union leaders' agony. As the roll call droned on, David McDonald, the president of the Steelworkers, left the dais to visit the corner benches where a delegation of Teamsters was huddled. He shook hands with several as if asking their forgiveness for voting with Meany.

Ed Miller, president of the Hotel and Restaurant Workers, torn between voting against his friend Hoffa and voting respectably for the expulsion, had an upset stomach about it the day before. In a weak and shaken voice he voted no (against expulsion).

The vote was tallied. A two-thirds majority was needed to expel. The vote was five to one against the Teamsters. Meany had carried with him the old AF of L craft unions as well as the new reformist CIO unions. One era had ended for the unions. Another had begun.

The vote on the Teamsters brought to the surface and dramatized the vast changes that had been seething since the AFL-CIO merger and the early corruption disclosures.

With the expulsion, Meany turned the ponderous, merged Labor movement around, changing its angle of vision from that of a self-centered introvert to that of an extrovert who looks outward and cares for the world's opinion. The government had intervened with the Wagner Act in 1935 to help the unions recruit millions of new members. By accepting this help and rocketing to great power, the unions could no longer claim they were voluntary associations, private clubs, and so exempt from outside regulation.

Meany shifted the balance of power from the great internationals to the Federation. No longer could the member unions dominate the Federation as the Teamsters and Carpenters once did. From now on the Federation would dominate them. The unions could no longer stretch the plea of autonomy to cover up evil.

When the late William Green dared speak out against labor crooks in 1929, Teamster Boss Dan Tobin took him aside.

"No more of that," said Tobin. There was no more of that.

This was because Tobin, as boss of the Teamsters, had a "power base," and Green, as Federation president, had none. A "base" in labor lingo is the membership power a union leader commands. Jim Hoffa, for instance, has a "base" of 1,500,000 members. Meany, technically, has no such power base. Actually, as the convention showed, he had the most powerful base of all—public opinion.

With this base he went on to hammer out new tools for coping with corruption. In the Teamster vote, the Federation showed it was master. No longer could any single union—nor any combination of unions—dominate the Federation and dictate to its president. In the case of another transgressor union, the Bakers, Meany went further.

James Cross, the president of the Bakers, dramatized this further change before the convention by appealing in person and with great emotion against the loss of his union head.

"The Federation has ordered us to hold a convention and elect new officers," Cross said. "But if the Federation doesn't like whom we elect, we'll be expelled. Let the members of my own union judge whether I should be president."

The plea failed. The convention voted to expel.

This vote showed Meany *could,* under certain conditions, dictate who could hold office in an International. He went on to demonstrate further that he could even put Federation "policemen" inside the once sacrosanct affiliated unions. These cops, known as "monitors," took corrupt unions in hand, called conventions, supervised elections. Six unions agreed to accept policemen named by Meany. Peter McGavin, Meany's troubleshooter, became a virtual caretaker of some of them.

Meany had sent the union world spinning along a new orbit.

Some six years after the decision to oust the Teamsters, James R. Hoffa still strives to whip up sentiment inside the AFL-CIO for the Teamsters' return. But to all overtures from Hoffa, Meany has said in effect: the Teamsters yes, Hoffa no. The Teamsters can return to the House of Labor only if they shed Hoffa. This is now a possibility because of Hoffa's conviction on jury tampering charges.

In six years, the once burning issue of corruption has yielded to other more urgent concerns: union membership erosion because of automation, the problem of organizing white-collar workers, and the further problem of developing the new men who will solve these problems. Which, as the first chapter shows, is where we came in.

Index

A & M Enterprises, 59
Adelstein, Bernard, 109 ff
Adonis, Joe, 113
AFL-CIO (American Federation of Labor-Congress of Industrial Organizations), 6, 10, 22, 24 ff, 77-78, 101, 106, 114, 117, 131, 156, 158, 169, 188, 213 ff; Department of International Affairs, 157; Ethical Practices Code, 38, 39, 219; Executive Council, 4, 15, 22, 26, 28-30, 38, 44, 67, 77-78, 84, 125, 157, 163, 193, 216; headquarters (Wash., D.C.), 25; Industrial Union Department, 78; merger, 25, 31-32; *see also* Meany, George
AF of L (American Federation of Labor prior to merger), 23, 24 ff, 77, 85, 89, 117, 121, 125, 156, 162-163, 166 ff, 174, 175 ff, 188-89, 190-92, 197 ff, 213 ff; founded, 31; merger, 31-32, 37-38
Albert, Sydney, 59
Alderman, Israel, 59
Alinsky, Saul, 198 *n*
Amalgamated Clothing Workers of America, 26, 37, 50
American Communist party (Lovestonites), 159 ff; *see also* Communism
American Federation of Teachers, 50
American Institute for Free Labor Development, 156
American Motor Company, 79 *n*
American Telephone and Telegraph Company (A.T. & T.), 9, 12
Anarcho-Syndicalist unions (Italy), 169
Anastasia, Albert, 28, 41, 92, 92 *n*, 107, 112, 113
Anastasia, Anthony, 28-29
Anti-Nazi Non-Sectarian League, 161
Anti-trust laws, 76
Ardmore Leasing Corporation, 60
Armenian Review (newspaper), 161
Attlee, Clement, 146
Automation, 1 ff, 9 ff, 103, 155

Automobile Workers Union. *See* United Auto Workers

Bad City, The (book), 88
Baer, George F., 179
Bakery and Confectionery Workers International Union of America, 29, 32, 49, 216, 221
Bates, Harry, 38
Beck, Dave, *ix*, 38, 45, 48, 52, 54, 124-126, 183, 216
Beirne, Joseph A., *x*, 9 ff
Bell Telephone Company, 10, 12 ff
Berger, Sam, 97
Bessemer open hearth process, 177
Bethlehem Steel Company, 151
Bill of Rights, U.S., 139
Blanc, Victor H., 119
Bridges, Harry, 155
Brindell, Robert P., 34
Brown, Irving, 166
Browne, George, 117
Buchalter, Louis ("Lepke"), 91-92
Building trades unions, 24
Bukharin, Nikolai, 159

Capone, Al, 60, 114 ff
Carey, James B., 154, 168, 217
Carpenters Union (United Brotherhood of Carpenters and Joiners of America), 38
Castro, Fidel, 61
Chapman, Alvah H., Jr., 58
Cheyfitz, Eddie, 50 ff
Chicago Restaurant Association, 114
China News Analysis (periodical), 161
Ching, Cyrus A., 147, 148
Cigar Makers Union, 185-88; *see also* Gompers, Samuel L.
CIO (Congress of Industrial Organizations prior to merger), 23, 24, 30, 37, 50, 69, 77-78, 166, 168, 194 ff, 213 ff; merger, 31-32, 37-38
Clinton, Stanford, 58
Collective bargaining, 13, 64, 69, 76, 146, 150 ff

223

Colorado Fuel and Iron Company, 180

Columbia University, 105

Committee on Equal Employment Opportunity, 104

Communications (telephone) Workers of America (CWA), 9 ff

Communism, 25-26, 28, 50-51, 64, 89, 156-70 *passim;* 193, 202, 208; in France, 156, 168 *n;* in Italy, 79, 156, 168 *n,* 169; in Japan, 156; in New York, 81; in Russia, 124, 156 ff

Confédération Général du Travail (France), 168 *n*

Conway, Jack, 70

Cooper, R. Conrad, 18

Corruption, union, 24 ff, 35, 37, 40-61 *passim;* 123-34 *passim;* 135 ff; *see also* Gangsterism; Hoffa, James Riddle; Teamsters Union

Costello, Frank, 41, 107

Cross, James G., 221

Curran, Joseph, 29

Dalitz, Morris ("Moe"), 59

Daly, Victor, 102

Darrow, Clarence, 53

Day, Virgil, 149, 154

De Gaulle, Charles, 196

Democratic party, 36, 49, 64, 71-72; *see also* Roosevelt, Franklin D.

Dewey, Thomas E., 83-84

Diamond, Legs, 120

Dio, Johnny, 119, 121, 133

Distillery Workers Union, 49, 113-14, 119, 121

Dobbs, Farrell, 47

Dorfman, Paul, 58, 117-118

Dranow, Benjamin, 60-61

Dubinsky, David, ix, 32, 35, 67, 68 *n,* 80-90 *passim;* 152-53, 162, 193, 196, 205, 208; background, 82 ff; and European unions, 164; and racketeers, 96 ff

Dulles, John Foster, 161, 162

Dunne, Grant, 47

Dunne, Miles, 47

Dunne, Vincent, 47

"Edge, the" (in garment industry), 94 ff

Edison, Thomas A., 177

Einstein, Albert, 83

Eisenhower, Dwight D., 161

Electricians Union (International Brotherhood of Electrical Workers), 5 ff, 139, 217; racial discrimination, 101

Englander Company, 130-31

English, John F., 216

Far Eastern Economic Review (periodical), 161

Fay, Joe, 35-36, 116-17

Federal Bureau of Investigation (FBI), 53, 92, 97-99

Feldman, Samuel (Shorty), 119

Fifth Amendment, 38, 83, 118, 126

Fitzgerald, George, 49, 71

Followers of Lafayette (trade union), 182

Force Ouvrière (France), 168 *n*

Ford, Edsel, 67, 68, 68 *n,* 82

Ford, Henry, 87

Ford Motor Company, 68, 75, 81-82; and Model T, 87, 145

Free Trade Union News (trade paper), 157

Gangsterism, 35, 40-61 *passim;* 65, 91-99 *passim;* 107 ff

Garment Center (New York City), 80 ff; gangsterism, 90-99 *passim;* 152; *see also* International Ladies Garment Workers Union

General Electric Company, 149, 154

General Motors Corporation, 70, 75, 76, 87, 144, 146-48, 154, 206-7

Giancana, Sam, 107

Gibbons, Harold J., 43, 50 ff

Goldberg, Arthur J., 16, 148, 154

Golden, Harry, 53

Goldwater, Barry, 183 *n*

Gompers, Henry, 181, 182

Gompers, Samuel L., x, 26, 31, 89, 143, 156, 171-92 *passim;* 193, 199-200, 203, 208, 213; Cigar Makers Local 144, 181; early career, 172 ff; enemies, 176; radicalism, 184 ff; Sherman Anti-Trust Act, 189-91

Green, William L., 25, 27, 162, 193, 204, 220-21
Greenbaum, Gus, 59
Guffey, James T., 128-29

Hamilton, James, 60
Harrison, George M., 26, 28-30, 32, 38
Harvard University, 50, 53
Haskell, Hannah, 82
Hayes, A. J., 39
Hillman, Sidney, 50, 166, 205, 209
Hired Broom, The (trade paper), 112
Hitler, Adolf, 161
Hoe, Richard M., 177
Hoffa, James Riddle, *x,* 12, 40-62 passim; 67, 71-72, 119 ff, 131, 136, 141, 214; alleged battles for Negro rights, 54; banking issues, 56 ff; Congressional investigations and legislations, 41 ff, 56, 61; early career, 46 ff; elected Teamsters president, 55; future of, 62; McClellan Committee investigations, 41 ff, 57, 58, 60-61, 116-18, 214 ff; model family man, 45; organizing Teamsters Union, 45 ff; trials and acquittals, 44, 51 *n*, 53-54, 62; *see also* Teamsters Union
Hoffa, James, Jr., 45
Hoffa, John, 46
Hogan, Frank, 81, 95-96, 113, 121
Holland, James, 101
Hotel and Restaurant Employees and Bartenders International Union, 48, 114, 115, 220
Howard, Charles P., 205
Hutcheson, Big Bill, 38, 204-5, 217-18
Hutcheson, Maurice, 38

Industrial Workers of the World, 180
International Association of Machinists, 104
International Association of Retail Clerks, 20 ff, 44, 129
International Confederation of Free Trade Unions (ICFTU), 158, 168, 168 *n*
International Federation of Trade Unions, 156
International Ladies Garment Work-

ers Union (ILGWU), 32, 33, 35, 37, 80-90 *passim;* 91 ff, 120, 147, 152; benevolent activities, 90; General Executive Board, 86; Management Engineering Department, 90; *see also* Dubinsky, David
International Longshoremen's Association, 28, 155
International Typographical Union, 149, 218, 218 *n*
Italian General Confederation of Labor, 168 *n*

Jackfert, Melvin, 140
Jewelry Workers Union, 132
John L. Lewis: an Unauthorized Biography (book), 198 *n*
Johnson, Lyndon B., 22, 26
Johnston, Eric, 52
Justice (trade paper), 80
Justice Department, U.S., 73, 94; and Corrupt Practices Act, 73

Kaiser, Edgar, 16
Kaiser Steel Company, 16-17, 155; and Long Range Sharing Plan, 16, 17
Kamenow, George, 127-28
Kefauver, Estes, 76
Kennedy, John F., 22, 104
Kennedy, Robert, 43, 50, 53, 108, 118, 127-28, 130-33
Kerrigan, Charles, 133
Kethly, Anna, 168
Kheel, Theodore H., 7
Knights of Industry (trade union), 182
Knights of Labor (trade union), 176
Knohl, Larry, 58
Korshak, Sidney, 131, 133

Labor Department, U.S., 57, 105, 138
Labor Relations Associates of Chicago, Inc., 126
Labour party, Great Britain, 170
La Follette investigations, 126
Landrum-Griffin Act (1959), 61, 135-136, 138-39
Las Vegas, Nev., 59

Laundry Workers International Union, 40, 48

Laurel, Ferdinand, 185-86

Left Communism, an Infantile Disease (book), 165 *n*

Lehman, Herbert H., 36, 153

Lenin, V. I., 164-65, 165 *n*

Levinson, Ed, 59-60

Lew, Abe, 130

Lewis, John L., *ix, x,* 26, 28, 68-69, 85, 88, 144, 147, 148, 171-72, 192, 193-212 *passim;* 213; admired by labor leaders, 196 ff; background, 198 ff; becomes president of UMW, 200; and General Motors, 206-7; political ambitions, 209; shuts down coal mines, 211

Lewis, Myrta Bell (Mrs. John L.), 198-99

Lieberman, "Scarface Louie," 96

Lincoln Leaguers (trade union), 182

Longshoremen's Union. *See* International Longshoremen's Association

Louis, Joe, 54

Lovestone, Jay, 157 ff

Luchese, Tom (Three-Finger Brown), 107

Lurye, William, 97

MacArthur, Douglas, *ix*

McClellan, John L., 124, 126-28, 219

McClellan Senate Rackets Committee investigations, 41 ff, 57, 58, 60-61, 64, 70, 108, 110-11, 114, 115, 116-118, 121, 124-34 *passim;* 135, 214, 219

McDonald, David J., 15 ff, 26, 154, 211, 220

McGavin, Peter, 221

McMahon, Eugenia, 33

Maloney, William E., *ix*

Manchester *Guardian* (newspaper), 161

Marshall Plan, 167-68

Mazey, Emil, 70

Meany, Eugenia McMahon (Mrs. George), 33

Meany, George, 10, 22, 23, 24 ff, 48, 77-78, 84, 101-2, 106, 157, 183 *n*, 193, 211, 213 ff; anti-Com-munism, 161 ff; bluntness, 27, 38; early career, 33 ff; Fifth Amend-ment issue, 38; and European unions, 164 ff; asks suspension of Teamsters, 38-39, 214 ff

Meany, Mike, 33

Michigan Fair Grounds Coliseum, 52

Mikoyan, Anastas, 25

Miller, Ed, 220

Miller, Marvin J., 16-17

Modica, C. Don, 112

Mohammed Ben Youssef, King, 169

Mollenhoff, Clark, 43

Molotov, Vyacheslav, 159-60

Moretti, Willie, 113

Motion Picture Association, 52

Movie Projectionists Union, 116

Mug, Joe, 41

Mundt, Carl, 183 *n*

Murder, Inc., 28, 58, 92, 108

Murphy, Frank, 207

Murray, Philip, 15, 27, 88, 150-51, 154, 193, 196-98, 206, 209-10

Musicians, American Federation of, 137

Mussolini, Benito, 169, 201

Name Is Hoffa, The (pamphlet), 46 *n*, 53

National Association for the Advance-ment of Colored People (NAACP), 103, 105

National Labor Relations Board, 31, 129, 130, 132, 133-34, 141

National Labor Union, 181

National Recovery Act, 202-3; *see also* Wagner Labor Relations Act

Negro rights, 54, 100-6

Neilsen, James T., 129

Nevada Gaming Commission, 59

Nevada Tax Commission, 59

New Deal, 36, 89, 192, 206

New York City Central Labor Trades Council, 35, 36

New York State Advisory Committee, 101

New York State Federation of Labor, 35, 36, 161

New York Times, 163, 208

Nitti, Frank (the Enforcer), 116

Norris-La Guardia Act, 191 *n*
Nunn, Guy, 73

O'Brien, Charles ("Chuckie"), 136
Operating Engineers, International Union of, *ix*, 116, 139-40, 204

Pacific Maritime Association, 155
Parisi, Joseph, 110
Pegler, Westbrook, 196
Pendergast, Tom, 36
Perkins, Frances, 209
Petrillo, James Caesar, 137-38
Pins and Needles (musical comedy), 90
Plumbers Union (United Association of Journeymen Apprentices of the Plumbing and Pipe Fitting Industry), 33; *see also* Meany, George
Political machine, union manpower and, 71 ff
Possehl, John, 204
Potofsky, Jacob S., 26
Potter, Charles, 73
Powell, Hyman, 133
Presser, William, 57
Promised Land, The (book), 88
Provenzano, Anthony ("Tony Pro"), *x*, 141
Puerto Rican workers, 103
Pullman, George, 117

Railway Labor Act, 203 *n*
Rauh, Joseph, 71
Reader's Digest (magazine), 118
Republican party, 28, 33, 49, 73, 206
Retail Clerks. *See* International Association of Retail Clerks
Reuther, Linda, 65
Reuther, Lisa, 65
Reuther, May (Mrs. Walter P.), 65-66, 67
Reuther, Roy, 73
Reuther, Walter P., *ix*, 22, 29-30, 32, 44, 49, *n*, 50, 63-79 *passim;* 87, 143 ff, 154, 215; attempts against life, 65-66; 115; becomes president of CIO, 37; anti-Communism, 64, 157-158, 165; Guaranteed Annual Wage

proposed, 145; police protection, 65; political ambitions, 71 ff
Ricca, Paul (the Waiter), 116, 119
Riesel, Victor, 52, 85
Rockefeller, John D., Jr., 179
Roen, Allard, 59
Roosevelt, Franklin D., 36, 37, 171 *n*, 194, 196, 202-3, 207, 209
Roosevelt, Theodore, 173-74
Rose, Alex, 191 *n*, 219
Rothstein, Arnold, 120
Ryan, Joe, 35

Safeway Stores, 110
Salinger, Pierre, 131
Scalise, George, 114
Scalish, John T., 107
Schnitzler, Bill, 29-30
Scotti, Al, 96, 108, 121
Seafarers International Union of North America, 97
Seaton, Louis G., 144, 148
Sevareid, Eric, 42 *n*
Shefferman, Nahan W., 124 ff, 131-32
Sherman Anti-Trust Act, 189-91
Shole, Christopher, 177
Smith, Alfred E., 89
Smith, Wint, 49
Socialism, 50, 75, 76, 87 ff, 183 *n*, 188
Solidarity (trade paper), 73
Solidarity House (UAW headquarters, Detroit), 67, 70
Sons of Vulcan (trade union), 182
Squillante, Vincent, 110-13
Staebler, Neil, 74
Stalin, Joseph, 159-60
Star Investment Company, 59
Steelworkers. *See* United Steelworkers of America
Steffens, Lincoln, 126
Strasser, Adolph, 185-86
Suffridge, James A., 20 ff
Sweatshops, 81

Taft, Philip, 203
Taft-Hartley Labor Act, 28, 102, 128-129, 211
Tammany Hall, 36
Taylor, Myron C., 207-8
Teamsters Union (International Broth-

erhood of Teamsters, Chauffeurs, Warehousemen and Helpers of America), *x,* 12, 28, 38-39, 40-61 *passim;* 109-22 *passim;* 124 ff, 135 ff, 183, 204; Central Conference of, 48, 130-31; Central States Pension Fund, 57-58, 61; expelled from AFL-CIO, 214 ff; Joint Councils, various, 47, 50; Southeast Area Pension Fund, 57-58; Southwest Area Pension Fund, 57-58; Western Conference of, 130-31; *see also* Beck, Dave; Corruption, union; Hoffa, James Riddle; McClellan Senate Rackets Committee investigations; Tobin, Dan
Textile Workers Union of America, 2
3-0-1 Corporation, 59
Time magazine, 199, 210
Tobin, Dan, 28, 126, 204, 217-18, 220
"Today" (television program), 21
Triangle Shirtwaist Company fire, 81
Triscaro, Nunzio ("Babe"), 61, 107
Truman, Harry S., 27, 36, 49, 211
Tyler, Gus, 99

Underworld, labor bosses in, 107-22 *passim*
University of Michigan, 51
United Community Funds and Council of America, 13
United Mine Workers of America (UMW), 2, 15, 85, 147, 194 ff; *see also* Lewis, John L.
United Nations, 24, 157, 161
United Rubber Workers (United Rubber, Cork, Linoleum and Plastic Workers of America), 148
United States Commission on Civil Rights, 101, 105
United States Rubber Corporation, 147
United States Steel Corporation, 18, 206

United Steelworkers of America, 15 ff, 20, 220; Human Relations Committee, 16, 17, 18, 19, 77; Long Range Sharing Plan, 16; *see also* McDonald, David J.
Upholsterers International Union of North America, 130

Van Arsdale, Harry, Jr., *x,* 5 ff, 104-5

Wagner, Robert F., Jr., 7, 153
Wagner Labor Relations Act, *ix,* 20, 171 *n*
Warren, Fred, 129
Washington Guards (trade union), 182
Weinberg, Nat, 68 *n*
Weiss, Phil, 132 ff
Western Europe, Communist penetration in, 156 ff
Westinghouse Electric Corporation, 149
White-collar workers, 3, 20 ff, 39
Williams, G. Mennen ("Soapy"), 65, 73-74
Williams, Paul, 95
Willkie, Wendell, 209
Wilson, Charles E., 75, 154
Winn, Frank, 69, 71
Winter, Herman, 216
Wirtz, W. Willard, 155
With These Hands (film), 90
Woll, Matthew, 164
Woodcock, Leonard, 70
Woodner Hotel (Wash., D.C.), 51
World Federation of Trade Unions (WFTU), 166
World War I, 157, 191, 200
Woxburg, Homer L., 60, 163, 191

Young Communist League, 51

Zwillman, Longy, 35, 117